# Ordinary Knowledge

For Julien Freund and Edgar Morin:

A Reminder of the Conflictual Harmony of All Thought

# Ordinary Knowledge

*An Introduction to Interpretative Sociology*

**Michael Maffesoli**

*Translated by David Macey*

Polity Press

Published with the assistance of the French Ministry of Culture.

First published in 1996 by Polity Press
in association with Blackwell Publishers Ltd

2 4 6 8 10 7 5 3 1

*Editorial office:*
Polity Press
65 Bridge Street
Cambridge CB2 1UR, UK

*Marketing and production:*
Blackwell Publishers Ltd
108 Cowley Road
Oxford OX4 1JF, UK

Blackwell Publishers Inc.
238 Main Street
Cambridge, MA 02142, USA

ISBN 0–7456–1118–4

A CIP catalogue record for this book is available from the British Library and the Library of Congress.

Typeset in Palatino in 10½ on 12 pt
by CentraCet Ltd, Cambridge
Printed in Great Britain by
T J Press Ltd, Padstow, Cornwall

This book is printed on acid-free paper.

# Contents

# Perspectives

When you speak to me of cathedrals, I cannot but be moved
by the intuition that allows you to divine something that I
have never told anyone, and that I am now writing for the
first time: I intended to give every section of my book titles
like 'Porch', 'Windows in the Apse' and so on . . . to reply in
advance to the stupid criticism that there is no construction
in books whose only merit I can prove to be the solidity of
their slightest parts.

Marcel Proust, letter to Jean de Gaigneron

Think of novels that are set in no particular place or time: Julien
Gracq's *Au Château d'Argol* (1939) or Hermann Hesse's *The Glass
Bead Game* (1943). Or think of Ernst Jünger's *Heliopolis* (1949). Of
course we can give them a setting, depending on our fantasies or
fantasms, but their main attraction is that they are suggestive and
evocative. They are primarily fertile matrices which the reader can
use to construct landscapes, situations and unexpected developments as the fancy takes him or her. The artist's task is simply to
erect guideposts for our intellectual wanderings. My ambition here
is rather similar. As far as it is possible to do so, I have cut out
allusions to concrete situations or historical references. Humour
alone tempers the cold logic to some extent. It is, however, possible
for anyone to use the outlines I am proposing for his or her own
constructs, as defined by the situations he or she has to live with
or analyse.

No legitimation, unless a debate with the theories that occupy
our intellectual field is a form of legitimation. Except, perhaps, that
given at the beginning of modern times by Savonarola in his

*Compendium revelationum*: 'I attempt to demonstrate and to per-
suade using probable arguments, figures borrowed from the holy
scriptures and other similarities or parables supplied me by the
present situation.'

At a time when another new age is beginning, placing oneself
under the tutelary sign of Savonarola is in a sense a symbolic
gesture. Not so much in terms of the content of his message as of
his ability to understand what was going to happen. That is a
whole programme in itself! Will this project – reflecting on the
modern modalities of knowledge – make it possible to write a book
which, without making concessions, does not lapse into the ratiocination that is all too often fashionable in academic circles? That
is the challenge. It is not a challenge that is easy to take up. Indeed,
one legitimate response to the essentially media-oriented charms
of the dominant intellectual output of the last few years is to begin
to measure scientificity by the standards of an obscurantism which
is often no more than a set of platitudes served up in indigestible
jargon. Diafoirus, the quack in Molière's *Le Malade imaginaire*, is
alive and well. Even intellectual journalists who once encouraged
those on the lecturer's dais are ready to sing the praises of gibberish
they do not really understand, provided that it is tricked out in
statistical or pseudo-economic finery. This is the context in which I
am daring to articulate a few ideas which are simple but which,
like all truisms, cannot be repeated too often. I am immodest
enough to believe that what I am outlining is congruent with the
*new art of thinking* that is beginning to emerge before our very eyes.

To speak in metaphors, we might say that it is is only natural for
a man who has reached his forties to wake up one fine morning
and wonder about the new rotundity of a body whose dashing
contours he remembers only too well. He then goes on a series of
diets in an attempt to regain his old slenderness. It is the same
with the mind. One's mental audacity, curiosity and liveliness
gradually decline as a result of a bad diet of laziness, institutionalization and, of course, the working intellectual's permanent itch to
act as a mentor to any individual with a modicum of power who
comes his way. All these things take us away from the basics
which, especially for a sociologist, provide the support for thought.
We might conclude that there is a periodic need for the collective
regeneration of a mode of thought which has become far too
listless. This is certainly what is happening today. Dogmas, certainties and convictions of all kinds are being given a rather hard time.

Is that a bad thing, in view of the epistemological excitement that results? Morin's (1977–80) encyclopedic research and the *necessary path – odos –* that Gilbert Durand (1969; 1979a; 1979b; 1980) is so patiently following encourage us to be daring (cf. Morin 1977–80).

Unlike the prudent managers who are in charge of research and those one might call the intellectual eunuchs, more and more people are attempting to restore a certain pugnacity to sociology, which I have described elsewhere (Maffesoli 1981) as the 'ideology of our day'. No one should have any hestitation about contributing in their own way to a debate which must be as wide-ranging as possible. It is with that purpose in mind that I propose to expound some possible *epistemological premisses for a treatise on 'common-sensology'*. True to form, I will remain allusive. And, to allude to an instructive example, I recall that, in the Middle Ages, *Lectio Divina* made it possible both to distance oneself from scholastic constructs and, by repeating a few home truths, to open up the way to a deeper interpretation of both divine reality and the world that was so closely bound up with it. We could undertake something of that kind: distance and repetition. An incantory retreat based upon scepticism and passion, which will allow us to get a better grasp of the most lively aspects of a multi-coloured *societal given* that still obeys specific 'forms'.[1] This interpretative attitude is somewhat mystical but, if we refer to the etymology of the word, we find that it is well suited to the confused and 'orgastic' atmosphere that characterizes our era. At a time when institutional sociology requires statistics, fieldwork and history precisely because it is lacking in self-confidence, it may seem paradoxical to adopt a deliberately speculative approach. Yet, in terms of the familiar conflict over methodology, it might not be pointless to go back to the epistemological preoccupations of the founding fathers to whom I refer: Simmel, Weber, Durkheim and Pareto. These reflections are also based on my own earlier work. Throughout my work on bureaucracy (Maffesoli 1976), revolution ((Maffesoli 1979a), violence (Maffesoli 1984), everyday life (Maffesoli 1979b) and the orgy (Maffesoli 1982), I have always tried to introduce a metaphoric note so as to avoid reifying my object of study. The following pages are intended to 'monstrate' the unity of this method. It exists, is as valid as any other, and it certainly inspires empirical research. Just as there are different ways of doing things, so there are various ways of thinking about them. I intend to outline one such way.

Given that knowledge has a number of 'interests' and that at a more trivial level time is inevitably restricted, this book is so constructed that it can be read on several levels:

1   In the introductory chapter I outline the *theoretical presuppositions* and the sensibility that have guided my reflections on epistemology.

2   The main body of the text elaborates certain categories that seem to me to constitute what I call a *sociological 'formism'*.

3   The final chapter and the conclusion underline the implications of 'formism', with particular reference to the interpretation of the increasingly important topic of everyday life.

4   For those who wish to go into specific questions in more depth, the bibliography and notes provide details of the books, research papers and studies on which these reflections are based.

As we all know, the world is unlivable, but we have to live in it. It is also unthinkable, but we still have to think about it. I suggest that we think about it in a minor key. Thinking in a minor key is a metanoiac process, as opposed to the usual paranoiac attitude,[2] but it will, it is to be hoped, allow us to approach the subterranean centrality that constitutes all sociality without violating it too seriously.

# Introduction

Have you ever observed, *madame*, as I have observed, that *monsieur* your son never utters any of those standard witticisms that are the laughing stock of our age? He declines to appear in a salon with a notebook, and his witticisms depend upon the feelings that are inspired in him. That is why fools are sometimes so displeased with him and why they do not approve of him.

Stendhal, *Armance*

## 1 First presupposition: critique of schematic dualism

When we look at the history of the recent discipline of sociology, we find that there is a constant oscillation between 'general' and much more specialized perspectives. What tends to be less clear is that, like any form of thought, sociology displays two complementary attitudes. It is difficult to define them with any accuracy but they coincide with the twin potentialities of reason and the imagination. To adopt a rather simplistic distinction, which can be seen as an ideal type (that is, as something which never exists in such a clear-cut way), we inevitably find, on the one hand, intellectual representations based upon *abstraction* and, on the other, representations which rely upon what a certain German tradition calls *Einfühlung*, a term which can be translated as 'empathy'.[1] The former stress construction, criticism, mechanicism and reason; the latter place more emphasis on nature, feeling, the organic and the imagination. This brings us back to the dichotomy outlined by

Tacussel (1982), which I am of course using metaphorically: paranoiac construction as opposed to metanoiac procedures.

It is necessary to insist on this division because, whilst it may
not put an end to all conflict, it does allow us to arrive at a
reasonable assessment of the findings obtained by the different
forms of investigation it implies. The opposition has always existed
and can be seen in all fields, and it would be instructive to list all
the terms it has borrowed, or all the systems it has generated.
Certain expressions coined in seventeenth-century Spain capture it
very well, and found a conflictual harmony between a *'conceptismo'*,
based upon ingenious rational proofs, and a *'cultismo'* that plays on
metaphors and verbal floweriness. Each attitude has its own rules
and therefore its specific efficacy, and it selects its objects accordingly. It is therefore obvious that the two are inevitably complementary. In a discussion of history, Renan (1921: 117, 122) remarks
that what he calls 'St Maur's erudition', or in other words painstak-
ing exhaustiveness, is complemented by 'the understanding of the
present', in which there is a considerable element of passion and
therefore partiality. With all due respect to disgruntled parties on
both sides of the debate, a subtle combination of the two is required
if we are to arrive at a more adequate vision of any particular
period or phenomenon. It is obviously unusual to find this combination in any one individual, but it may exist in the broader context
of the 'republic of letters', which should permit the workings of the
simple mechanism whereby intuition inspires more exhaustive
research, which in turn provides a more informed view of a given
contemporary situation. In short, there can be an exchange between
those who snuffle around at the subterranean level where things
begin to be instituted and the 'taxonomists' who classify institui-
tionalized and official forms and situations.[2] To cut a long story
short, we can say that there are various 'types' of knowledge, and
that their existence is quite in keeping with the immensity of the
social spectrum and its multiple variations. We find the same
eternal dichotomy in sociology too. We could therefore apply
Mannheim's comments on ideology to sociology; some are 'situationally transcendent' and others are 'situationally congruous'
(Mannheim 1936: 175). The outcome is obvious: critical and utopian
outlooks on the one hand, and the legitimation of the established
order (whatever it may be in nature) on the other. It goes without
saying, of course, that no normative value-judgements will be
passed here; our sole concern is to note certain major articulations,
which are themselves subdivided into many parts. The specializa-

tions that characterize the various academic sociologies are in this respect suggestive. Thus, whilst I agree with Balandier when he warns (1981) against a deceptive oscillation between two poles, the classification he proposes – *utilitarian sociology* and *sociology of knowledge* – remains pertinent, though it may require some qualification. We do in fact find this division in the various specialized sociologies mentioned above. This classification allows us to state that the normative attitude can have both conservative and revolutionary implications; the same can be said of the interpretative model and of the concern with knowledge for the sake of knowledge. It is not so much the object as the intentions of the sociologist that determine the issue.

Without wishing to pursue the examples he gives to illustrate his argument, it is interesting to note Boudon's (1979) distinction between *interactionist* and *determinist* paradigms. The distinction, which is eminently clear, obviously underlines the essential characteristics of the assumptions behind the respective methods of sociological analysis. It should, however, be noted that within this dichotomy the individual is still the essential point of reference. The individual, either as an individual or as an individual interacting with others, remains the irreducible monad that allows either explanation or interpretation.

Adopting the terminology used by Windelband and Rickert in their analyses, Ferrarotti (1983), on the other hand, has no hesitation in asserting that there is a radical divorce between 'nomothetic and idiographic intentionality'.[3] The distinction is certainly not devoid of interest at a time when it is obvious that the great explanatory systems are becoming saturated and when we are witnessing the renaissance of biographical exploration. Biographical exploration and, more generally, anything to do with everyday life and its analysis inevitably stresses the limitations of sociological instruments designed to explain macroscopic social forms rather than to interpret all that is meaningful but purposeless in everyday life. When sociology attempts to analyse everyday life, the result is therefore either a critique of its alienated aspects (Lefebvre) or a 'time-budgets' type of accounting which, whilst it is not uninteresting, merely reinforces the economistic vision of the social given.[4] This is another example of the dichotomy we were discussing, but this time it is a divorce between a *positivistic sociology*, for which everything is merely a symptom of something else, and an *interpretative sociology* that describes lived experience as it is, and simply identifies the goals of the various actors involved.

To adopt a fairly pejorative expression used in North American sociological debates to describe the non-determinist approach, we are not far removed from a certain 'romanticism' which, as R. H. Brown (1977) points out, derives from intuitionism.[5] Perhaps we should proudly adopt the term 'romantic' sociology, but give it a wider meaning and use it to refer to a very general attitude which refuses to choose or to state what is and what is not important or meaningful, and which rejects a division that has provided the substratum of critical philosophy since the eighteenth century. From this point of view, the thinker or 'he who speaks of the world' cannot stand back from it: he is part of what he is describing. He is inside it and can therefore see it from the inside: '*in-tuitively*'. It is certainly possible to explain Schutz's 'typicality' in these terms.

*The aim of this book is to outline a sociology from the inside.* This would not have been alien to either Weber or Simmel, nor of course to Nietzsche, who was the source of their inspiration. It should further be noted that the global approach we are describing could also be related to the holism which, according to Durkheim, is the essential characteristic of sociology. This does of course imply a metaphoric reading of Durkheim's thought, but it is always useful to upset classic exegeses of canonical authors, if only in a hypothetical mode.


## 2  Second presupposition: 'form'

Sociological 'romanticism' must of course absorb an element of rationalism if it is to achieve a balance that allows it to perceive both the logical and the 'non-logical' that permeates the social given. The refusal to discriminate at the level of the object and the rejection of dualism at the methodological level in fact imply social and natural organicity. With that in mind, I will later (chapter 4) propose the notion of 'formism'. The neologism is intended to be a tribute to the sociology of Simmel, who used the term *formal* and not *formell*. The former term designates the form of a problem; the latter, its formal aspect. The distinction is important. In an obvious attempt to invalidate it, Gurvitch (1967: 5, 55) speaks of Simmel's 'formalism'. Simmel's position is, however, quite clear: 'Sociology studies forms of social life insofar as they are containers, as opposed to their content' (Simmel 1898).[6] The notion of formism does not allow the misunderstandings that are so often introduced by the idea of 'form'. It seems to me that it is an adequate way of describing from within the contours, limits and necessity of the situations and representations that make up daily life. We can thus temper the rigidity of structuralism and at the same time retain the pertinence of its comments on invariance. And that well-tempered modulation will allow us to understand the lability and warm currents of lived experience.

This too is a concern with a respectable ancestry. A separate study would be required to trace this notion back to what the Aristotelian-scholastic tradition calls the 'formal cause' or 'substantial cause'. In their various ways, Leibniz's simple substances, Kant's categories of the understanding and, of course, all *Gestalt-theorien* are all ways of dealing with this problem. The Western tradition remains, however, very unsure about all this, and a triumphal iconoclasm does tend to displace all interpretation towards a rationalist formalism. As Durand remarks, it is 'Eastern' thought or, in a very different perspective, modern biology, which has really come to terms with the characteristics of '*Forme*' (Durand 1961; cf. Corbin's analyses). Thus, Wadheim's definition of the morphogenetic field as a *chreode*, Portmann's *Urbilder* and the very real 'morphic causality' established by the English sociologist Rupert Sheldrake all open up important perspectives for formist thought. Having no particular competence in these areas, I am merely suggesting some possible lines of research.[7] On the other hand, Dumézil's functions/structures, Durand's anthropological structures (or the metaphor of 'semantic basins' that he now uses), and the idea of limits and 'constraining forces' (the mythical setting for *La Chartreuse de Parme*), are all of great relevance to sociological analysis in that they demonstrate that 'form' is not something formal, but a matter of 'forming'. It is also instructive to note that, in addition to 'formism' (Simmel), we can also make reference to 'essential characteristics' (Durkheim), 'ideal types' (Weber), 'residues' (Pareto) and 'typicality' (Schutz). All these notions stress the need for a specific focus if we are to bring out the variety of societal phenomena. As Habermas (1968: 159) remarks, 'Hermeneutic understanding must employ *inevitably general* categories to grasp an inalienably *individual* meaning.' For the qualitative perspective we are adopting here, this emphasis on typicality is in a sense a guiding principle that allows us to use metaphors in a comparative way and to give them a real cognitive value. In this connection, it should be pointed out that attempting to note the incoherence, lability or polysemy of the social given does not mean that we will be unable to find structuring forms within it. It is increasingly recognized that there is a very close connection between order and disorder; the point is therefore to find a way to find an epistemological explanation for the organic link between the two (cf. Maffesoli 1978 and Dupuy 1982). It seems to me that a combination of 'the minuscule' and 'form' is the best possible approach. It allows us to avoid the accusations of anomie or dilettantism that are all too often directed against research that attempts to get away from the beaten tracks of positivism (or at least means that our more honest colleagues will not make such accusations).

I am less concerned here with expounding a method than with outlining the assumptions behind formism and, more specifically, with demonstrating that it may quite literally have a *cohesive* function that still leaves the object of its analysis intact. It is important to stress this twofold function. It is a third way which will, in my view, characterize sociological thinking in the decades to come. Without abdicating any of its intellectual responsibilities, the metanoiac attitude makes, as I have said, every attempt not to constrain or reduce the real. It should also be pointed out that, after a few centuries of iconoclasm, a methodological return to 'form' is very a pertinent way of looking at a sociality which is increasingly structured by the image. All these dimensions are well captured by what Durand calls 'constellations of images' (Durand 1969: 40f; cf. Spengler 1922–3). Constellations of images allow us to bring together and describe disparate elements that can later be analysed and compared. We can thus create 'groups of morphological affinities' (Spengler) around a number of types identified on the basis of experience, chance or the subjectivity of the researcher. The subject matter itself is of little importance, as we are not dealing with a closed system, but with heuristic and probable propositions which can (must) be compared with constructions elaborated from different 'points of view'. Once again, this involves the organization of morphological constellations, and it corresponds to the mutual organization of societies or micro-societies.

We find a similar preoccupation in Max Weber. Just as polytheism is often a polite form of atheism, his pluricausalism is in my view an elegant way of rejecting or relativizing (which amounts to the same thing) causality itself. When, for example, he argues (Weber 1904: 78–9) that when we are analysing a phenomenon, the 'question of causality is not a question of *laws* but of concrete causal *relationships*'; it is not a question of the subsumption of each event under some general rubric but of its imputation (*Zurech-nungsfrage*) as a consequence of some constellation', he demonstrates that, because it is a crystallization of the complexity of the world, any phenomenon is amenable to multiple explanations, but is also an element that explains other constellations. To that extent, we see once more the importance that has to be given to what is all too often regarded as 'frivolous' or 'secondary'. The articulation of constellations, or in other words the interplay of forms, allows us to take stock of the efficacy of the anodyne or the minuscule. Whilst it has nothing to do with the oneiric connotations that are inevitably introduced by the 'constellation' metaphor, it should be pointed out that in Weber's interpretation (1913) one of the golden methodological rules states that in order to untangle real (*wirkliche*) causal relationships, we establish unreal (*unwirkliche*) causal relationships. This ability to use the non-real to understand the real is extremely important, and it corresponds to one of the functions we can ascribe to 'form'; it allows us to grasp both the image and its significance within the social body. To borrow an old philosophical expression, this function can be regarded as a 'condition of possibility' for both existence and cognition as a whole. And the observable fact that the world has once more become 'enchanted' gives this faculty a new contemporary relevance that sociologists cannot ignore. Indeed, they must make it a major element in their arguments. Defined in their broadest sense, spatial frameworks ('countries', territories, nature, localities, etc.) are real *a priori* forms of sociality, and the *Umwelt* and its relational correlates require the establishment of invariable categories that escape the influence of historical specificities.

Invariance, in the modified perspective I have outlined in connection with constellations, is also a component element in any scientific attitude. It establishes regularities, and it is impossible to understand the crises, changes and modulations we can observe without referring to intangible structures. *A fortiori* anything relating to normal life, which abounds in repetitions and latent or manifest references to archetypes or stereotypes. In my analyses of bureaucracy, violence and everyday life, I bring out the importance of paroxysmal categories such as power, might, ritual, theatricality, duplicity, tragedy and so on. To the extent that they do not exist or are unreal, these categories are to be understood as so many modulations of 'form'; their unreality does not detract from their methodological importance, as they allow us to illustrate, to visualize all the meaningful little bits and pieces and all the macroscopic structures that make up our societies. To answer Bourricaud's objections (1981: 230), form allows us to pay attention to the particular without ignoring essential characteristics. It helps us to avoid both prophecy and conservatism. These are, then, the categories that provide the main themes of this reflection on epistemology. The ten (or twelve) 'labours' Hercules performed in his initiatory quest for immortality covered the broad social spectrum of his day. If we update that goal, it is possible to imagine the modern scientific community diversifying its own 'labours': monographic, empirical, thetic, dogmatic and so on. Other labours can be carried out by the speculator or the 'formist' who is content to create what I have termed 'conditions of possibility'; this is not an empty or meaningless game, but an exacting approach which has far-reaching implications for the interpretation of the *experience* of societal being-together (cf. chapter 8 below).

## 3  Third presupposition: a relativist sensibility

It is quite clear that the 'convergence' method (Piaget, Durand), the establishment of 'typicalities' and the comparative study of forms are all based upon a methodological relativism. This is true in two senses. On the one hand, nothing new ever happens in human history; we simply see the same values returning in cyclical fashion. The only thing that changes is their technical weighting. On the other hand, the mode of approach does change and accentuate one or another aspect in accordance with the dominant values of the moment. The familiar oscillation between the Dionysian and the Promethean is instructive in this respect. There is no such thing as a single Reality; there are only differential ways of conceptualizing reality. The *contradictoriel* (Lupasco, Beigbeder) that is at work in the social given refers to contradictory versions, and it is pointless to attempt to reconcile them.[8] The terms of the current debate over the end of the great explanatory systems – Marxism, Freudianism, positivism – that have marked our period (and perhaps it would be more accurate to speak of their 'saturation') have been badly put. The point is not to invalidate them because of what they are, but to demonstrate that they derive from and explain (and can be explained in terms of) a given period. They were elaborated during a period dominated by the homogenization of an expanding civilization, and are no longer adequate to a description of the process of heterogenization that results from the decadence of that civilization.

I will therefore attempt to demonstrate in chapters on 'the

fascination of positivism' (chapter 1) and on 'the experience of relativism' (chapter 2) that whilst the hypothesis of *homo oeconomicus* may well have once been pertinent, it is now in danger of producing a totally reductive vision of social life.[9] Appearances to the contrary notwithstanding, social life cannot be explained in terms of a set of economic laws. It can be understood in terms of the broader system of communication (correspondence, analogy, sociality), which has been given a powerful boost by the technological developments with which we are all too familiar. Boudon's cautious admission that there are factors that go beyond the economic dimensions of social life is no longer acceptable. He does of course speak of 'psychological dimensions ... which are more difficult to identify ... but no less important' (1979: 12).[10] We must, however, go beyond this and accept that classic psycho-sociological instruments modelled on the *principium individuationis* (economy of the self, economy of the world) can no longer in themselves describe societal constellations in which the image and the symbol have pride of place. To adopt the categorization we employed earlier, we might say that, as the world becomes more heterogeneous, our systemic interpretation must be applicable to a wider spectrum.

That said, it is quite obvious that pluralization and the relativism it induces are far from being widely accepted or recognized. Many academics and research workers prefer established certainties or reassuringly quantitative studies. For their part, the research bureaucrats, or the self-appointed guardians of 'the social demand' prefer studies with an immediate application; the international 'crisis' exists in order to justify their recourse to the 'dancer' known as speculation. Such moralism is, however, short-sighted; some things have to be called into question, if only in discreet terms. And utilitarianism, be it academic or bureaucratic, is one of them. It would take a separate study to demonstrate that methodological relativism is gaining ground in every area of social life:

| Domain | Symptom |
| --- | --- |
| politics | lack of commitment |
| labour | diversification of personal investment |
| religion | minor forms of the sacred |
| family | casual sex |
| social | multiplicity of networks |
| intellectual | interdisciplinarity; confusion |

| ideological | cynicism |
|-------------|----------|
| consumption | hedonism |
| technical | archaism |
| national | local |

I suggest that we call this 'The Conquest of the Present', or 'tragedy replaces drama'. It is, however, clear that our schema, which is incomplete, is an appeal for an open sociology which can integrate specialized knowledges into a plural knowledge which is constantly in the making ... and constantly being unmade. As Max Weber reminds us in a classic text: 'Every scientific "fulfilment" raises new "questions"; it *asks* to be surpassed and outdated. Whoever wishes to serve science has to resign himself to this fact' (Weber 1928: 139). We might add that this is now a collective fate and that as the debasement of social values accelerates, we would do well to produce 'local' theories which, like a continuous dissolve, fade into other configurations which are themselves destined to vanish in their turn.

When it comes to a sociology which stresses sociality, the imaginary and the everyday, elaborating a 'content' is therefore less important than establishing a perspective. Sociology as points of view.[11] This attitude has nothing to do with claims to absolute knowledge, and still less to do with claims to being immediately operational, and for that very reason it can pay attention to all aspects of the social given. In that sense, we might speak of a 'stereoscopic vision', as opposed to the monocular vision of specialists. If we identify a variety of different angles of approach for every object of analysis, we will come much closer to understanding the contradictory element at work in sociality.[12] This may seem paradoxical, but the defining characteristic of any society – and all societies are made up of heterogeneous elements – is precisely that it is paradoxical. And a systemic reflection that attempts to describe a complex order and the interaction that sustains it must at least look at this stereoscopy and the paradoxes it generates.

This is why I will, throughout this book, make a critique of concepts, or at least of the conceptualism that hypostasizes the instruments it uses. It is perhaps unnecessary to attach excessive importance to words, which, according to R. M. Rilke, 'kill what they name'. In its attempt not to overlook any part of the social whole, the relativist sensibility prefers a cautious approach to what I have described elsewhere (Maffesoli 1976: 12) as 'the terrorism of coherence'. It implies proceeding by concentric approaches, and successive sedimentations. All these approaches respect the incompleteness and the gaps which, on the one hand, we can observe empirically and which are, on the other hand, a structurally necessary part of existence because, as is well known, perfection means death. All this take us on what Popper (1992) calls an 'unended quest'. The unended quest appears to me to be the motor behind the causal pluralism that means that the analysis of forms and empirical observation are inextricably connected. And to dismiss the speculative approach as obscurantist, or to establish a strict divorce between description and theory, is the classic positivist delusion.

This interaction, which is not necessarily the doing of a single researcher and which must be understood in the broader context of the scientific community, takes us out of 'classic epistemological frameworks' (Ferrarotti 1983: 56). We can generalize from the formula Ferrarotti applies to the biographical method by stressing that, because it relies upon an interplay between 'formist' analyses and descriptions of the frivolous, the relativist sensibility makes redundant the taxonomic fantasy we have inherited from the nineteenth century. It also knows that the truth is always fleeting and factual. To adopt a moralistic stance, we might say that the researcher's fidelity to his object is serial rather than constant. What is more, when we look at the social given as a complex whole, it is not inappropriate to recall that the hallmark of scientific humility is the occasional admission that there are degrees of truth and that 'we do not know'. If we take the view that the social whole is no more than a modulation of the divine (Durkheim), it is not irrelevant to liken sociology to the apophatic theology that challenged the positivism of the schoolmen. According to this view, God can only be discussed by not discussing God, by approaching the question tangentially; rejecting the dogmas and norms that reduce the very thing of which they speak, it uses metaphors that can actually describe the life-force in all its expansiveness. As it happens, many scientists, politicians and industrialists understand that an *indirect* search for the truth is much more productive than a direct approach (cf. chapter 8 below).

As Boudon pertinently points out, there is indeed a dichotomy between a theoretical work based upon the idea of absolute knowledge and employing a universalist notation, and more intuitive projects that pay attention to finitude and take care over their style. The relativist sensibility is closer to the latter attitude. In my view, the 'aestheticism' (this was one of the criticisms addressed to

Simmel[13]) that characterizes it does have a place in the academy, especially at a time when, because values are changing, we have to be able to hear the grass growing. *Managing* established knowledge and *sensing* what is coming into being are, after all, merely the two poles that make up the conflictual harmony of all knowledge.


## 4 Fourth presupposition: the search for a style

I have already pointed out (Maffesoli 1981b) that sociology can be regarded as the 'ideology' of our time. It is true that in every era one set of representations (a plural discourse) becomes a point of reference. In saying that I was rather crudely reproducing Renan's (1921: 104–5) much more subtle analysis, which demonstrates that each century has 'a particular literary genre which it uses as a pretext for saying everything'. Thus, 'history appears to be the hallmark of the nineteenth century . . . just as philosophy was that of the eighteenth.' It could also be argued that, in other periods, theology acted as an intellectual matrix. Whatever the truth of the matter and with due respect to all those who equate scientific work with a rebarbative style, sociological 'literature' does need a specific form of expression that can describe its period adequately. Everyday life (cf. chapter 7.2 below) has a style made up of gestures, words, theatricality, and major and minor works. We have to be able to explain that style, even if doing so means having to content ourselves with merely stroking its contours and adopting a stochastic and light-hearted approach. In that respect, the aestheticism we require is a corollary to 'formist' thinking. It is possible to imagine a sociology based upon a constant feedback between form and empathy.

Whether we like it or not, any intellectual approach implies a 'stylization of existence'. Simmel makes the point with regard to Marx and the economic dimension (which gives his work its familiar aspect). There is, however, no reason why 'stylization' should not take into account 'the complex intertwining of sequences of events'. The result would be a much more fragmented, polyphonic and therefore more self-reflective style of writing. Now it has to be admitted that this is not widely accepted in our discipline. And yet the problem has not been completely overlooked. There are of course the pedants and the schoolmen, with their constant accusations of 'dilettantism' but, coming from those whose ambition is to regulate the sociological profession, and especially from their chorus of epigones, the anathema simply does not have the desired effect: not everyone can be a self-proclaimed defender of the Law. What is more, the same reproach has been directed at everyone from Montaigne to Freud and then Weber! Essayists who care about style are really criticized for their attempts to allow as many people as possible to share a storehouse of knowledge the clerics would like to monopolize. Pseudo-complexity at the level of expression masks contempt for others and banal schematicism. This is obviously true at the level of language too. Words too are tools. They are part of our instrumentation, and there is a knack to using them. And without claiming that there is any one answer to the problem, we must try to ensure that our reseach, our books and our papers do, without losing any of their scientific rigour, appeal to a range of social protagonists.

In a discussion of methodological problems, one disciple of Auguste Comte refers to outrageously complicated hypotheses as 'scientific gongorism' (Lemos 1924: 215). On this point at least, we can endorse a positivist analysis: 'gongorism' is widespread in the human sciences, and its sole effect is to discredit the disciplines and practitioners in question. Bertaux (1979: 725) describes the writing of sociology as one of the most urgent tasks confronting us: 'We are beginning to find out what we want to say ... we have yet to find a *form* to say it.' His article on the subject is extremely clear and, whilst I do not share his optimism about serving humanity, his arguments about unreadability and his critique of a certain pretence at scientificity, namely the overdevelopment of the quantitative method and of the hegemony of the *'normalien'* model, do ring true. All the more so now that our small intellectual world is beginning to suffer from fatigue. It is a well-known fact that almost no one reads their colleagues' articles. Rumours, gossip, accusations of dilettanteism, and fame itself – it all helps to encourage intellectual laziness and autism. As for students, they took refuge in textbooks and anthologies long ago.

We can no longer ignore the work of writing, or work on writing. And it cannot be confined to the novels, autobiographies and newspaper articles that academics 'produce', with varying degrees of success, from time to time. It is with this in mind that I will (in chapter 5) describe metaphor and analogy as essential elements of our methodology. Allegory can be an epistemological category, and the same could be said of metaphor or even of 'the aphorism that strikes at the heart of the real' (Bertaux). Once we take into account the fact that the given world is made up of heterogeneous elements, and once our analyses take into account physical and social 'correspondences', we have to find a way of expressing the polysemy of sounds, situations and gestures that makes up the social fabric. Walter Benjamin (1928: 61) thought that there were three stages in the production of good prose: 'Work on good prose has three steps: a musical stage when it is composed, an architectonic one when it is built, and a textile one when it is woven.' The metaphor could usefully be applied to both sociality in the making and to the work of reflection that tries to express it. Just as everyday life is a fabric made up of thousands of interwoven threads, thought must on occasion become slippery, dynamic and multicoloured; and all this is bound to upset the certainties of dead dogmas.

Yet whilst sociology is under an aesthetic obligation to pay attention to what is going on, and whilst it has to be able to take account of the lability of society, it would be regrettable if the result were, as we sometimes find, the hyper-sophistication that sees metaphoric procedures as ends in themselves. Scientistic dryness and haughtiness are constant temptations, but they must be resisted if we are to escape both Scylla and Charybdis. Commonsensology must do all it can to remain in close contact with social banality. Resisting the intoxicating platitudes of jargon (psychoanalytic, linguistic, philosophical etc.) and keeping our feet on the ground are also prerequisites for a sociological search for a style. It may sound simplistic and repetitive to say it, but these are 'forms' which are deeply rooted in popular modes of being. Once again, this is a challenge. Perhaps as a result of our iconoclastic tradition, which tends to distrust images in general and images in the intellectual realm in particular, expressing one's thoughts in a clear and suggestive manner is far from universally acceptable.

It is, finally, quite obvious that 'speaking properly' is not synonymous with 'saying everything'. Lack of precision can sometimes be a way of acknowledging the complexity of things and of respecting the reader. Such evasions are by no means an abdication of intellectual responsibility, but an invitation to a deeper understanding. Leaving a problem unresolved (after having outlined it) is a way of stimulating contradictory debates and suggestions, all of which is perfectly in keeping with the diversity of society. Those who require certainties will obviously find this open-ended procedure unsatisfactory. The spiral movement of reflection is disturbing; throwing up ideas – which are often adopted, after having been attacked or described as hare-brained – is no more reassuring. Yet, just as there is an existential style of walking through life, there is a form of intellectual audacity which rejects petty-bourgeois caution and intellectual conformism. Excessive scruples or, more usually, misplaced pride, prevent us from introducing into the debate elements, reflections and research which could benefit everyone (it is true that this does have something to do with the chronic laziness that prevails in research circles). Making suggestions is dangerous, and that is the way it should be. The problem is that those who are most critical are those who have nothing to say, and that those who have no real academic talent become apparatchiks on the innumerable bureaucratic committees that try to manage intellectual research in the same way as a factory or an adminstrative department is managed. In their view, any reflection which, like the 'essay' in living that is sociality, takes the form of an 'essay' in thinking, is open to every possible reproach. And especially the supreme insult: aestheticism.

## 5 Fifth presupposition: libertarian thought

Intolerance and quarrels between schools have always been with us, and the history of ideas shows that they can even lead to bloodshed. Given that we live in a civilized society, the only blows that are permitted are the ones that land below the belt, even when the least honourable of men deliver them. It is this intolerance that makes the intellectual task of speaking from nowhere and in the name of no one so difficult. And yet that is the ambition of this book. Our fidgety Parisian intelligentsia (which, as it wears itself out in minor intestinal quarrels, is heading towards inevitable extinction) does not tolerate the offhandedness, the absolute irresponsibility and the *gaya scienza* that earned Nietzsche such unfair treatment. A word of warning to those who, being free of all ties, wander at will as chance encounters or opportunity arise, to the *kairois* of ancient memory that keeps us in tune with what is going on or going by. Everything will be used to discredit them: silence, then insults and finally intellectual invalidation. All in the name of science, of course (and without having read a line by those who are being judged and sentenced). Conformism rules in our small intellectual world, and it takes time for impertinent or untimely propositions to gain acceptance. And yet sociologists should be familiar enough with the law that states that not all the effects of institutional gravity are pleasant, especially not in the intellectual domain. Does it have to be pointed out that concealing your work behind a mask of frivolity makes you a veritable intellectual aristocrat? To pursue the Dionysian metaphor, here is a little fable: 'The god Pan is jealous of his miracles. In order to accomplish his conjuring tricks, he has to feign frivolity, but I suspect that he spends whole nights working on them, like any *polytechnicien* who works on algebraic equations with several unknowns. As you surely know, all gods keep their secrets to themselves' (Drot 1971: 37).

We will, therefore, adopt a libertarian approach. Founding a school is both easy and boring; it is much more fruitful to struggle for the right to look freely at things. This is an insolent, naive, even trivial stance, and it is to say the least uncomfortable, but it does open up gaps, and allows intense exchanges that shopkeepers and bureaucrats cannot even begin to imagine. An insolent thought, then. I have spoken of wanderings and caprice, and this brings us back to the preoccupations of Balandier (1972) and Touraine (1985), who speak of 'not respecting limits' or of the interaction between different schools of thought.[14] It also brings us back to the invigorating impertinence of Edgar Morin who, as early as the 1960s, established prolegomena for a daring approach that was in keeping with our times in his *L'Esprit du temps* (Morin 1979). It is more than necessary to destroy, or at least to laugh at, intellectual baronies, not to mention the little thematic constituencies within them that are guarded all the more jealously in that they are inconsistent and, to put it mildly, outdated. Innovators upset institutional *gravitas* because they distrust the collective drowsiness that results from the establishment of specialized bodies of knowledge [*savoirs*]. To take only one recent example of some importance, it is not a neutral matter when the anthropologist Pierre Clastres attacks the State in the name of 'Society' (Clastres 1974). He discomfits the intellectual conformism and narrowmindedness that is usually known as scientific caution. Does it have to be said yet again that all the human sciences are based upon a gamble, and that we are all to some extent aware of that fact?[15] It is also possible that the quality of the gamble can be gauged by the audacity that gave rise to it. Thought that can retain the flexibility and even the clumsiness of its adolescence often provides a wealth of unexpected new developments. The Nobel prize-winner Szent-Györgi makes a distinction between the 'Apollonian' researcher who reinforces and refines earlier discoveries, and the 'Dionysian' reseacher who opens up new paths. The latter is less sure of himself: he does not know the direction in which he wants to go in his search for the unknown (cf. Hall 1977: 123). It may well be an obvious question, but what would become of science without intellectual adventurism, without the Dionysian approach?

All this implies a certain partiality at the level of analysis. Pluralism has never meant unanimism. Polytheism in general, and epistemological polytheism in particular, involves relativization, misrecognition and ignorance, and all this has an effect on creativity. In the realm of cognition, we therefore have to remain deaf to certain commentaries if we are to hear the efficacy of the situation, configuration or structure we are attempting to analyse.[16] I am not suggesting that we should rule out other approaches; on the contrary, by both avoiding 'contamination' and completing the pantheon of knowledge we can at once strengthen the scientific community and improve our understanding of particular objects. For the specific 'objects' that he or she approaches, it is important for the sociologist to wake up innocent every morning. Amnesia is a force that allows us to look at things in a new way. Forgetting theories and 'off-the-peg' thought is primarily a way of getting back to our *materia prima*: the realm of banality. In a research programme that is both disabused and demanding, forgetting what we have learned can be a guarantee of originality.

By adopting this logic, which is inspired by Alfred Schutz – whom French sociologists have either ignored or, which is worse, used *in pectore* for too long – libertarian thought can make use of the notion of typicality. Typicality can be defined in various different ways, and I will return to the point later. For the moment, we will simply stress that it implies involvement on the part of the intellectual. It is pointless to go on taking refuge in the citadel of objectivity – Morin (1979: 18) speaks in a similar context of a cultural Montségur [a mountain fortress]. That is a process of disavowal that could not be further removed from concrete reality. To put it in a nutshell, let us say that, although the sociologist does not, as certain methodologies demand, necessarily have to be a participant or an actor, a certain interaction does take place between observer and object of study. They connive, and sometimes collude, and I would even go so far as to speak of empathy (*Einfühlung*). *And it is perhaps this that defines the specificity of our discipline.* Understanding implies generosity of spirit, proximity and 'correspondence'. It is because we are in a sense 'part of it' that we can grasp or sense the subtleties, nuances and discontinuities of a given social situation.

Any authentic work always contains an element of extrapolation;

of course we have to keep a firm grip on the reins, as an authentic work can be mettlesome and intemperate, but it should not be reined in too tightly. There is a price to be paid for true inventiveness, or the ability to find something that already exists.

This too is a matter of typicality: we are involved in what we are talking about, either at the fantasy level or at the level of reality (not that it makes much difference). That is why the critical perspective gives way to assertions. When we no longer have to choose between good and evil, we can rest content with talking about what exists, safe in the knowledge that, in various ways and thanks to differentiated modulations, we are an element of the real world.

It is very difficult for intellectuals to adopt this attitude because they are, as I have already said, quite 'paranoiac'. And it is because they reject correspondence that they put all their trust in the divine power of criticism. They 'are not involved'. They are above it all. Thanks to a quite understandable ruse of reason, the rejection of typicality leads to its pathological exaggeration. The situation was well analysed by Paul Valéry, and then in a work of fiction by the sociologist Gilbert Auclair (1973: 56): 'megalomania is the right word. We are all brilliant, and unfortunate to have a vocation for the demented professions: *we all want to be unique.*' The intellectual tries to make sense, to talk Sense by refusing to be one signifying element amongst others. Windbags have to be deflated. We are always talking about ourselves to some extent, and we are always talking to someone. And, as a result, we become integrated into an overall architectonic where 'scents, colours and sounds correspond' in what I call a conflictual harmony.

If we transpose Baudelaire's vision into the order of social representations (*ex-pressions*) we can see the true richness of typicality. This is particularly obvious for the human or social sciences, which attempt to see things as they evolve rather than to classify things that have already evolved. Spengler's argument that scientific experience is equivalent to spiritual self-knowledge deserves to be taken to its ultimate conclusion. Montaigne showed the way in his eminently human solitude. So too did Schopenhauer (1819: vol. 1, p. xxi), who, in his mystical misanthropy, valued only 'that which one has thought out and investigated for onself'; as that alone is 'afterwards of benefit to others; not that however, which was originally intended for others'. Those who try to teach others lessons would do well to contemplate this bitter wisdom. If we inject homeopathic doses of subjectivity into our analyses, we can protect ourselves from an invasive eruption of subjectivity, and we can also be certain that our findings will inevitably find their place within the social polyphony. The resultant convergence between individual typicality and social typicality obviously has its effects on the development of research in the social sciences. As Goethe puts it, no one can judge history unless he has lived through it. What is, on the other hand, clear is that the aggressivity and, more curiously still, the moralism that prevail in intellectual circles are bound up with the undeniable frustration of those who claim to be able to make sense of social existence but are quite incapable of exercising the slightest control over their own lives. Which means that they can understand absolutely nothing of the 'duplicity' that structures sociality (Maffesoli 1979b: ch. 7). The richly meaningful situationist expression 'Mind seeks work' might have been coined with them in mind. Today's teachers were once the wretched students who, before 1968, divided their lives between protests that got them nowhere and a bad conscience that knew no limits. Their status may have changed, but their underlying 'qualities' remain the same, and we should be writing a new *On the Poverty of Intellectual Life*. That salutary task can be left to others; for the moment, we need only stress that rich, original and forward-looking books are always written by *free spirits* who short-circuit schools, dogmatists and fashions. They combine thought with passion, and they are not afraid to turn the combination of the two into a real adventure. It should also be recalled, if only briefly, that the academic establishment has adopted the old ecclesiastical practice of protecting itself from intellectual innovations by resorting to *ad hominem* criticisms of their authors. Thanks to the dominance of the media, such dirty tricks can now be left to the rank and file, but the technique has not changed. Many universities and science laboratories have become workshops that turn out rumours and slander. 'Knit one, purl one. . .' As they knit their identical sweaters, the new lady patrons keep a good lookout, and they always denounce anything that dares to stray from the straight and narrow.[17]

Serenity may well be the appropriate response, as books last longer than dirty tricks. And it so happens that books are always the product of nonconformism on the part of free spirits. The title of a French anthology of texts by Max Weber (1983; see in particular pp. 45, 49 and the notes by M. L. Martin, pp. 52, 62) is a good illustration of the libertarian thought I am describing: *De la liberté intellectuelle et de la dignité de la vocation universitaire* ('On Intellectual

Freedom and the Dignity of the Academic Vocation'). It is also interesting to observe that many authors whose thought is indisputably original and who are now recognized were once harassed by the malevolence of the petty-bourgeois bureaucrats of their day. Werner Sombart, for instance, had to put up with what Max Weber called 'lamentable gossip'. His aestheticism and his 'bohemian manners' inevitably shocked those of his colleagues who also found his interest in fashion as social phenomenon pointless. The same could be said of Robert Michels, who was driven out of the German academic community because of a life-style which was, according to his detractors, 'lacking in sobriety'.

The technique is the same in both cases: criticisms of a man's private life are used as arguments against themes and methodologies which upset established certainties and intellectual conformism. Vilfredo Pareto suffered the same fate when he was criticized for his cynicism and his penchant for a Machiavellian ethics. It was in fact his polemical contempt for intellectuals who 'drone on' that could not be forgiven. And despite the praiseworthy efforts of Busino and others, he still languishes in purgatory. We still hear talk of Scheler's 'immoralism' and Simmel's 'dilettantism', to take only two examples (see Busino 1983: 1126; Freund's preface to Simmel (Freund 1981: 11), and Dupuy (1959, vol. 2: 726, 730). The anger of the frustrated and the philippics of professors of private or political morals in fact often mask an unspoken anxiety about the perpetual evolution of the social world.

It cannot be said too often that intellectual wandering is no more than a replica of social wandering. Both relate to a stochastic model which, rather like a Mahler symphony, combines harmony and discord, brings together autonomous elements and, in short, uses contradictory devices which simply reproduce the polysemy of the given world. Its polyphony is usually denied and it is not surprising that the intellectual vivacity – the goddess Metis, daughter of Oceanus – that it inevitably inspires in some should displease the established intelligentsia, 'all the pseudo-intellectuals, and the sage managers of knowedge and of the *polis*; this is because it contravenes the logic of the One, the injunction to have an identity, the fact of being either this or that. Like Nietzsche's *gaya scienza*, men who follow Metis dance, and are not satisfied with established functions. They are multiple, like everything that lives' (Maffesoli 1984: 157f).

In *Les Fleurs du mal*, Baudelaire speaks of a 'Satan Trismégiste' who, we can assume, inspires a demonic wisdom that is eminently capable of explaining the nocturnal dimension of existence and all the 'residues' that so stubbornly resist asepsis and attempts to restore order. Libertarian thought shares that wisdom. The way of the world is also the way of the spirit. That is the justification for intellectual nomadism. Spiritual errantry requires a spirit of adventure that can sometimes make us look like traitors or opportunists. To those who believe in nothing, who have no loyalties to anything because they are merely passing through and because everything passes, everything else (discoveries, 'invention', a career) is an unexpected bonus. And that, amusingly enough, will always outrage the intellectual bureaucrats. If we emerge from this career both disillusioned and serene, we will at least have learned the lesson that illusions (or complacent conformism) are the only things to be ashamed of. As the Ancients knew: *turpe est illudi*.

# 1
# *The Fascination of Positivism*

I may have doubts, but not about the facts themselves. I do have doubts about the extreme degree of trust that is placed in them.

Theodor Fontane, *Der Stechlin*

## 1 Positivism in its environment

Strictly speaking, positivism is, perhaps, a myth. In the sociological world that concerns us here, reference is made to it and it is challenged unhesitatingly, sometimes without qualification. Perhaps this is inevitable. Having presided over the birth of our discipline, it stands there like the Commander's statue, offering comfort to the faithful and denouncing those who stray from the straight and narrow. A foundation myth brings a community together and gives it what Durkheim calls 'a feeling of itself', but at the same time it generates interpretations and quarrels, and it is that which encourages heresy.

Whatever its true nature, and whatever self-image it attempts to project, sociological positivism is protean. Like any mythological form, it has its doublets, exists in multiple versions and teaches multiple lessons. Ironically enough, its fragmentation can be seen as an index of the slow, stubborn work of life which, even within a reductive interpretation, brings about the resurgence of a causal pluralism.

I therefore have no intention of providing a new definition of positivist sociology here – many other studies do so in exemplary fashion. If we regard it as a mythical referent for anyone who wants to do scientific work, it is more relevant to demonstrate that our discipline must go beyond it in many different ways, and that it has a lot to gain by doing so. It is possible to show, tangentially, that the social given can also be interpreted by means of an endless movement that leads, as we have already said, from nominalism to empathy, from objectification to participation, from cold analysis to warm interpretation. It seems to me that such an approach allows us to avoid both dogmatic rigidity, or the critical pretensions of the 'should-be' (in any realm), and 'metasociology', which is primarily Parisocentric and whose circumference or extension is nowhere to be found. Besides, it is by no means certain that this 'metasociology' can escape positivism, even with the aid of structuralism or semiology. In that respect, the intolerance it so often displays is instructive. Once more, I would like to adopt the relativist stance that snaps its fingers at certainties and fashions and which can adopt the words of the disillusioned but *redividus* Mephistopheles: 'Gray . . . is all theorizing, and green, life's golden tree' (Goethe 1808: lines 2028–9).

As a starting point for the process described above, we can agree on, if not a definition, a characterisically positivist intellectual stance. As we are referring to an attitude, we will concentrate on its most banal aspect. Although it is familiar, this aspect is often masked or misread, and yet it does profoundly influence the most lively analyses and the most sophisticated research.

On numerous occasions, Durkheim stresses that 'social facts are objective' (see in particular Durkheim 1895, ch. 2). In his view, that proposition is, it should be recalled, 'the fundamental principle of the sociological method' (Durkheim 1897: 310). That he should adopt this position is not surprising; it is consistent with his general perspective, which attempts to subordinate every element of nature and society to reason. In that respect, Durkheim's approach is quite logical; given that its task is the specific exploration of a *terra incognita*, sociology must obey the guiding principles of the Science of the day. Social facts can be measured. Their power and magnitude can be measured, as is 'done with sources of light and electric current' (Durkheim 1897: 310). Durkheim's celebrated proposition has often been the object of pertinent and rigorous criticisms. But not enough emphasis has been placed on the fact that it is an expression of the fantastic synergy of the Promethean vision which, from the nineteenth century onwards, gave every individual science a specific role in the investigation of the *system of realities*. In that sense, Durkheim, Comte and Marx all subscribe to the same epistemology, and it is not surprising that their distant descendants, who appear to be divided over their ideological options, in fact have a great deal in common when it comes to defending the same cultural values.

Without taking our critique of the equation of social facts with objectivity any further, we will simply point out its historical inscription. Every period has its own system for investigating and interpreting the social and natural environment, and it is always difficult to escape the dominant tendency. For the great taxonomic movement inaugurated by the philosophy of the Enlightenment, it was, for instance, only natural that the science of societies should strive to identify the same 'necessary laws' that had been shown to govern natural phenomena. The disenchantment that had emptied the forests and the countryside was now making transparent the obscurities and mysteries of life in society. Hence the 'necessity of resorting to the laborious methods of the natural sciences to gradually scatter the darkness' (Durkheim 1912: 27) that still surrounded social realities. For the triumphal march of Progress that characterizes the late nineteenth century, the rational and the quantitative were and had to be the motors behind life in society.

The prize was a perfect society. Society would no longer be based upon a religious or imaginary fantasy, but would be grounded in reason. The millenarian utopia in fact remains the same, but the key idea on which it is based is displaced. Numbers and the reflections they inspired played an important role in ancient Greece, and in both Gnostic and then Kabbalistic thought. The development of the natural sciences gave them a similar role. As one protagonist in this epic put it, mathematical equations could provide soaring bridges between the various elements of nature and society. The laws of nature could be understood by the human mind, and the methods that were applied in order to identify them would – must – provide a model for what was then called the moral life. The human sciences were fascinated by the development of the 'hard' sciences. Transferring the observable successes of physics and chemistry into the realm of human thought was a matter of urgency. Bouglé speaks (1904: 712) in this connection of a 'temptation', and sociology was only too eager to succumb to it.

We therefore have to explain, if only briefly, the attraction the natural sciences had for the emerging discipline of sociology. What is more, we know that, in order to exist, sociology had to differentiate itself from philosophical thought or metaphysical speculation. Looking at life in society *more geometrico* was certainly a noble ambition and it is quite understandable that this ambition should have inspired legitimate enthusiasms. The transformation of the laws of physiology into social laws demanded by Sainte-Beuve was a project which would draw many thinkers into a new-style crusade that reached its apotheosis at the end of the nineteenth century.

But what seems legitimate in the climate of a given period becomes suspect when attempts are made to make it an experimental *sine qua non* or an essential reference for the intellectual world as such. This is one example of the widespread attitude, whose effects on sociology are well known, that turns a local truth into a universal truth which has no boundaries in either time or space. In their day and in their own way, both philosophy and theology were both eternal modes of thought. Every society has to modernize its specific discourse, and it does so by flying in the face of a dominant ideology,[1] or an institutionalized body of thought. The imperialism of positivism was all the more deep-rooted in that it seemed that nothing would be allowed to escape it. It was part of the 'bourgeoisism' which, with the help of science and technology, was to channel and control the whole of social existence. Everything was subject to reason; everything had to give a rational account of itself. In that respect, the work of Michel Foucault is a remarkable demonstration that there is a close connection between the injunction to know and social control. In terms of our own concerns, we should note that this universal and perennial 'will to know' can affect sexuality itself. As Foucault's book on the subject (Foucault 1976) is sufficiently eloquent on that subject, we need only note in paroxysmal fashion that it is obvious that nothing escapes the will to truth.

No ambiguities are permitted, no equivocations; sexuality itself is called in for questioning. It is important to use psychoanalysis to eliminate even 'the obscure instant' (Bloch) that constitutes each of us. In that sense, 'telling the truth about sex' can be seen as the essence of positivism: nothing must escape it. This is not a trivial matter. It pertinently underlines the full extent and depth of the mathematization of the human mystery; it is a clear demonstration of how to give a new meaning to qualitative research. Carried away by its own logic, positivism forgets just how much it owes to experience. Now, if there is one sector in which experience cannot be ignored, it is human existence. Every generation and all individuals rely upon their own experience to understand, largely by trial and error and with the help of others, what they are living through. Social erotics implies a collective aesthetic, a sensation and an experimentation that largely escapes absolute knowledge.

The above comment on erotic experience is verifiable for other aspects of life in society and of life in general. And it is fortunate that contemporary developments in the 'hard' sciences mean that we have to be more modest. It is also amusing to note that our human scientists are once more behind the times. Whilst they cling to a one-dimensional model of the sciences, physicists, astrophysicists, mathematicians and logicians seem to be adopting a much more relativistic approach and appear to be much less self-confident. The nineteenth-century obsession with the hard sciences has become an obsession that prevents the analysis from integrating parameters that go beyond the classic rationalist model. And, if there is one domain in which it is a mistake to reduce knowledge to science, it is surely that of social existence. To borrow an image from computing, social existence supplies a mass of 'soft' data, and it is both impossible and pointless to quantify it. The open-minded Lussato, who teaches information technology at the Conservatoire National des Arts et Métiers with great competence has, for instance, no qualms about stating (Lussato 1981: 148) that 'if we attempt to formalize life, we will probably see only shadows and noise'. His book is living proof that, whilst neophytes become obsessed with the very things they fail to understand, a lucid specialist can easily see the limitations of formalization and quantification, even at their most sophisticated.

Social existence contains a surplus. Pareto called it a 'residue', and it can and must be taken into account without necessarily going through the Caudine Forks of positivist rigour. We simply have to recognize that, if they are to be expressed, the lability, mobility and imperfection of societal dynamics mean that we must have instruments which are themselves supple and flexible. A proposition of this kind is naturally not intended to be hegemonic, and it cannot be hegemonic; it simply implies a rejection of the all too frequent reduction of knowledge to science. It stresses the fact that sociology *also* deals with passion, the non-logical and the imaginary, which also structure the human activity of which we are either the actors or the observers (see Maffesoli 1982). This is not an empty *petitio principii*. As the contemporary techno-structure was established, sociologists gradually adapted their discourse to the dominant utilitarian practice so as not to be out of step with history. And thanks to a curious mimetism, those who claimed to be keeping their critical distance began to model their critiques on the very ideology against which they were struggling. As the etymology of the term indicates, their contestation (*con-testare*) remained with the positivist field they wanted to subvert.

The problem merits attention. The fact that in many ways our *fin de siècle* shows that a certain theoretical practice has become saturated should encourage us to be be audacious enough to look for an alternative and more adequate approach to everyday life. It is important to recognize that positivist science is merely one modality of knowledge. As Habermas (1968) notes, a scientism based upon the hegemonic ambitions of the nineteenth century is ill-equipped to grasp the multiple 'communicational activity' that now swarms everywhere. There is no notable difference between scientism and the functionalism of the techno-structure: they reinforce one another. And whilst it may once have been true that most intellectuals regarded their development as inevitable, either so as to legitimize them or criticize them, that is no longer the case. Many intellectuals in all disciplines are now reverting to the relativism that allowed some of their number (Simmel) to grasp the casualness of social existence.

At the risk of appearing to repeat myself, I have no hesitations about stressing in various ways the immense sociological import-ance of the idea of contradiction. Hegel, who is, either explicitly or implicitly, the reference point for all the systems that came after him, was lucid enough to make contradiction the basis of his analysis. With the help of the dialectic, he did, however, find a synthetic resolution. In doing so, he legitimized the building of the perfect societies that religion had been wise enough to project into the beyond. The relativism we are talking about here recognizes, for its part, that contradiction is a constituent element in being and that it therefore cannot be transcended (cf. Durand or Beigbeder). There is such a thing as a contradictory logic, and it comes into conflict with the principle or logic of identity. And the reappear-ance of archaic values like territory, ecology, regionalism and hedonism is in that respect instructive. All the things that positiv-ism hoped to erase, smooth away or make one-dimensional are returning in force, as though to point out, in relatively trivial ways, that there is no such thing as absolute knowledge. Just as we are obliged to come to terms with alterity or death, so we have to accept that both the statics and the dynamics of societies are contradictory.

Defined in its broadest sense, the study of war is simply a reminder that, just as we have a plurality of divine figures, we also have a conflict of values. It is pointless to deny it. The contradiction at work in any given conflict in fact creates a balance of tension. And just as matter is made up of the tension between its various elements, so the 'being together' that sociology takes as its object results from the attraction/repulsion the members of the social body exert over one another. It is worth recalling these banalities because, in the context of a discussion of epistemology, they are a reminder of the futility of the all-seeing and domineering positivism that attempts to reduce socio-economic forms to the concepts it manipulates. The heterogeneity of the world denies us absolute knowledge. With his usual caution and intellectual sophistication, Adorno (1966: 10) said that 'The cognitive utopia would be to use concepts to unseal the non-conceptual with concepts, without making it their equal.' The intention is a noble one, and we know that Adorno pursued it modestly and circumspectly. The fact remains, however, that the production of concepts often results in the absolute knowledge which, for my own part, I regard as one of the harbingers of totalitarianism. Once it believes it has found the key that explains existence – be it the existence of race, history, a subject of history or happiness – absolute knowledge, with greater or lesser sophistication, grounds political tyranny in reason.

The concept of a particular object is One, or at least combines with other neighbouring concepts to form a unity. It determines the truth and what the truth must be. Everything that escapes its grasp is Error, and does not have the right to exist. Such, in schematic terms, is the logic of the 'should be' that characterizes the conceptual attitude. And if we think of the political effects of logical error or non-existence, this is no laughing matter. Throughout human history, forcing the heterogeneity of life to fit in with the unicity of the concept has always had serious consequences. Which is why we would do better to contrast the softness of notions with the rigidity of the concept. The softness of the notion satisfies our desire to know, but at the same time it relativizes the fantasy of power that slumbers in every intellectual. The distinction between scientist and politician that Max Weber held so dear stems directly from the polytheism of values that is at work in any society. It is a structural dichotomy that cautiously institutionalizes contradiction, and puts it on stage for the greater good of all. In epistemological terms the notional attitude takes account of heterogeneity, looks at the same object from different angles and shows that it is both one thing and another. It avoids turning local truths into universal truths. Once we accept the bankruptcy or at least the relativization of Promethean excess, of which the concept is one modulation, we have to accept the modesty of the notion. That in no sense affects our status as intellectuals. On the contrary, it restores it to its place in the organic score of sociality.

In short, we can say that all the great explanatory systems of the nineteenth century felt a need for legitimation and scientific justification. From Marx to Durkheim, from Comte to Freud, they all, quite understandably, displayed an enthusiasm for the attitude that transcends contradiction through conceptualization. They thus vested new powers in the religious or, rather, fideist matrix which, because of its finalist goals, overlooks the incoherence of the present and the structural imperfection of the world. Tragedy is the most reliable index of contradiction, but they opted for drama, or in other words for something that unfolds with varying degrees of pathos, but which inevitably leads to a solution or resolution. As the activist period draws to an end and as productivism and progressivism run out of steam, it is not surprising that there should be no great popular enthusiam for science. What Sorokin calls the saturation of a cultural value is contagious, and it gradually contaminates everything around it and everything that is bound up with it. There is such a thing as a logic of experience, and it can effectively undermine scientific fideism. Such critiques were once made by marginal figures or prophets – the work of Nietzsche is a case in point – but the lassitude is now universal. We therefore have to accept that throughout history we regularly observe that mobilizing myths collapse at the height of their power and give way to other myths which had, or so it was believed, been definitively defeated. It would seem that the same is true today. The monovalency of a value with a universal destiny is crumbling away and giving way to polytheism. Hard and rigorous conceptuality is giving way to the soft polysemy of notions.

## 2 In praise of pluralism

Without wishing to accept the whole of his analysis, and especially not his remarks about the 'collective body', we can agree with Bernard de Jouvenel when he states (1972: 43) that the human mind 'prefers unity to reality because it is possessive and because it is easier to possess unity than diversity'. It would be pointless to turn this into an absolute statement, but it is clear that the need to possess is an anthropological constant, and that it has a natural counterpart in the representations or discourses that man in society uses to legitimate his 'being-in-the-world'. The process of reification, which has been well analysed by modern and contemporary German philosophy, is a good explanation for this constant. Yet as early as the Middle Ages the ambitions of this fantasy of the conceptualizable One had been spelled out in the famous quarrel over Universals. And for every Abelard who pointed out the schematism of such a vision, there were many supporters of the official line: their only concern was to make the intellectual machine run smoothly.

The Reality of Universals, Reification and the fantasy of the One are simply so many examples of the attitude of mind that tries to see social or natural facts as objects (*Gegenstände*) so as to control their riches and their workings. It has to be stressed that the process of reduction is always utilitarian. The imposition of a theocratic social organization or the justification of the exploitation of nature and society is always the result of reductive thinking. It is indeed easier to use a body of thought based upon a single value than one which brings into play a multiplicity of nuances and which is therefore difficult to use. When Durkheim describes (1928: 148f) the benefits of a 'positive sociology', demonstrates how it fits into the 'circle of the social sciences', notes the difficulties that punctuate this difficult trajectory and states, finally, that positivism has fulfilled humanity's old aspiration towards 'unity of knowledge', he makes it clear that this is a 'productive' operation. From his point of view, this is beneficial because the productive operation fits in perfectly with the triumphal march of socialism, which will finally realize the unified and transparent society that will bring about social happiness.

Unity of knowledge and utilitarianism go hand in hand. But we now have to look beyond this monovalent functionalism and demonstrate the existence of what might playfully be called a *functional plurality*, or in other words a plurality which finds its meaning and end within itself, which does not project itself into hypothetical radiant futures or into the realization of perfect utopian societies or other paradises, lay or religious. When literature and fiction describe creators in any domain, they portray them as being full of contradictions. And these are dynamic contradictions which cannot be overcome, contradictions which in fact guarantee the richness and fertility of the genius in question. In that respect, the character portrayed by Thomas Mann in *Dr Faustus* (1947) is truly exemplary. For Mann, antinomy is a sign of fullness and any attempt to unify being is a threat to the pursuit of either an authentic work of art or an intensely lived life.

We can learn a lot from the paroxysmal side to this fictional figure. Indeed we can, at least hypothetically, generalize and say that the genius of the social body, the tiny creations that make up the fabric of sociality, depend upon this functional plurality. That the normal life of our societies is made up of a multiplicity of situations, intersections, and communicative and instrumental activities, each with its own importance and efficacy, is an experiential fact that no abstract construction can conceal. It is of course possible to hypostatize any one of these elements, and it is possible to propose and impose a hegemony, but it will not stand up to the ravages of time. I have explained elsewhere (Maffesoli 1979b) that the survival of society is definitely the result of an active pluralism which, despite the monovalent justifications of theorizing, provides the foundations for everyday life. The polytheism of values is a veritable storehouse of acts and discourses which, because they relativize one another, ensure a powerful conflictual equilibrium.

Whilst this pluralism does have a future, it also has a noble ancestry. In a way, it was his open and plural vision of society that made Gurvitch's work so original. This is not the place to develop the point at length, but his work, which has had a powerful influence on French sociology, is a constant polemic against all forms of positivist monism (Bossermann 1981). If one does not have a fetish about 'levels' and 'landings', his 'in-depth' sociology represents an attempt to explain the interdependency of every element in the 'total social fact'. When he borrowed that notion from Mauss and updated it, Gurvitch was trying above all to emphasize the complexity of society. Nothing can be excluded from the interpretation. From that point of view, the economy is certainly important, but collective representations, juridical realities, social roles and relations, and everyday life itself are all important elements and they are meaningful only because of the way in which they relate to other elements. This '*Gestalt* sociology' obviously cannot accept any reduction to a single factor which can be described as determinant or overdetermining, and which will therefore give one a schematic vision of society. There is a generosity of spirit to this pluralism that puts it in touch with the pulse of society, which always manages to resist attempts to force it into an intellectual and/or political corset.

We find similar preoccupations in the work of Georges Balandier. In his introduction to Gurvitch, Balandier (1972) demonstrates that the latter's 'support' for pluralism stems from his deep insight into 'the fabric of social life'. In the same text we find references to the notions of equilibrium, integration and participation, which all relate to the organicity in which the various elements of the social whole complete one another, form an architectonic, and both attract and repel one another. In his *Sens et puissance*, Georges Balandier (1971; cf. Balandier 1972) suggests an eloquent formula to specify what is meant by pluralism: 'Society is plurals.' His argument is close to the argument I have been developing: because it was based upon progress, the nineteenth century emphasized continuity; we are now obliged to emphasize all that pertains to 'social discontinuities' (Balandier 1972: 68f; 1971: 46f). Balandier therefore stresses the problem of the heterogeneity that is found in every aspect of social life. Anyone who speaks of 'differential dynamics' or who emphasizes the play of differences that is at work in all human aggregates must inevitably stress the 'approximative' aspect of the theory that tries to account for them. There is a structural link between contradiction, heterogeneity and sociological approximation. Despite all its precautions and attempts to construct a pure object, scientism makes the mistake of forgetting the ambivalence of the specific object known as the social. If we are too reductive, we find ourselves dissecting a dead object, unless we content ourselves with looking at social life from such a height that we fail to see anything of its concrete nature. Certain of our contemporaries fall into this trap in their attempts to define, or even regulate, 'the profession of sociology', but one of the dangers of the intellectual life is that one can become divorced from the existential dynamic and apply one's understanding and knowledge to purpose-built objects. This is what Guy Debord called 'intelligence looking for work'. That some should succumb to it is only to be expected. Just like children who have been left to their own devices in their bedrooms, they play with their toys in certain academic establishments and thereby add to the contempt in which the backward students known as intellectuals are, not without reason, held by the general public.

Yet whilst there is a danger, it is far from being inevitable. And it seems to me that modesty in the face of pluralism is an effective defence. The idea needs to be developed in more detail, but for the moment it is enough to point out that whilst the cognitive utopia does exist, and whilst it is legitimate, it must not be forgotten that, although knowledge claims to be exhaustive, it comes up against the harsh reality of the complexity of the social world, which always slips through our fingers just when we think we have finally grasped it. It is certainly not the principle of identity that constitutes the structuration of individuals or collectivities; it is contradiction or alterity. It is therefore pointless to attempt to formalize or quantify the situations, social relations or multiple activities that bring alterity into play. If it were possible to measure it, and if it were possible to master the dynamics of change, we would see constant progress in our mode of being or in the quality of life. Now, whilst it may be possible to see progress in scientific and technological developments, their multiple applications in everyday life do not seem to have brought about any greater fullness. Talk of the 'good old days' is pointless; we have to accept that our individual and collective lives are always ambivalent. They are a mixture of intensity and banality, excitement and boredom, adventure and monotony, happiness and unhappiness.

If it were possible to understand the laws of social development in quantitative terms, we would no doubt be able to improve things. Yet, whilst things may not be getting worse, there has been no qualitative improvement in our lives. They simply pose the eternal problems with which we are confronted in new terms. This eminently trivial scepticism is the best way to relativize the insane hopes of Marx, Comte or Durkheim, to mention only the social reformers. Has scientific progress allowed us to reform death? It seems not. The same could be said of contradiction and alterity, which are the minor forms of death that we experience every day. It may seem banal to say so, but this is the stumbling block that frustrates all positivist triumphalism. The popular scepticism that finds a variety of different expressions – and which we are all too quick to describe pejoratively as 'common sense', 'good sense' or 'false consciousness' – must be taken into account when we look at societies. If we take these precautions, our 'sociological facts' will not be too far removed from the 'social facts'.

It was clearly with this problem in mind that sociologists like Weber and Pareto tried to explore what has been termed 'causal pluralism' (cf. Freund 1978: 223f). Having weighed the implications of the polytheism of values whose workings are to be observed in social life, and having noted the 'interdependence of social facts' (Pareto), these authors, who deserve to be better known in France, attempted to combine intellectual rigour and attention to the lability of events, and showed that a single social fact can have multiple causes. Even though they were influenced by the positivist climate of the day, these sociologists did not, fortunately, forget the aesthetic, the religious, the non-logical, passion or the imaginary; all this was included, together with supposedly more rational forms, in the interpretation of all social phenomena (cf. Maffesoli 1981a). The *'hiatus irrationalis'*, to borrow an expression from Max Weber, is present in every social form, and if we wish to take lucid account of it, we must be able to integrate as many parameters as possible into our analysis, even if some of them do at first sight appear to be useless or superfluous.

The following quotation from Weber's admirable essay on '"Objectivity" in Social Science and Social Policy' (Weber 1904: 78–9) provides a good description of this 'causal pluralism':

> An exhaustive causal investigation of any concrete phenomenon in its full reality is not only practically impossible – it is simply nonsense. We select only those causes to which are to be imputed, in the individual event, the essential feature of an event. Where the *individuality* of a phenomenon is concerned, the question of causality is not a question of *laws* but of concrete causal *relationships*; it is not a question of the subsumption of the event under some general rubric as a representative case but of its imputation as a consequence of some constellation.

One could not hope for a better, or at least clearer, definition. Quite apart from the fact that it is an index of a certain intellectual scepticism, the reference to causal connections is a good explanation of the complex architectonic of passions and situations that typifies the social. When a phenomenon can be reduced, either directly or in the last instance, to a single explanation, a rationally grounded political tyranny is not far away. When intellectuals attempt to determine unambiguous situations, they may well be displaying great naivety, but their naivety often has unfortunate consequences. Fortunately, and as recent history proves to us, in political philosophy a succesion of contradictory positions and analyses can be adopted without being too concerned about coherence. Successive loyalties. This is an admirable ruse (perhaps on the part of reason?) which reintroduces into political practice the pluralism that the intellectual rejects at the theoretical level when he elaborates the conceptual system that provides the only explanation for a given social phenomenon.

Pluralism relativizes, and it is adequate proof that nothing is more fragile than the mechanism of rationalization or justification. Despite its universalizing claims, it has to be recognized that reason is remarkably unstable. Ever since the seventeenth century, moralists have often stressed that it is subject to historical and geographical variations and fluctuations. And political life provides more than adequate proof that constraints also change, even though they are always rationally justified. What we call reason is in fact often an attempt to justify and reduce active passions. I have attempted elsewhere (Maffesóli 1979a) to demonstrate how much we can learn about this from the revolutionary process over the last two hundred years.

This is simply another way of saying that the sociologist must pay attention to both the univocity of reason and the polysemy of gestures, or to what information technologists would call the soft data of lived experience. Everyday life is always full of possibilities, and is never univocal. This creates a further difficulty for an interpretative sociology: how can we use terms which, no matter how we try to qualify them, are always cold, to express the warm current of existence? Schematism or a pre-established interpretative grid may well be able to describe the monumentality of great social and economic forms. The same cannot be said of the bits and pieces, the tiny breaks and the minor creations that make up our daily lives. Like threads that are woven to make a piece of cloth, they form the greater part of the societal fabric, but they are difficult to grasp and analyse. We know, however, that political revolutions are announced, prepared and made by apparently minor events. And minor events certainly play a major role in such manifestations of sociality as basic solidarity and the theatricalization or organicity of passions, gestures and discourses.

It is therefore pointless, or quite illogical, not to take into account what has been termed the *hiatus irrationalis*, contradictions and the heterogeneous, and pluralism is certainly their most complete methodological expression. If we agree that, as I have tried to say, sociology is the ideology of our era, it is essential for it to talk about its every aspect openly and generously, and to recognize what exists before it pronounces on 'what must be'. In his incisive critique of psychoanalysis, James Hillman (1972) demonstrates the gradual appearance of a dichotomy between scientific language and the objects it attempts to describe. He shows how the abstract images and metaphors used by scientific language gradually destroy its ability to explain the density of existence, and how the darker side of the individual soon needs only to be described as such for it to become pathological: a clinical object which has no specific efficacy. A similar critique could pertinently be applied to the social sciences, and to sociology in particular. Sociology must be able to account for the present and events without becoming trapped into a purely quantitative vision, but it cannot do so in the same way as the literary novel or poetry. It must be able to show how gestures, walking, cooking, sexual peccadilloes and amorous passion, fashion and cosmetics all combine to make up our specific field. Mythology was perfectly capable of expressing this in its own form; we have to learn to do the same. The work of certain contemporary sociologists – I am thinking here of Durand, Balandier, Morin, Duvignaud and Baudrillard, though the list is far from exhaustive – have shown the way. They have made a *de facto* break with the dominant positivism and with the quantitative fantasy that was once the 'sign' – in the strict sense of the word – of scientificity. We have to continue in that direction and, as I noted earlier with reference to Gnosticism, we should emphasize the magical or symbolic aspect of numbers, if only to relativize it. If we can do that, we can go beyond a purely quantitative vision or, to borrow a phrase from Sorokin, a 'quantophrenic' vision of the social world, and at the same time admit that it does have the power to fascinate.

Such an exercise in relativization would allow quantity and quality to complement one another, albeit in a conflictual way. A similar complementarity could in fact be seen in the work of Durkheim, until such time as his epigones took it upon themselves, as they so often do, to establish irreducible dichotomies. If we ignore his positivist convictions or methodological pronouncements, his *Suicide* is in that respect exemplary, and it is the subtle combination of the quantitative and the qualitative that makes it a standard work. The same is true of the *Elementary Forms of the Religious Life*, which interweaves elements typical of, respectively, the religious life and socio-economic analysis. I am not suggesting that we take them as models, or even that we analyse Durkheim's work in detail, as to do so would require a separate study. I am simply pointing out, purely for further research, that the founder of the French school could be more subtle than we think. Culture, like the return of the repressed, leads to the reappearance of elements that have been overlooked by his intellectual heirs. His insistence on constantly 'connecting ... the reason to the senses, or the mind to matter' (Durkheim 1912: 447) is another way of expressing the interconnections I have just described. Intellectual honesty, or quite simply open-mindedness, requires us to recognize, without begging the question, that a great deal of passion is at work in the life of societies, and this means that we must corect over-rigid laws by referring to facts, events, and the factual. In that sense, 'situationism' is a good antidote to the totalitarianism of theory.

In the realm of the political, as in the realm of thought, the law is the prerogative of those who believe they can change the world, and improve both morals and men. A long line of thinkers from Pelagius to Marx has always believed that the scientific rectitude of their theories and their 'correct lines' of action would influence the evolution of the world. It would be interesting to analyse positivism as a *pelagianismus redivivus*, and to see it as a modulation of the intellectual optimism that typifies Promethean ideology.[2] It takes a very different intellectual temperament to look at the facts, to attempt to relativize the great systems that try to explain the social given, and to note the connections and interconnections that exist between all the elements that go to make up any one social phenomenon. To put it metaphorically, we can say that initial causes and final causes are merely modulations of the same deistic principle: the fantasy of the One, of which monotheism is the classic expression. Causal pluralism, which certainly negates causalism (the various causes neutralize one another), derives, in contrast, from pagan pantheism, from a polytheism of values which in fact denies the existence of the gods. To go back to the activism/ theoreticism dichotomy we were discussing earlier, we find ourselves dealing with a mild Dionysianism which argues that there is nothing new under the sun. It is a tragic sense of existence, and above all it is common amongst the people. Men of culture, bourgeois activists, politicians and public servants are always *believers*. No matter which paradise they dream of, they put their faith in the perfectibility of man and society. A man of the people may well have his illusions, and he may well act them out and play with them, but he is still an unbeliever at heart. He is a religious infidel, or in other words a political infidel.

This digression is simply intended to demonstrate that it is in sociology's interests to look at this disorganized and pagan social life. Concepts unify, simplify and reduce; life explodes, and bursts all the fetters that we try to put on it. Hence, perhaps, the importance of *notions* which, as I have already suggested, express an intellectual desire and concern which neither ignores nor constrains social life; it merely traces dotted lines between things that are already in fragments.

## 3 The obscure instant

One of the tasks of a qualitative sociology might well be to protect the singularity of acts and situations from the steamroller of positivism. There are obviously classical techniques and instruments for doing that, but they may have to be forced to express their full potential. In a sense, we must therefore go back to the method that moves from explanation to interpretation. Without wishing to rule out explanation, we must resolutely think through the notion of interpretation. Commentators on Weber (Aron, Freund) have of course tried to do so but, as I have just said, interpretation's full potential has, perhaps, not been fully explored. The development of 'life stories' (D. Bertaux, C. Lalive d'Epinay, E. Lazega and *Cahiers internationaux de sociologie*, 69 (1980), is one indication, and the multifaceted interest in everyday life (M. de Certeau, C. Javeau, H. Lefebvre, P. Lucas, M. Maffesoli, J. Rémy etc.) is also highly instructive. At all events, discourse *on* the social must, as a matter of urgency, listen closely to the discourse *of* the social, even if its incoherence does shock rigorous minds shaped by the rationalism of the Enlightenment. Excessive rigour takes us too far away from the real, and Leibniz's warning has a contemporary meaning for the sociologist: *cave a consequentiariis*. Do not trust those who are too logical; they will blind you to the lability of things and to their chaotic aspect.

'Interpretation', on the other hand, implies a certain sympathy towards existential pluralism, and I have already spoken in this connection of the empathy that brings us into contact with social events. It is not a question of justifying everything or excusing everything. That is not our role. Our convictions may lead us to condemn, but our generosity of mind must accept everything. In order to do so, we have to remember that the principle of identity, the *principium individuationis* around which a certain logic and therefore a certain ethics or politics pivots, has become saturated. Ambivalence is no longer merely something that has to be recognized within the ego; we have to accept that it also has its effects on the collective body as such. Once we recognize that, the underlying correspondence that exists within culture and nature, basic solidarity, conflictual harmony, or in a word what we call sociality, will begin to become perceptible on a large scale within sociological discourse. Sociological discourse will no longer be content to be a more or less rebellious ally of the contemporary techno-structure; it will be the mythology of a period, the plural representation that a community always needs to strengthen its sense of itself.

If it is to explain the coincidence or coexistence of opposites that structures the given world, 'science', as conceived by positivism, must, in a word, adopt certain parameters which it overlooked or ignored in the ardour and schematism of its youth. Life and its fertility cannot be constrained by reductive mechanisms and injunctions about identity. We must reformulate and widen the alliance that exists between 'thought and movement' to cite the title of an essay by Bergson (Bergson 1955). Some will inevitably see this line of thought as inconsequential and irresponsible verbiage. My answer to them is that we do not have to be intellectual bureaucrats who think orderly thoughts to order. Indeed, I believe I have demonstrated that a sense of order is the one thing that will alienate us from our object of study. There are professionals who are paid to be responsible and logical. There are famous schools that train them, and they are very well known to be very good at it. We would do better to gamble on marginality, as that is the quickest way to the centre. The shrewdest public figures and industrialists often have a very good idea of how to turn things to their own advantage. As Adorno remarks (1951: 81), 'Every thought which is not idle ... bears branded on it the impossibility of its full legitimation.' The lesson is worth learning. It comes from an intellectual who spent his entire life thinking about the conflict between critical rationalism and social evolution. It seems to me that such an attitude, which makes no claims to being the conscience of an era or a mentor to this or that social stratum, will allow us to avoid the twin dangers that lie in wait for any intellectual: the obsession with rigour that characterizes the positivist *'plenum'*, and paranoia, which all too often characterizes the vacuousness of intellectual fashions.

Sociology is a form of thought that means nothing to our declining productivism and it is of little practical use, but it can help us to grasp the dynamic of cultural values. No matter whether they are macroscopic or minuscule, it is essential to understand both their invariance and their modulations, and it appears to me that we can understand, or at least approach, *the multiplicity of the games* (economic, political, cultural, administrative, quotidian) that make up the greater part of the social fabric. We will then be in a position to interpret a whole series of social situations without destroying the mystery that surrounds them. The intellectual is part of the organicity of people and things because he naturally wants to explain daily life in his own way. His contribution, together with other modes of verbalization or other gestural expressions, can be of real importance, if it becomes part of the great impressionist self-portrait that is painted by every era. This is obviously far removed from the universalizing vision of an all-conquering positivism. Unlike the vision from on high which thinks it can take in everything, the interpretative sociology that is being outlined here is part of what I call the immanent transcendence that is secreted by the body social itself.

Our task is to ask questions which are so obvious that they have been forgotten. The texture of the world is complex, and the text that describes it must not be irreproachably perfect; it simply updates the myths that allow us to live in society as best we can. If sociology is the ideology of our era, it must participate in and partake of the mystery of existence. It should be recalled that, according to the ancient tradition, a mystery is something that binds initiates to one another. If he recalls that, the sociologist who deals with the problems of sociality can indeed become, as Mallarmé puts it, 'a seeker after a mystery which he knows does not exist, and which he therefore pursues beyond his lucid despair, for it might have been the truth.'

# 2

# *The Experience of Relativism*

Seeking means: to have a goal; but finding means to be free,
to be receptive, to have no goal.

Hermann Hesse, *Siddharta*

## 1   The plurality of reasons

We can now develop the argument that founds sociological relativism and at the same time stress the fact that it is by no means an abdication of intellectual responsibility, but an approach that allows a better understanding of the richness of the social experience. Let me put it metaphorically. I am thinking of a text by Eddington which describes the complicated business of entering a room through a door: 'First of all, I have to fight against the atmosphere, which exerts a 1 kg force on every square centimetre of my body. I then have to try to land on a plank which is revolving around the sun at a speed of 30 km per second; if I wait for a fraction of a second, the plank is thousands of kilometres away . . . What is more, the plank is not solid. Landing on it is like trying to stand on a swarm of flies . . . It's true. It is easier for a camel to pass through the eye of a needle than for a physicist to cross his own threshold' (cited, Benjamin 1966: 761). The parable is a good illustration of the impossibility of living by scientific preoccupations or representations alone. At every moment of our existence, we have to use the power of forgetting simply in order to exist. All comparisons are of course misleading, but it is often helpful to demonstrate the weakness of a rational argument by taking it to extremes. This is of course a commonplace experience, but it is useful to recall it when we are attempting to study the epistemology of sociology.

We could also cite texts by Durkheim which contradict his usual positivist triumphalism. I obviously have ulterior motives for citing these texts. The point is not so much to make excessive demands of him as to demonstrate, as I have already said and as I will later argue again, that Durkheim is less self-confident than he seems to be, which is something his epigones and disciples appear to overlook. It is in fact striking to note that all his great books contain caveats, reservations, qualifications or simply *lapsi calami* which clearly demonstrate that it is impossible to elaborate one universal theory that can explain and/or change the world. This is obvious in *The Elementary Forms of the Religious Life*, but the same point is made in texts dealing more specifically with the contemporary world. *The Division of Labour*, for instance, expands (Durkheim 1893: 300) on the theme: 'Any general proposition lets slip from its grasp a part of the subject-matter that it is attempting to master.'

It is the increasing number of 'special sciences', and the multiple laws, methods and techniques they generate, that leads Durkheim to this conclusion. The positivist ideal of arriving at a single vision or a unitary science proves once more to be a structural impossibility precisely because all social situations are grounded in the concrete, or in other words in difference. The situations and forms that structure any society can, of course, be classified, but the taxonomy is always abstract. And the aporia that the sociologist comes up against is that 'there is too great a gap' between his syntheses and his 'detailed research' (Durkheim 1893: 300).

We have, perhaps, not paid enough attention to a distance specific to our discipline, which takes as its object the nature and the impact of the collective feelings that shape any social aggregate. Durkheim expressess similar doubts at several points in his Latin thesis. The syntax of Latin may lend itself better to doubt, as his formulations are less abrupt and often come close to scepticism. This is all the more remarkable in that it is the constitution of social science that is at stake. One comment is particularly symptomatic. The author notes that 'the subtlety of things' is incommensurable with the 'subtlety of the human mind': 'We are not claiming that social phenomena as such are illogical. But though they may have a *certain* fundamental logic, it is *not the logic* to which our deductive reasoning applies. It has not the *same simplicity*. Perhaps it obeys other laws' (Durkheim 1892: 54, emphasis added).[1] One could not hope for a better definition of what I call sociological relativism. In this text, we see the art of ellipsis at its finest. We must not disillusion those who use the concept in their work, but at the same time we have to admit, in restrictive parentheses, that the 'certain' logic of things social is not to be confused with the deductive constructs that make us ascribe an identity to people, things and situations.

To exaggerate a little, we might admit that, whilst the society studied by the sociologist is not 'illogical', it is not reducible to one truth, or that we are dealing with fragmented truths which are multiple and unstable, and which elude the grasp of an over-reductive approach. The principle of identity of the supporters of the Enlightenment and the Revolution of 1789, together with the objective principle of identity of the nineteenth-century socialists and reformers and then of the founding fathers of sociology, become uncertain, inadequate or quite archaic when we abandon conceptual overviews and when we are confronted with the insignificance – in the strong sense of the word – of everyday life. To go back to Durkheim's reservations, one wonders – bearing in mind the way he establishes it – if he did not intuitively realize that this principle is inadequate, or even that it could have deadly effects. In his classic work on suicide (1897: 280) Durkheim says of Hartmann's analysis of the development of consciousness and the wakening of the will to live that: 'ideation and movement are really two hostile forces, advancing in inverse directions . . . This is why the absolute reign of the idea cannot be achieved, and especially cannot continue; for this is death.' This brings us back to Eddington's parable; ultimately, thinking prevents me from moving.

Once again, a paroxysmal exaggeration reveals how the imperialism of theory comes up against the stumbling block of the incoherence, or at least the unevenness, of social existence, and how its turmoil frustrates all attempts at reductionism. The logic of the conceptual method is such that it can only work with bodies that are already dead. Taxonomic dissection, discrimination and analysis require the relaxation and immobility of which death is the ultimate expression. These are of course extreme examples which never exist as such, but it is interesting to note that Durkheim does provide us with the means to go beyond the absolutism of theoretical overviews. The point is certainly worth stressing, as it has to be said that intellectuals, even intellectuals who pride themselves on being free thinkers, are very often clerics who project their nostalgia for religion or their desire for a totality on to 'the work of the concept'. Belief is deep-rooted and it always finds an outlet, either in the plenitude of positivism or in the void of catastrophism. And for the benefit of those who do not find comparisons offensive, I would point out that in our religious tradition institutional Thomism and marginal negative theology are there to remind us that the spectrum of fideist attitudes can be very broad.

It should not be forgotten that according to Greek wisdom – and it is difficult to improve upon it – the interest of intellectual or spiritual research lies less in the content or the answers one expects to find than in the way the questions are asked. *Kalos aporuesthai*: posing the problem in beautiful terms. We have here a balanced mode of thought in which mind and sensation remain in intimate contact, in which the aesthetic and the intellectual are not contrasted. What matters is not the elaboration of an overall truth, but the articulation of truths that are 'local' in every sense of the word and that allow us to situate ourselves in the present.

It is clear that a parallel can be established between Durkheim's unspoken relativism, the overt relativism that we regularly find in the ancient world, and the variability of theory and dogma that has been stressed so often. From Pascal to Voltaire and Rousseau, it has often been noted that religious, political, moral, economic and aesthetic systems of reference are historically and geographically contradictory; the insight can be either a cause for scandal or a reason to rejoice in the name of other values. It has also been noted that, even in given periods and places, systems of reference alternate between two extremes. To be more specific and to adopt an epistemological point of view, empiricism gives way to rationalism, and idealism to materialism. Picking up one of Gilbert Durand's insights, I have demonstrated elsewhere (Maffesoli 1982) that the same is true of the great cultural values that mark any given civilizational space. We can, for instance, observe the great Promethean values giving way to their Dionysian opposites, and vice versa. The sociologist Sorokin speaks in this connection of the mechanism of saturation. These observations, and ultimately they are banal, should inspire us to be more modest or, given that modesty is never easy in matters intellectual, more cautious. The diversity and death of civilizations and of their systems of reference invalidate the pretensions of positivism; what is more, scepticism

– and it is pointless to deny its existence – should draw the sociologist's attention to the futility of excessively rigid theories.

Indeed, I take the view that the variability and plurality of organizational systems and social representations are grounded in the fragmented, plural, collective and polyphonic aspect of the social body. Human histories are an eloquent demonstration of the fact that it is impossible to unify, standardize or reduce difference. Sooner or later, either directly and violently or through the indirect use of cunning or passivity, difference always reappears. This is the explanation for the polytheism of values that finds expression in all domains – even in what seem to be the strictest forms of religious monotheism. It would be a mistake to think that intellectual constructs, no matter how brilliant they may be, spring spontaneously from the brains of individuals or groups of individuals. They express, with varying degrees of distortion, specific desires, illusions or social practices. Even the most aberrational constructs, which seem to have no connection with so-called normal existence, do have something to do with the social fabric. The relationship between canonical and popular works, which has still to be studied, would appear to show that creativity and genius are primarily collective. Of course ideologies become institutionalized and sclerotic, and they do lead to totalitarianism, but in the dynamism, fertility and generosity of their founding moment all ideologies are necessarily organic.

It is this process, and we can now agree that it does exist, that explains and justifies the plurality of reasons. A unitary explanatory system can be used to control a dead body, but it is, by the same criterion, impossible to place univocal restraints on the exuberance of social life as it evolves. It may be crudely expressed, but it is in that sense instructive to cite a comment from a spokesman for the Enlightenment. In his 'Reflections on the use and abuse of philosophy in matters of taste', d'Alembert states: 'We usually acquire new knowledge solely in order to dispel some pleasant illusion, and we usually gain enlightenment at the expense of pleasure.' The mechanism of disenchantment that is affecting our various positivisms is a restoration of order, a call to order, and a call for a purge – in the strict sense of that term. All this applies to the social object, but also to the process of cognition, which strives to forget the substratum on which it is built (or to deny its existence). Forgetting the popular genius of which it was born, it remembers only the individual genius (or talent) that produces an *abstract* body of work. D'Alembert's 'pleasant illusion' can be understood here as meaning everything that makes up the richness of normal life. Its richness is a potential threat to the reductive spirit, and it therefore has to be pruned back.

It is impossible to overemphasize the *ludic element* in sociality. It is difficult to integrate it or even to subsume it into a strict finality. If, as Silesius puts it, 'a rose exists without knowing why', the same can be said of the tumultuous present that is actualized in moderation, but also in incoherence, passion and turmoil. The creative imaginary, whose social importance is now beginning to be recognized, abounds in elements which should encourage us to interpret societies in terms of a multiplicity of reasons.

## 2 'Learned ignorance'

The result of all this has always been a methodological scepticism which acknowledges that the given world is ambivalent. There are a number of ways of elucidating its ambiguity. Poetic intuition well captures the plural aspect of truth: 'You are a lamp, you are night ... prisoner, bride' (Char). Because it rejects the rather simplistic imperialism of reductive reason, scepticism introduces nuances, relativizes things and stresses that every situation is structurally polysemic. The key figure in this relativist tradition is the anti-Christian polemicist Celsus, who clearly demonstrates the dangers inherent in a religious monotheism which crushes and flattens the multiple potential of human beings. Celsus stated the problem with great clarity. The object of his scepticism is not any particular article of faith, nor perhaps any truly theological debate; he is primarily concerned with defending the popular, or in other words differentiated and pluralistic, aspect of the religious representations of antiquity. Paganism's rituals, objects of worship and representations are all fragmented. Paganism is the protean expression of the multiple potential of human beings. There is a lot to be learned from the saga of the gods: it gives free rein to every impulse, situation and reason. In that sense it is the paradigm for a rich social turmoil.

A few centuries later, with Nicholas of Cusa and his 'learned ignorance',[2] we find the same relativist distrust of the hegemonic reason that claims to be able to explain the complete otherness of the deity. Leaving aside the theological aspect, the remarkable thing about Nicholas of Cusa is his refusal to allow Alterity to be reduced to a single dimension. Alterity has at various times been crystallized in the form of a god or gods, but even when monotheism predominates, the intellectual stance of a Nicholas of Cusa is a reminder that it is dangerous to claim to know everything about a deity. For the record, it might be pointed out that it is on the basis of that claim that inquisitions are founded and that stakes begin to be erected. The drift into the political realm then beomes obvious, as the possession of positive knowledge of complete otherness, and of the next world, naturally encourages those who possess it to rule this world or at least to give princes competent advice on how to manage it. The same claim has been made in all ages and in all parts of the world, and the outcome has never been a happy one. To take only one example to illustrate the point, it will be recalled that, when Latin America was being colonized, the Jesuits established villages called 'Reductions'. The term was well chosen. In his description of these Jesuit 'Reductions', the sociologist Gilberto Freyre demonstrates (1974; cf. Baeta Neves Flores's (1984) important thesis on the subject) the full extent to which they controlled existence.[3] Everything was put under surveillance, normalized and standardized: politics, education, costume, food, culture, sexual life ... Time and space were of course planned in the image of what the Fathers assumed to be life eternal. Socio-economic life was organized on the basis of their positive theological knowledge. Whilst a host of other examples could be given, and whilst the term 'reduction' is highly significant, it suffices to note that any social organization based upon absolute knowledge will be very restrictive.

Having referred to Nicholas de Cusa's 'learned ignorance', we can now emphasize the need for localized truth and the reality of localized truth. The Universal is contradicted by the existence of a multiplicity of singularities, just as the plurality of representations short-circuits generalized and total knowledge in the real world. That knowledge can exist only in a restrictive form. It is in that sense that political totalitarianism and absolute knowledge are so closely related. If we ignore politics and quarrels between schools, we always find that the relativism of learned ignorance is central to sociality. In its popular form, it obviously does not concern itself with sophisticated arguments, but so-called minor works of literature, collections of rural proverbs and sayings, and banal discussions of everyday life are all reminders of the futility of talk of a Universal Reality and, therefore, of any Knowledge that claims to explain it. The sociologist who overlooks the interplay of difference and alterity at work in existence may be directly 'usable' in social management, but he will therefore be unable to understand anything of the complex organization of people and things. Learned ignorance makes it possible to contrast forms of thought which promote 'being-together' with a utilitarian science which is less interested in existential perambulations than in finality, or in the goal it wants to achieve. It is striking to note that this utilitarian science can be found amongst both our contemporary technocrats and fashionable advertising executives or vulgarizers. In their haste and thanks to their contempt for erudition, they overlook everything about the complexity of human situations that has no direct application, and are concerned only with ideas that 'sell' well, or with the normalization of supposedly eminently rational socio-economic practices.

Appearances to the contrary notwithstanding, the technocratic secular arm and its spiritual equivalent are no more in touch with social reality than intellectual abstractions. If we ignore their specific jargon, their point of view is that of the absolute, be it absolute reason or an absolute moral ideal. Socio-economic life is not analysed as such, or for what it is, but in terms of *what it should be*. Whether they intend to do so or not, they therefore establish or encourage the techno-bureaucratic tyranny whose soft totalitarianism will represent a major threat for decades to come.

Modes of thought which are not primarily concerned with a goal, which do not have a pre-established finality, and whose primary concern is to stimulate thinking rather than to have a purpose may well be irresponsible and may perhaps be no more than a manifestation of popular wastefulness. They do not try to manage, reform or revolutionize social life; they attempt to give a jerky and incomplete description of social life as it takes place, with all its meanderings and halts. In short, they are fully involved in a journey which is anything but predictable, which is lived from one day to the next, and which is intense precisely because it is precarious. Because it does not determine any 'should-be', such an intellectual attitude lets the multiple potential of sociality 'go' or 'lets it be', but it can also explain it whilst taking part in it in its own way. It integrates itself into the polyphony of social discourse without trying to orientate it or give it a meaning.

For my part, it seems to me that sociological notions like 'form' (Simmel), 'ideal types' (Weber) and 'residues' (Pareto) are all expressions of this attitude. These authors are aware of the plurality of values that is at work in social structuration, and do not try to construct 'reductions' or elaborate systems which rule out contradictions. And they are therefore fully aware of the ambiguity or equivocity that we always find in the life of a society. The various problems that sociology deals with are not subsumed into an explanatory system or into an analytic grid which allows nothing to escape. On the contrary, the various residues analysed by Pareto are left to develop as the tensions between them allow them to develop. Every situation and every social form is, in varying degrees, a composite of heterogeneous but articulated elements.

Admitting that this is a *de facto* state of affairs is not a dereliction of intellectual duty; on the contrary, it is a way of coming to terms with the 'dynamic logic of contradictories',[4] which constitutes culture's micro-creations and great achievements alike. This is the spirit of learned ignorance, the polytheistic spirit which refuses to introduce clear-cut divisions into the turmoil of social life. This is the tragic spirit which feels it does not have the right to reduce the structural aporia of the world. Taxonomy, perfect order and dissection are no longer regarded as essential categorical imperatives for any science worthy of the name. Because it takes the view that many of the spirit's manifestations are aberrational, that the ludic has its place in even the most supposedly serious actions, and that madness has its role in the social organizations and works that punctuate human histories, learned ignorance is lucid enough and perhaps realistic enough simply to to trace the jagged trajectory that characterizes our human condition.

At the end of his blackly humorous book about 'the little father of the peoples', François George recalls (1979: 177) that Stalin took the application of a 'scientific world view' to its ultimate conclusion, and argues the case for a moratorium on concepts, and a bracketing out of beliefs. Personally, I would also argue the case for a moratorium on absolute and positive knowledge. It might then be possible to take into account the situations, effects, passions and frivolous things in our social life. Now that the great systems are ending their careers in disaster and derision, perhaps it is time to turn our attention to the minuscule, incoherent, punctual and frankly demented phenomena that make up the greater part of individual and social structuration. The way in which positivist ideology ostracizes them is all the more dangerous in that it encourages perverse and paroxysmal (i.e. bloody) manifestations of those very tendencies. If we accept that they do have a place, and admit that they have their own social efficacy, we will not give societies a smoothly homogeneous image. We will therefore come closer to their reality. Because it refuses to project a pre-established, perfect schema on to existence, learned ignorance can be a real initiation which allows us to interpret the mysterious and irrepressible social will to life.

# 3
# *The Ideological Function*

I will leave you to choose the lie which seems to you most
worthy of being the truth.

Paul Valéry, *Mon Faust*

## 1  The world represented

The critique of positivism results, then, in learned ignorance. This
is not a dogmatic proposition but a working hypothesis designed
to re-adapt our discipline to an unstable and unstructured object:
sociality. This attitude does not result in complete 'indifferentism',
to borrow a phrase from Kant (1781: 2). All things considered, it is,
rather, a matter of going back to and updating the great philosopher's project of sanctioning reason in its legitimate aspirations
and at the same time denouncing its unfounded presumptions.
The project is of course, as the reader will have realized, to be
understood here in a specific way, but it remains Kantian in spirit
and stresses the futility and rigidity of dogmatism.

In the present case, the point is to demonstrate that what we call
ideology cannot be understood in a univocal way. Whilst it cannot
be judged by the standards of science, it does contain riches of its
own. If we take away the term's pejorative connotations, ideology
is, in a certain way, a veritable repository of the social will to life.
For the moralist, the politician or the religious leader, of course,
not all social representations are equally valid. Some are to be
condemned, and others are erroneous or even dangerous. But to

the extent that it is not for the sociologist to decree what society or one or another of its members 'should be', he must be able to evaluate for what they are all the stories, justifications and legitimations which constitute the polyphonic discourse of the social, without judging them on an *a priori* basis. I have analysed the duplicity of ideology at greater length elsewhere (Maffesoli 1976, esp. ch. 5). In referring to its duplicity, I mean that our relationship with these various representations is totally ambivalent. We simultaneously believe and do not believe. Attitudes towards religious or political doctrines are exemplary in this respect. We act 'as if', and we do so in order to avoid a pointless expenditure of the energy required for the daily confrontation with destiny that makes up our existence.

It is this attitude, which can be confirmed daily, that makes it so difficult to discriminate with any certainty between true and false, or between science and 'ideology'. We should perhaps take the view that our knowledge of the world is a combination of rigour and poetry, reason and passion, logic and mythology. Many thinkers have stressed these antinomies, but we have yet to draw the full conclusions from this. Where sociology is concerned, it is important for its various analyses to be able to take into account this structural bipolarity. By recognizing the existence of what Parmenides of Elea called 'the way of truth' and 'the way of seeming' we can take cognizance of the twofold, ambivalent or dual way in which we understand the world and situate ourselves within the environment. By going beyond the characteristically reductionist attitude of modern and contemporary epistemology, we can then agree to describe social life as an inextricable combination of the intelligible and the tangible, of *sapiens* and *demens*. This is a line of research that reintroduces into social analysis the mythical and imaginary dimensions that Western rationalism thought it long ago eradicated for ever.

Now it so happens that the combined contributions of anthropology, sociology and ethnology reveal that these imaginary elements are still present, or are even currently re-emerging with new strength. Looking to the future, one might even take the view that they will become stronger still in the decades to come. It is therefore important to be forearmed if we are to grasp their contours or understand their manifestations. It might also be pointed out that this interpretative approach to social facts is rooted in an old tradition which, from Max Weber and his 'ideology' to Vilfredo Pareto with his 'residues', strove not to reject anything that contributes to societal specificity. With its insistent concentration on economic development alone, sociology in its Marxist or functionalist variants has, curiously enough, minimalized or even ignored the realm of representations. The term 'ideology' thus gradually came to mean 'false consciousness' or spontaneous and imperfect 'opinion', or in any case something that specialists in the social sciences must transcend, or even reform and revolutionize. Taken as a whole, the masses were *naturally* ignorant and childish, and truth could result only from an external intervention.

These dismissive conceptions, which can be found right across the political spectrum, are therefore based upon the determination of society by the economic order, and have as their corollary the individualism that is the essential notion found at the beginning and the end of all studies of society. Once we take into account society's collective consciousness, we restore to it what might, following Louis Dumont (1966: 23, 56f), be termed its 'holistic' character. In doing so, we may come closer to the spirit of the founding fathers and their project of attempting to understand society as a whole, to understand it on the basis of the whole. Indeed, it is increasingly obvious that a society based upon individualism is no more than an intellectual mirage and that, when we go beyond economic ideology, sociality has always, more or less surreptitiously, been experienced as a whole, if only because, as Dumont notes, 'individuals live by social ideas'. Thanks to the dominance of the Promethean myth, this reality became obscured, but as the myth fades we are beginning to appreciate the efficacy of such 'ideas', whatever their order may be. It is striking to observe that, in the domain of politics and economic organization, not forgetting bureaucratic or administrative organizations, we always find an element of mythical discourse in the founding act; whatever their role, these various aspects of social life require a symbolism. The conventional view is of course that this is something to be resisted, that these 'non-logical' references are to be regarded as retrograde residues, but the fact that it is impossible to do without them is a constant source of illumination and should encourage us to pursue our research in that direction.

There are of course some scientists specializing in the 'hard' sciences who have no qualms about building bridges between their research and the social sciences, and there are of course sociologists like Edgar Morin who try to respond accordingly in their own work, but suspicion is still the general rule, and the dominant rationalism is still ossified by powerful prejudices. It is in fact difficult to accept that a metaphorical description of unstable social phenomena can contain precious data, simply because it is not possible to generalize or codify such data. 'Soft' data, to use the language of information technology, is at best regarded as a spiritual indulgence, or as a poetic variation which can be tolerated so long as it is confined to the nebulous domain of culture. The budget that a productivist society allows itself to spend to enliven its relaxed after-dinner conversations is rather like the 1 per cent of the cost of constructing a public building that must, according to French law, be allocated to art.

As Barel remarks (1973: 417), it may seem paradoxical that a 'strong argument' like science should constantly look to a weak argument like ideology for support.

Basically, the attractive thing about ideology is its weakness. Its weakness conceals its great strength: its ability to answer an indeterminate number of questions. It is interesting to note that in his unusually dense book, Barel, a specialist in futurology and science policy, has no hesitations about recognizing the social function of ideology. To pursue the logic of his argument, I would add that we should not be trying, in a dialectical manner, to transcend ideology or to regard it as a mere support which we can use and then ignore or negate. It should be recognized as having a specific role as a possible mode of social knowledge. In sociological terms, the existence of ideology is an indication that the interpretation of society must make *simultaneous* use of all possible approaches. Depending on the circumstances or the situation, ideology may be affirmative, negative or interrogative, and to that extent it is very close to the dynamics of sociality. Perhaps we should describe it as a chameleon which can take on all the colours and forms that structure life in society. The various manifestations of intellectual creativity are pertinent only when they have their roots in popular creativity, when they consent to be no more than one expression of that popular 'genius'.

Because it uses a variety of instruments, refuses to be confined to criticism, and goes beyond positivist reductionism, the method I am proposing will be able to put its finger on the social pulse, which never remains the same and which varies in accordance with the mood of the day. The intellectual, cultural, economic and even technological mood that is now emerging has little in common with the mood that was dominant from the end of the last century until the 1960s. The powerful mechanism of social unification and the intellectual fantasy of reducing everything to One have had their day. There are many indications that customs and ways of life are becoming fragmented, and we are seeing the resurgence of supposedly outdated attitudes whose symbolic is hard to conceptualize, as it centres on the individual or collective body (territory). All this requires the elaboration of an *ars coincidentiarum* which does not see truth and living as completely watertight entities. It will become increasingly difficult to carry out satisfactory intellectual work if we are not broad-minded enough to integrate the polysemic contribution of ideologies.

## 2 Ideology and sociality

The best way to come to terms with this proposition is to refer once more to Durkheim. It may not be the easiest way to do so, but the detour is still illuminating. It is well known that Durkheim is ambivalent about how to analyse representations. On the one hand, he puts his faith in the linear progress of reason; on the other he cannot ignore the fact that a 'mental point of view' is no more than a 'system of representations'. The ultimate goal is of course still a reformed society which can be managed by positivist science, but the observation itself escapes the imperative of an intellectual 'should-be'. In *The Elementary Forms of the Religious Life*, for instance, Durkheim (1912: 431) admits that: 'Science is fragmentary and incomplete; it advances but slowly and is never finished; but *life cannot wait*. The theories which are destined to make men live and act are therefore obliged to pass science and complete it prematurely' (emphasis added). Despite the positivist hesitations and qualifications, we have here a real recognition of the pre-eminent role of ideology in the social will to life. It is of course a provisional recognition, and the supplementary aspect of Durkheim's representations, which could open up an interesting line of investigation, is deemed premature. The fact remains, however, that, insofar as it is a matter of living and doing, human action is based upon histories, upon discourses which always outstrip their scientific justifications. If we pursue the logic of this analysis, we have to admit that the ideological function has a power to anticipate and to inspire that nothing can escape.

If we look at some historical examples and, more specifically, at their tumultuousness, we find that revolutions and their institutionalization in social organizations are ideological through and through. To take only the last two centuries, both the French Revolution of 1789 and the Russian Revolution of 1917 are more than adequate proof that the economy, law, culture and even spiritual life are organized around ideological references. No matter whether the starting point is the rights of man or the dictatorship of the proletariat, political life is organized around a representative value. That the rationality accorded to the value in question is described as progressive, or even scientific, alters nothing: if people are to be motivated, convinced or deluded, recourse to an ideology is always necessary. What is true of these paroxysmal examples is also true of minor political changes and of everyday life. In a metaphorical sense, the 'foundation of the *polis*' always requires a specific mythology. When the collective bond that is inherent in any human structure becomes weaker, society needs to reinforce the feeling it has of itself or to recall the basis of its 'being-together', it falls back on and reactivates its foundation-myth. In that respect, symbolic manifestations have not changed greatly from the cult of Aglaurus in ancient Athens to our modern Republican festivals.

Be that as it may, it is important to recognize that passion and acts of passion are still the essential pivots around which social life revolves. Justifications, theorizations and rationalizations come after the event. The primal element is the impulse to act and speak that presides over various aggregates, that encourages attraction and repulsions, and organizes alliances, or in short all the 'non-logical' elements (Pareto) which we cannot ignore here and which are basic to our mode of being. According to Durkheim (1912: 227), for example, 'nearly every collective representation is in a sense delirious'. A phenomenon to be observed in religious belief can be regarded as 'one particular case of a very general law'. It would be difficult to put more emphasis on the importance of the sensible universe, or on that of irrepressible and unstructured feelings in what we call society. Once we are agreed (at least in problematic terms) as to their importance, and, once we accept that *homo demens* is also an irreducible element in our object of study, we have to accept all the implications. If we fail to do so, we will see representations as archaic, or even pathological. Sociology has taken that view for decades. Yet, even with a purely causalist framework, how are we to explain altruistic attitudes, political commitments and the sacrifices that are made in the name of transcendental values? How can we account for the enduring presence of patriotic, cultural and religious symbols? The list is far from exhaustive.

Once we break with a narrow rationalist schematism, we realize that collective representations inform even the most supposedly scientific actions and discourses, not to mention the great works and minuscule creations that make up the fabric of human histories. The totemism described by Durkheim may well have disappeared, but the important thing about his analysis is that it reveals the existence of a 'very general law' which, with specific modulations, can be applied to many contemporary situations. The mechanism of 'participation' which, thanks to the mediation of a totem, makes me part of my environment is still relevant. It is the *ultima ratio* of all sociality. The various ludic manifestations to be observed even within the realm of politics are in that sense instructive (cf. Balandier 1980 for an anthropological analysis). We do not need to privilege these paroxysmal examples, as we can see the same mechanism at work in the basic solidarity that is so central to the life of a neighbourhood or village. Without it, the conformism or conformity of gangs, networks, teams, clubs and various social groups would be incomprehensible. We have only to think of the contemporary resurgence of political or religious ideals, of the loyalties inspired by notions of territory or country, of the reappearance of large families, of musical gatherings and people's festivals, or of the importance that is now given to ecology and wholefood co-ops, to be convinced that it is futile to attempt to reduce social life to its economic substratum or physiological base. 'Ideas are realities . . . collective representations are forces that are still more active and efficacious than individual representations' (Durkheim 1898: 91).

It is representations, or the beautiful stories that we tell ourselves, that structure collective and individual development. To put it in metaphorical terms, we might say that they act as a counterpoint, as the music that accompanies the sinuous progress of human existence, as an antidote to the rigours of destiny, to the harshness of social or natural tyranny. This is not a negligible function, and it is certainly one which confuses traditional political and social analyses which are quick to dismiss it or give it a minor role. From this point of view, theorization is one element in the representative attitude. It tends to be imperialistic or monopolistic, but by its very nature it emphasizes only one aspect of the human mind: the ability to discriminate and to generalize on the basis of the lowest common denominator. To use the vocabulary of philosophy, theory has a tendency to hypostasis: something that is no more than an image, or an aid to interpretation, becomes an entity that cannot be transcended, a substance which *must* exist as such. According to this view, the pure concept gives a surplus-being to what it describes. It makes it exist as a plenitude. The pretensions of the concept, which we find regularly in the history of ideas, seem to make it forget, on the one hand, that its perfection is abstract because the concept selects the most conspicuous element in a whole mass of data, and that, on the other hand, it appears *post festum*, when the socio-economic situation no longer exists, when the event or the phenomenon is over.

This last element is extremely relevant to the sociological approach because it is pointless to tell the Truth about phenomena which are, to say the least, intangible. At best, we can analyse how such phenomena have been interpreted. That is (or should be) the object of a sociology of knowledge. Once again, there are texts by Durkheim that relativize the conceptual claims I have been discussing. *The Division of Labour*, for example, contains analyses (do we have to see them as aberrations?) demonstrating that social development is neither a conscious process nor something that has been foreseen, that it is at best used 'after the event'. It is interesting to find Durkheim writing that men walk 'because they have to walk': this is a reference to the impulse we mentioned earlier. Social life and its discourse about itself are in no sense programmed; they arise, then are always more or less imperfect and their various elements cancel one another out in a somewhat mysterious manner. For Durkheim, it is only 'after the event' that we can tell which element was dominant, which was useful and which was being used.

I have already spoken in this connection of the *social coenaesthesia* which ensures that, despite their incoherence and their uneven progress, and despite the vicissitudes and the catastrophes, the carnage and the crimes that regularly punctuate history, social aggregates do survive. They put up an organic – or perhaps we should say 'vegetative' – resistance that is a constant source of wonder. This resistance is not necessarily active. We have to assume that it stems from representations, from the imaginary, which are in no sense rigorous but which do structure a community as such. It is this that leads Durkheim to remark (1893: 277): 'Individuals are much more a product of common life than a determining factor in it.' At this point, the author's progressivist optimism fails him. The development of civilizations is not the result of concerted, resolute and premeditated action. It simply occurs and, as it does so, it determines and retroactively structures the individuals who make up the social aggregate. This conception, which is unusual in Durkheim, stems from a form of vitalism which regards existence as primary, and intellectual constructs as secondary, especially when compared with the imaginative ideologies that go hand in hand with existence.

This does not mean that every moment of social development is not accompanied by theoretical elaborations. Every age and every civilization secretes a more or less abstract body of thought and, from Plato to Aquinas and then to Comte, there is no shortage of examples of how the great interpretative systems left their mark on the next age and the next generation. But what I am trying to say here is that, regardless of their inherent scientificity, these systems are to a large extent ideological. It so happens that it is after the event that we discover or recognize this mythological dimension. The scientism of the nineteenth century is no exception to the rule. Not only are we beginning to recognize the ideological element within it; we are also beginning to assess its impact on social organization itself. By that I mean that it is its mythical dimension that makes an idea dynamic, that allows it to inspire enthusiasm and to generate projects and achievements. In that sense, it was because it was a myth that the scientism of the nineteenth century could inspire the techno-economic achievements with which we are so familiar. Referring to Saint-Simon, Durkheim clearly demonstrates (1928: 91) that knowledge can be the 'moving power of progess'. Given that he is talking about his own times and that he starts out from the principle that 'A society is above all a community of ideas' (1928: 91), he therefore has to recognize that ideas can be the impetus behind social development. Yet at the same time, institutions are 'ideas in action' (1928: 91), and he implicitly admits that ideologies are valid only if they bring together and establish communities. Which is tantamount to admitting that they are ephemeral and mortal. It is this that gives representations their grandeur. They change from generation to generation, and express the ideas, nostalgia and projects of a generation. And, like generations of men, they die, become outdated and give way to other imaginaries. It is because they become exhausted as they are actualized that it is impossible to regard them *a perennis*. To extend our metaphor, an ideology shares in the act that founds a society, and it also develops as society develops, but it is always life and its development that triumphs. This aspect is important, as it clearly demonstrates that the important thing about a representation is not so much its content as its ability to unite people. The power of religion resides less in theological subtleties than in its ability – or inability – to give an impetus to aggregates. The same is true of the great revolutionary movements and of the various ideals which have, at one moment or another, shaped communities. For vitalism and its pendant gnoseological relativism, the accent falls on the strength of 'being-together'. 'Common sentiments' (Durkheim 1893: 330) are of interest to the sociologist only because they are an index of the birth, apotheosis and death of a social aggregate. For our present purposes, nothing is true unless it helps us to grasp the vitality of a period, the vitality of specific and particular events and situations. Whilst the formula should not be understood in too utilitarian a sense, we can say that understanding exists only by virtue of the collective use that is made of it.

If ideology is so important for any reflection on the art of thinking, if it has to be given back its letters patent, if it is necessary to rescue it from the hell of false consciousness and the curse that lies on common sense – which is supposedly artificial and naive – it is because ideology is our prime source of information about the degree and strength of sociality, and because these appear to be essential problems for sociology. Common sense, popular intuitions, the discourse of everyday life and sometimes political oratory (I refer to saloon-bar politics) tell us much more about the 'non-logical' element that is at work in societies than rationalizations which are primarily stratifications. To be more specific, they should be described as an expression of a sort of hyper-rationalism which almost intentionally integrates elements that are essential to an overall equilibrium but which tend to be overlooked by intellectual rationalism. At several points in his study of suicide, Durkheim stresses the importance and specificity of 'common consciousness'. He demonstrates that the latter is not reducible to an arithmetical sum of individual consciousnesses, and that their combinations generate the new situations that are the specific domain of the sociological discipline. The objectivity which, according to Durkheim, characterizes social facts implies, of course, that common sense is not to be trusted. One wonders, however, whether this might not be a way of begging the question, as the emphasis on 'collective sentiments' does relate, whether we like it or not, to a shared passion and it is very difficult to quantify its effects.

The collective consciousness, or in other words ideology, produces, to go on using Durkheim's terminology, 'a psychical existence of a new species' (Durkheim 1897: 310) which thinks and acts autonomously. This metaphorical description of society is not without its audacity, and it certainly underlines the solidity and primacy of the symbolic bond. The resultant association is 'also an active factor productive of special effects' (1897: 310). The important thing about representations is that they both found sociality and guarantee its specific efficacy. Whether or not the 'special effects' in question can, as Durkheim would have it, be scientifically quantified and analysed is a different question, but it is quite clear that we have to recognize their irreducible existence. It has always been possible to measure their impact on the course of history. Upheavals and upsets, unpredictable social events, the fragility of laws and kingdoms, are all to a large extent the result of these 'special effects'. And those who have attempted to govern peoples on the basis of strictly rational principles or tried and tested economic laws have learned to their cost that the power of the mind is not something that can be ignored. Unless we take it into account, many political situations and upheavals would be incomprehensible. Be that as it may, and this is what we can read between the lines of Durkheim's text, sets and combinations of representations are prime social movers. Being both causes and effects of sociality, they are the repository to which we have to turn to understand in qualitative terms the incessant interplay of human passions.

This approach may seem metaphysical and some researchers who, like the sociologist Gilbert Durand, have looked at the structures of the imaginary, have been criticized on those grounds. And yet a refusal to segment reality does allow us to see overall tendencies within society in terms of their specific diversity. The essential or specific thing about human associations is indeed the collective consciousnesses described by Durkheim. Yet, whilst it lies at the origin of the various social domains (the economic, the ethical, the cultural and the political) and is present throughout their evolution, it cannot be reduced in a one-dimensional way. It extends beyond – far beyond – the limits that nineteenth-century positivism imposed upon it. If we interpret it in an open-ended way, it is this 'interpenetration' that founds the myths, ideologies and representations that explain the survival of sociality. If we are to interpret it, we must therefore plunge into the bizarre, noisy, impassioned and polyphonic aspects of everyday life.

With his dazzling style and the characteristic generosity of mind that shines through all his work, Edgar Morin speaks (1980: 84–5) of ideologies as 'noological beings' with a vast field of action. They 'possess those' who possess them. He accords these entities 'certain properties of living existence'. By proposing an ecology of ideas, Morin displays his kinship with those who want to give human representations their full dimensions. To speak of 'ecology' (I am using the term metaphorically) is to speak of retroaction, reversibility and co-organization. And we can never place too much emphasis on what I call the *efficacy of ideal forms*. Unless we refer to these forms, we will understand nothing about utopias, religions (classical or secular), enthusiasms, conquests or human achievements in general. The gods, 'the most accomplished spirit-beings' (Morin), have always been the motive force behind the actions and discourses of society, and they are the expression of an immanent transcendence which is secreted by the collective body and then acts upon it. The resultant polytheism of values allows us to understand a complex world which it is difficult to reduce to either economism or culturalism. Polytheism in fact allows us to understand the varying intensity of ideologies, their lives and their deaths. In other words, something that was dominant in a certain period falls into abeyance in another, or acts only as a counterpoint.

These 'spirit-beings', which go by a variety of names and exist in different modulations, are a representative expression of the multiple potentialities running through sociality. Just as the gods of the Pantheon took part in the life of mortals and shared their loves and their sufferings, spirit-beings are present in economic struggles, political issues, bloody warlike jousts and bitter intellectual polemics. If we fail to take their intrusions into account, we will fail to understand the vagaries of events and circumstances. They may burst in violently and noisily or they may, as Nietzsche remarked, come as softly as a dove, but they never miss their appointments. The voluntarism of politicians and the 'scientific' activity of experts may of course have some influence on the course of events, but the fact remains that it is the popular passions inspired by the 'spirit-beings' – representations – that make the decisions, either actively or passively. We cannot act for very long without them or against them. That in itself may explain a new form of 'learned ignorance' on the part of intellectuals.

In the course of the general transition from monotheism to critical philosophy the impact of 'idea-forces' was gradually relativized or eliminated. The reduction of the gods to a single omniscient divine entity, the conversion of the divinity into profane substances like Nature, Spirit, History, Progress or Science, and then the production of the historical subjects who were to realize man's purpose, all facilitated the emergence of an individual whose essential characteristic was the constant assertion of his intellect. *Identity* was shaped in a personal relationship with God or, from the eighteenth century onwards, his secular avatars. According to this view, there is no need for collective representations; to put it more accurately, they are tendentially destined to vanish. All that matters is the formation of a critical spirit, and its application in various professional skills (intellectual, technical and artistic). This is the basis for scientific positivism and for its inevitable correlate: utilitarianism. It is therefore not surprising that sociology should regard representations or ideologies that do not fit into the individualist schema as inconsequential, or even as crude errors and survivals from another time.

It seems, however, that the trend is beginning to be reversed. As a result of the first stammerings of ecology, and of the new Dionysian values and the importance they give to space, the principle of identity is crumbling (see Maffesoli 1982). Is this to be viewed as regression? It is not for us to pass judgement on an emergent movement which, like anything human, is a combination of good and bad. What is clear is that the intellectual attention is once more being directed towards the dynamic roots of ideologies, and that this gives a much more complex and perhaps more exciting vision of social existence. Neither the individual nor equality are on the agenda; community, and the architectonic it inspires, are.

It is well known that many social achievements and even technical and scientific developments started life as utopian representations. This is not the place for a discussion of utopianism, and many studies have already been devoted to that topic. We can on the other hand stress that a utopia is an ideological form pregnant with social aspirations and desires, and often with future achievements. Utopias are always present, in either a latent or explosive form, in the life of societies. Utopias therefore show us the potential efficacy of representations. Arguing about or describing a utopia refers us to a non-real world that allows us to see or think the hidden potential – or simply the potential we hope to see – in any given social structuration. Associations of individuals, be they voluntary or compulsory, are surrounded by imaginary projections: national utopias, family utopias, communal utopias. And it is not possible to understand them at all if we do not try to comprehend this rich ideal activity *for what it is*. I am not suggesting that we have to overevaluate it, but nor, as is so often the case, should we regard it as an inconsistent projection which is primarily an expression of a lack of being. We simply have to accept that it is an index of human finitude, in all its incompleteness, its clumsiness and grandeur.

From the epistemological point of view, taking account of representations or ideologies therefore means thinking in a non-real mode. The productivity of this mode has been well demonstrated by sociologists like Max Weber. Insofar as this approach still has a heuristic function, it allows us to keep a close eye on the tumbling of the social dice. No matter what we call it – ideal type, form, archetype, residue – it allows us to focus on both great deeds and minuscule creations, and at the same time to give them every opportunity to express themselves. In a word, its rejection of the 'should-be' gives us access to the qualitative aspect of sociality.

# 4
# Towards a Sociological 'Formism'

Don't ask me what 'form' is. It's like asking a centipede
how it can walk with so many feet.

Wolfgang Koeppen

## 1 The Pre-eminence of the whole

The so-called formalism of certain authors has often been misunderstood or misinterpreted. The term itself is not unambiguous, as
it seems to refer to an abstract attitude that has no connection with
the world as given. In order to speak of the framework that will
allow us to bring out the characteristics of social life without too
much distortion, I therefore suggest that we use the term 'formism'.
It is well known that the generally iconoclastic tradition of the
Judaeo-Christian West has always distrusted the disorder of the
image, or in other words the expression of meanings. It has often
had no alternative but to come to terms with it, but it has done so
with great reluctance. When it had to come to terms with the cult
of the saints and their images, Catholicism made it clear, with a
pained expression, that this was a mere *dulia*, whereas its *latria* was
addressed to the one invisible God who combined and completed
the attributes that had wrongly been ascribed to the old idols. This
trend reached its logical conclusion with the Reformation and the
Enlightenment, and the baroque of the Counter-Reformation is,
ultimately, no more than a parenthesis that social catholicism was
anxious to close from the nineteenth century onwards.

This later provided the basis for the 'secular' and theoretical critique of cultural and political forms, appearances and spectacles of which we are the belated heirs or protagonists. It is therefore quite understandable that thinkers who insist on observing the play of social forms should seem paradoxical, or to be going against the dominant analytic trend. And yet it seems essential to preserve because analysis now shows in more and more ways that both political life and everyday life are to a great extent made up of theatricality, superficiality and spectacular effervescence. Taking stock of it is important. Perhaps, to borrow a phrase from Nietzsche, we can say that depth is hidden on the surface of things and people. We do tend to forget the banal truth that it is thanks to form that there is something rather than nothing. The phenomenon is certainly a limit, but it is a limit which conditions our existence. The Latin word *determinatio* refers to the stone that marks the boundary of a field, but it is a type of limit that permits life, as opposed to non-definition or the formlessness of a limitless desert. Things exist because they are inscribed within a form. Creative artists of all kinds are well aware of this, as they are initially confronted with a form; the content comes later. It might be more accurate to say that content is not comprehensible unless we study form. Developments in philology have clearly demonstrated that even the freest and most unrestrained poetry obeys unavoidable and readily identifiable formal rules.

The same is true of social existence. It is both rule-governed and 'hidden'. I have attempted elsewhere to show how much paroxysmal situations such as anomic violence, state violence and even Dionysiac values owe to conformity or rules. To say nothing of banality, or everyday life. The rituals that make them up are so many collective scenarios that express our encounter with destiny. It is at this point that banality coincides with an epistemological project: *what we can know* is what can be seen, what is depicted in gestures or acted out. But we must show none of the contempt that is conventionally reserved for appearances. It seems to me that we will then have the basis for a fair assessment of the pertinence of sociological 'formism'. Formism is far from being a static world view, and the classic authors who adopted it were able to explain the changes and forces to be seen in the life of societies. To take a more contemporary example, the whole of Georges Balandier's work – both his sociology of Africa and his social anthropology – clearly reveals the 'generative' dimension that structures all social life (see e.g. Balandier 1971: 9). For my own part, I believe, as I will argue below, that formism and vitalism are the most reliable poles for the structuration of an interpretative sociology.

Thus the 'frames' we construct allow us to reveal more clearly the various facets of life as it develops. The object is in a sense, to borrow a phrase from Spengler, to reveal the historical 'physiog-nomies' of the handful of social forms that we find throughout history. According to this perspective, modulations or derivations of institutions, cultural facts or daily rituals can be both grasped in all their precariousness and credited with having an undeniable efficacy in the here and now (Maffesoli 1980). This may help to explain the mechanisms of belief and illusion, which are at once so fragile and so deep-rooted (Maffesoli 1979b).

Of all the lessons that are be learned fom Durkheim, it is perhaps the emphasis on holism that is most worthy of attention. He returns again and again to the idea that the specificity of social facts cannot be reduced to the generalization of individual facts, and stresses that sociology can expect nothing from an analysis based upon the arithmetical sums of individual characteristics. The defining characteristic of the individual is a concern for the self, in every sense of the term. Deep down inside and at the conscious level (or the unconscious level, which amounts to the same) and not forgetting private space, an individual strives to reach perfection, to reach a completeness measured on the scale of his or her possible autonomy. Autonomous individuals may form *contractual* associations in order to undertake collective actions, but even in such cases collective action is governed by individual wills. Stressing the specificity of the social whole means giving collective form precedence over individual content, and recognizing that individual consciousness is the product of the group rather than vice versa. In that respect Durkheim (1893: 287) has no hesitation about asserting that: 'It is indeed rather the form of the whole that determines that of the parts.'

Whatever the influence of the individualist ideology of Durkheim (or the French sociological school), his occasional holistic remarks do allow us to think through the importance of the *structure-effect* in societal interpretation. In a period like ours, which has seen the resurgence of the organic function, his remarks are not without their contemporary relevance. The pre-eminence of the whole over its parts, which has been well analysed by various 'gestaltist' theories, is clearly present in every moment of the life without qualities that makes up the greater part of the social fabric. We are dealing with an intersection of existences which, over and beyond or despite individualist ideologies, expresses itself force-fully, and sweeps aside the barriers we erect and the various obstacles it encounters. There exists, so to speak, an impulse to 'be together' which can be empirically observed and which never misses an opportunity to manifest itself. Even in the most aseptic places, and in the spaces for gregarious solitude that the contem-porary techno-structure has contrived to construct, we inevitably see a collective reappropriation of space that ploughs its furrows deep. Sporting events, musical or political gatherings, the sounds and hubbub of the streets of our towns, and festive occasions of all kinds all forcefully underline the pre-eminence of the whole. What is more, its pre-eminence increasingly tends to result in a fusional reality, or in what I have termed 'the return of Dionysiac values', with individual characteristics being replaced by organicity or by what Fourier called the *'architectonic'* of the whole.

In an architectonic, the gestural is dominant. The imaginary is active in fleeting and multicoloured situations which owe more to the polyphony of meanings and affects than to the calculating and economic vision of reason, and they are the focus for both attraction and repulsion. As we can see from these brief remarks (which may perhaps be premonitory), what I am calling 'form' is a polypod with aesthetic, ethical, economic and political implications. It naturally has gnoseological implications too. The one thing that is clear is that civilizations or cultures based upon the individual monad are circumscribed in time and space and that, even though they may appear to be strong, their dominance seems to be porous and about to make way for something new. Before long, individ-ualism and the related notion of 'inwardness' or consciousness will exist only for intellectuals. Intellectuals are eminently solipsistic, if only because it is easier to explain things in terms of conceptual reduction than to interpret them in terms of the dissemination of images.

It is because of the existence of this solipsistic tendency, which has deep psychological – and partly philosophical – roots that I think it necessary to identify everything in our cultural tradition that can serve as a touchstone for its transcendence, if only to liberate our thinking from the tranquil quietism of preconceived schemata and the arrogance of rather moralistic pedagogic dog-matisms. If we interpret it in a heuristic sense, formism may allow us to grasp the exuberance of social appearances. Not directly, as that would indeed be pretentious, but transversely, by establishing limits or 'determinations'. The true sociological approach would then mean, to borrow a phrase from Tönies, understanding 'pure forms' and not 'singular realities' (see Tönnies 1887). This is simply another way of saying that because it is content to grasp structures and their development such an approach allows singular realities to exist as they are. They are not something to be judged as conforming or failing to conform to our expectations as to what they 'should be'. They are to be accepted as incomplete, partial and ephemeral. Paradoxically, the formist attitude respects the banality of existence, of popular representations and of the minuscule creations that punctuate everyday life. It does not give them a meaning. It is not inscribed within any religious, political or economic finality. It does not formulate categorical imperatives. It is happy to talk about its own times in its own way and it is therefore inscribed within the polyphonic discourse a society pronounces upon itself. Perhaps this is what is meant by the term 'the organic intellectual'.

Literature – from poetry to science fiction, from the novel to drama – has traditionally had the function of transfiguring everyday banality. There are of course exceptions, but on the whole writers have bowed to this demand. The theoretical approach is modelled on it, and may even exacerbate it, as concepts will not tolerate approximations and will have nothing to do with redundancy. The real is therefore no more than a base raw material to be transcended as quickly as possible. More accurately, it is a raw material that has to be controlled by an abstractly elaborated project or programme. In a novel or poem, this transfiguration does in principle have the virtue of stirring the emotions, but at the level of theory it becomes arid and etiolated, like a plant which has been uprooted. In its attempts to break down or get around what it sees as an obstacle, namely the world of appearances, theory becomes a mere list of prescriptions when it is bound up with power, and a list of pious wishes when it attempts to reform or revolutionize power. In both cases, it is imbued with the resentment that characterizes every kind of 'lack of living'. Theory's fear of impure images, its fantasies of transfiguration and, in a word, its iconoclasm lead it to propose a new world in place of the 'facticity' of the present. We have only to look at the great schools of thought we can observe down the ages to see the same process at work in the theology that transcended a multiplicity of magical or religious practices, in the philosophy that rationalized popular wisdom, in the psychology that attempted to subsume empirical knowledge about the mind and the body and, more recently, in the sociology that took such a haughty view of popular common sense and of the incorporated skills that structure all societies.

In all these cases, the spontaneous will to life is considered inconsequential, even though its images and representations organize time and space, and thus allow a collective response to the tragedy of the passage of time and our anxieties about finitude. It is also striking to note that the theoretical constructs that derive from the modes of thought in question are all designed to save the individual, to ensure the fullness of his mental life, to cure him of his psychological malformation and to ensure his optimal integration into the social ensemble. The object of these multiple attentions is always the individual monad. It would seem that, if it is to work, the mechanism of transfiguration has to be addressed to an isolated individual. A collective adventure is inverted into the individual adventure that is so well described in a *Bildungsroman* like Goethe's *Wilhelm Meister* and Mann's *The Magic Mountain*. In some mysterious way – and it is well known that a mystery is something that provides a bond between initiates – civilization is based upon functional collective values in which the consciousness of individuals counts for little. There is of course 'Cleopatra's nose' and there are individuals who succeed in organizing the chaos, furies and upheavals of history, but those individuals are 'acted upon' rather than being sovereign actors. We do not necessarily have any clear awareness of this structure-effect or movement, but at an intuitive level we know them for what they are. Perhaps that is why the masses are described as being volatile, indifferent and sceptical. Personally, I tend to think that they are quietist, because the masses 'sense' that, whilst charismatic individuals and political authorities may come and go, there is no great variation in their treatment of the masses.

Even so and whilst there is a structure-effect, and whilst the individual is, ultimately, no more than a more or less perverse avatar of collective organicity, it is important to find a way to explain the handful of forms that structure that organicity. The stakes are high: this intellectual instrument must not become a new way of programming 'what must be'. Ultimately, it has to be content with having observer-status, in the full knowledge that social passions, political turmoil, struggles and conflicts, attraction and repulsion will take place, no matter how acute or accurate its observations. It does not have to transfigure anything; it simply has to reveal the mulitiplicity of figures that make up the social game.

## 2 'Formist' invariance

Whilst a certain *gravitas* does mean that the intellectual attitude tends to transfigure what exists, or in other words to ignore appearances in order to look for the deeper meaning of things, certain authors do have the ability to think in terms of form by using stipple or by speaking *mezzo voce*. They have in a way succeeded in getting away from a very vague notion of individuality as an initial or final explanation. It would seem that they are therefore in a better position to understand the indifference of the masses towards the individual, or in other word their withdrawal from politics. The sociologist who has to deal with what he sees and neither what lies behind it nor the future *polis* – though in other respects he is quite entitled to place his hopes in it – might find it helpful to adopt the same attitude.

It is not surprising that all those who find appearance attractive should have taken their inspiration from the Greeks, who had a great fondness for figures. I am not speaking of structured philosophy, but of the polytheistic substratum that is inseparable from Greek civilization. Hence the adage *pollon onomaton, morphe mia*: 'many names, one form'. This hints at something that might shed light on our reflections: the recognition of a 'formist' invariance that exists throughout the multiplicity of its modulations. Although the sociological observer must be wary of conceptual abstraction, this does not imply that he must abdicate his intellectual responsibilities. On the contrary, by trying not to give the minor actions of everyday life any specific finality, and by accepting appearances for what they are, sociology can integrate them into the small number of great structures which have, without any noticeable changes, informed social life throughout human history. Conceptual formalism attempts, by definition, to give a meaning to everything it observes: it gives reasons, and subordinates everything to reason. 'Formism' merely describes the great configurations which, without reducing them, encompass the pluralistic and sometimes antagonistic values of normal life. In a perpetual to-and-fro movement, invariant forms, and the acts (or discourses) that modulate them, echo one another, articulate one another or come into conflict. In doing so, they shape the simultaneously aleatory and solid equilibrium that I call social coenaesthesia. As Gilbert Durand puts it, archetypes and stereotypes are part of the same dynamic.

As we can see from the domain of creativity, great and mediocre works are not basically heterogeneous, and each can interpret the other in its own way. The link between archetype and stereotype is an excellent metaphor which makes it possible to specify the heuristic value of form: form is an empty set, and does not exist as such, but it does make it possible to interpret appearances that do exist. It makes it possible to interpret them in qualitative terms because, when they are neither judged on the basis of something else, nor rejected, nor marginalized, the stereotypes of the moment appear in a new light and can therefore take their place in the great play of illusions that structures the given world. Whereas science must reduce, eliminate and prune back the non-essential in order to exist, the 'formism' I am outlining here offers a more generous scientificity which can integrate into its research parameters that have traditionally been neglected. Everything is important: anecdotes and minor events have their place in identifiable configurations. Whereas the function of the concept is to exclude, the function of form is to bring together. It helps things to germinate. It gives birth to a multiplicity of rootlets which then spread to infinity. Once again, we have the metaphor of a vitalism which, without being too discerning, unfolds, spreads and gives birth to good and bad alike.

From this point of view it is obviously difficult to formulate value-judgements about the situations and acts we are observing. But is not what Max Weber called strict 'ethical neutrality' one of the ambitions of scientificity? As it develops, life secretes all sorts of things. It uses its own forms to maintain its own equilibrium. The same is true of social existence, where order and disorder, functionality and dysfunctionality are always articulated in such a way as to ensure its permanency. Once we accept this schema, we have only to identify the form or forms around which this exuberant growth is organized. The term used by Pareto in this context is eminently pertinent: the intangible 'residue' around which its various 'derivations' move has connotations of 'germination'. And whilst no specific causality is involved, if we can identify the seed, we will be able to shed a new light on the blossoms that follow.

Before we look at this 'formism' in modern sociology, we should briefly recall its philosophical origins. And we should begin with that positivist *avant la lettre*, Thomas Aquinas, according to whom 'Within all sensible things, we find something intelligible: form.' The precise interpretation of the question is a task for specialists in medieval philosophy, but for our purposes we can accept that all sensible things being potentially linked to a form opens up a vast field for investigation. This means accepting that all things share in one way or another the divine charcteristic of form. Ultimately, evil itself is a derivative of the deity. In that sense, the case of the biblical Lucifer is instructive. And, to take only one example, it is not surprising that the Thomists who became Fathers of the Society of Jesus should, unlike more rigorous minds, have tried with their well-known indulgence to negotiate with the sins that beset members of the Christian community. Everything can be used *ad majorem Dei gloriam*, even evil. It is all a question of one's point of view. And the use they made of the baroque is quite logical: *appearances*, whatever their form, are not to be rejected, because they 'potentially' refer to the divine form. The architecture and the iconography of the Jesuit churches of the Counter-Reformation, with their sensual and somewhat intoxicating aspects, can be interpreted as an index of an acceptance or an affirmation of all worldly situations. Not for nothing were the Jesuits greatly sought after as confessors in a society which was to say the least libertine. Because they accepted the world for what it is, they produced a truly pantheistic version of Thomism. Anyone who doubts this has only to look at a few well-known sculptures, like that of St Ignatius in the Gesù or that of St Teresa in Santa Maria della Vittoria.[1]

Another medieval philosopher also developed ideas which are relevant to our concerns. Occam was of course the great enemy of Thomism, but it seems to me that his nominalism can be interpreted in terms very similar to what we have just been saying. In Occam's view, the Universal, which is another name for form, is merely the 'sign of a plurality of singular things' (cited, Jeanneau 1963: 118). The things that we understand are singular realities, and the universal word that designates them is ultimately no more than an instrument which, without exhausting those singularities, brings them into the framework of our intellectual inquiry. Nominalism thus brings us back to the idea of the 'empty set', of which we were speaking earlier. Occam's position allows us to clarify our approach in that he rejects intellectualist reductionism, but does not overlook the desire for knowledge. Without going so far as to establish an irreducible dichotomy between words and the things they designate, we can recognize their respective antinomies and, which is more important for our purposes, accept that the plurality of things to which a single term refers is, as everyday experience indeed teaches us, an index of the extraordinary richness of social appearances or phenomena. In that sense, nominalism is another expression of the polytheism that governs all life in society. No matter what is said by grumblers, by journalists who are short of copy, positivist intellectuals and the politicians who play second fiddle to them, the polytheism we are describing has nothing to do with a reactionary nostalgia for some lost religiosity; it refers to an essential characteristic of any societal aggregate that uses a few figures to typify the underlying pluralism of values, situations and passions that bring it to life. In that sense, there is a close connection between nominalism and empathy. The two complement one another: nominalism builds the stage, the set and the scenery for the magic theatre in which, thanks to empathy, our normal existence can be played out.

To continue our rapid survey and to go on tracing the tenuous but constant thread of 'formism' we can refer, for the Renaissance period, to the philosophers Georgias Gemistos Plethon and, of course, Nicholas of Cusa. Surprisingly enough for a writer of the fifteenth century, Plethon was a theorist of the plurality of gods, and he too supplies elements that allow us to grasp both ends of the chain. The gods, who are 'symbols of formal causes', have a 'creative' function within the order of the cosmos. Nothing is excluded from this symbolic order, not even 'the gods of Tartarus', who also have their place in the order of beings. Plethon's paganism, which has been described as a 'figure of rhetoric', led him to devote all of his attention to what he calls 'common notions' (*koiai ennoiai*) or 'anticipatory attributions' (*prolepsies*). A comparative study of the creative aspect of 'formal causes' and the importance of 'common notions' is certainly illuminating (see Gandillac 1973: 37f and the bibliography: 350f). It reveals, in a somewhat esoteric form, the to-and-fro movement described earlier, which does so much to delineate the articulation between the few invariant archetypes and the multitude of figures (both practical and representative) that make up social life at its most banal.

It is also interesting to note that Plethon had a far from negligible influence on the thought of his day, and particularly on Nicholas of Cusa, who, in my view, displays the same trust in ordinary existence and at the same time tries to understand more fully the 'intellectual spirit' which circumscribes the elements of that experience. It was certainly not for nothing that Nicholas was accused of pantheism; preferring 'the Book of the world to that of the erudite' (Gandillac 1973: 25–7) has always succeeded in annoying the clerics who control knowledge and sanction power. The importance he gives to the 'coincidence of opposites' and his wish to go beyond Aristotle's *'ratio'* because it is too closely bound up with the principle of non-contradiction, is, of course, of considerable contemporary relevance. All these things clearly relate to a vision of a complex world whose various elements correspond at some deep level, even though it is not, strictly speaking, possible to establish any causal relation between them. Nicholas's *unitas multiplex* implies interaction and continual reversibility. 'Unity' may be no more than a word that allows us to trace its complexity in outline form, without exhausting it. From the epistemological point of view, a correspondence in which everything has a place cannot but be relevant to an interpretative sociology which, as I have already said, lucidly *states* that a plurality of acts and values results *de facto* in a societal equilibrium which, if one thinks of the forces of natural and social tyranny, is a constant source of wonder.

If we refer to a precursor of the Enlightenment such as Vico, we also find that this equilibrium, or in other words the survival of the human race, does indeed result from the intimate connection between banality and form. Interestingly enough, this view was expressed just as the high tide of modern rationalism was in full flood. What Vico calls 'the property of sociability' is in part based upon the existence of 'fantastic universals'. These are neither abstract nor isolated in some distant empyrean; on the contrary they influence existence at its most concrete. They constitute so many mobilizing myths around which the various skills and discourses that structure being-together can cohere. For Vico, of course, humanity's destiny leads from primitivism to rationality, but it does seem that his rationality is neither narrow-minded nor clearly defined. What he calls *divinitas* must result in a balanced and rational social life. The deity in question is certainly not far removed from what we understand by the divine in a sociological sense; it is a product of what Durkheim calls the 'collective consciousnesses'. It is clear that these fantastic constructs make it possible to reconcile the great invariants that provide the substratum of social life with the concrete situations of normal existence, and that is how I analyse them. The latter are supported and legitimized by the great mythological figures which, in one way or another, still sustain political, economic and social life. Although the disenchantment of the world that Max Weber describes so well has greatly influenced modern and contemporary thought, it is now a declining force. We are now seeing the re-emergence of the great agglomerative figures that integrate every individual into an endless chain, and into a sociality whose effects are now being studied once again.

What I am calling 'formism' is, then, in a sense a new way of posing the eternal problem of Universals and Particulars. Every era's 'ideology' has to deal with this problem and, as far as I am concerned, sociology cannot ignore it. Georg Lukács puts it well in an early text, or in other words in the most open way possible: 'There are, then, two types of reality of the soul [*seelische Wirklich-keiten*]: one is *life* and the other is *living*; both are equally effective ... Ever since there has been life and men have sought to understand and order life, there has been this duality in their lived experience' (Lukács 1910: 4). And although it may in his eyes be no more than an aesthetic category, Lukács does add that form alone allows us to experience both types of reality. The comment is of considerable interest, especially if we recall how much Lukács owes to Simmel, who also had a great influence on Max Weber. It is certainly possible to extrapolate, and to extend these comments on artistic creativity to social creativity as a whole. 'Life and living': the essence of being together and concrete existence are an inextricable combination of the two, and it does us good to appreciate both elements. At all events, and this is its primary interest, formism is above all a global form of thought. Unlike any totalitarian (and monovalent) world view, what classical sociology calls 'holism' never privileges any one element. In view of technological and scientific developments and the diversification of modes of knowledge, it is more important than ever to demonstrate the complexity of the world, which always (again) escapes the fantasy of enclosure. Every era goes through a period of optimistic scientism, in which it claims to have found the universal key or the totalizing explanation. The history of ideas demonstrates more than adequately that no civilization and no culture has escaped this ambition. This is a constant, or a sociological burden, and it is both pointless and futile to attempt to deny its existence.

And perhaps this mechanism does have its uses. Precisely because it is so simplistic, such optimism does permit a renewal of enthusiasm. It reinforces mobilizing myths, and prepares the way for the many discoveries or rediscoveries that structure and determine all social life. It is, however, also important to stress the relativism of this world view. The alternative is the mechanistic schemata which – from China's mandarins and eunuchs (cf. E. Balazcs 1968) to our modern technocrats – has always legitimized quantitative management and social controls, and justified the techno-bureaucratic tyranny whose harmful effects on basic sociality are plain for all to see. Thanks to a perverse effect (which Jules Monnerot would call 'heterotelia'), progressive optimism, the scientific Truth and the technological Whole become more and more abstract and simply deconstruct 'society's feeling of itself', and that is what allows the societal aggregate to survive.

Formism makes us wary of all this. As many observers have pointed out, an emphasis on 'form' leads quite naturally to a polytheism of values, privileges movement and takes into account the multiple aspects of every element in social life. When, for instance, they describe the 'formism' of Simmel – who was, at the beginning of the century, the first to reveal its advantages – Georges Friedman and Bernard Groethuysen point out that it resulted in a 'sort of extremely subtle and sceptical pluralism' and that it led him to see 'things as whole'. Opening up an extremely important line of investigation for the sociology of knowledge, Friedman goes so far as to establish (1936: 12) a parallel between 'formism' and the 'refusal to choose' or the *disponibilité* and the artistic freedom that we find in the immoralism of a Wilde or a Gide. I am obviously not suggesting that we extend the comparison, but we can underline its pertinence and demonstrate its contemporary relevance, as we are indeed now re-evaluating the complexity of the world and rediscovering the importance of the play of difference. Taking forms into account makes it possible to reveal the multiple creations or situations of everyday life without confining them within the narrow limits of finalism. In that respect, formism is a reaction against rationalist monovalency. It brings out the polysemy of gestures, the multicoloured aspect of normal life, whereas concepts attempt to purify, to reduce, and to cram the complex into brevity.[2] Paul Valéry's Faust tells Mephistopheles: 'Spirits are as brutal as the pure acts that are their essence.' And there is certainly something both simplistic and brutal about rationalism, if only its claim to exhaust everything it touches, and to make the object of analysis express all that it contains.

The refusal to choose and the aesthetic *disponibilité* we have just mentioned are much more respectful of the sensible aspect of social life, of its structural pluralism, or in short its irrepressible hedonism, which it is pointless to attempt to reduce. It is not irrelevant that, when he developed an analysis of forms, Simmel was also arguing the case for a 'sociology of meanings'. In his view, the essential characteristic of formism is that, like a picture frame, it brings out the colours, the complex architectonic, the intense but humdrum atmosphere, or in a word the appearance in depth of everyday life. Combining depth and appearance is not an empty paradox. Others have done the same (Nietzsche). The point I am trying to make here is that the greater part of existence is constituted by and in *seeming*, and that 'seeming' is anything but unified, pure and coherent. If we break with normative conceptions of every kind (conservative, reformist and revolutionary), we can give the most ordinary and obvious forms of 'seeming' credit for expressing the density and pluralism of existence.

Unlike those who hand down 'scientific' lessons, we are in a position to admit that it is not the fact that a social object exists but the way in which it reveals itself to our gaze that should guide us in our research. That sums up the ambitions of formism. There is therefore no question of abdicating our intellectual responsibilities; it is simply a matter of finding the best possible match between relativism and existential pluralism, and the intellectual approach. This is a perfectly legitimate practice, and it has something in common with what Pareto calls 'descriptive theorems', which are less concerned with elaborating laws than with indicating tendencies. Those researchers in the 'hard' sciences who are currently demonstrating the fecundity of error and rediscovering the importance of 'successive approximations' are in that sense very close to the 'logic of form' that I am trying to outline here.

Whenever it comes to the fore of the debate, the logic of form allows us to think the essential link between experience and the essence of things, between the social lived experience and its representations. It is also instructive, as I have already pointed out, to note that the great proponents of the emergent science of sociology all, in one way or another, raised the question of the constants, invariants and archetypes that help to reveal normal situations. A comment made by Kant may shed some light on this: 'My place is the fruitful *bathos* of experience, and the word transcendental ... does not mean something that goes beyond all experience, but something which, though it precedes (*a priori*) all experience, is not designed for anything more than solely to make knowledge by experience possible' (Kant 1783: 144n). He adds that 'if concepts step beyond experience, their use is called transcendent' (ibid). I am not qualified to analyse this remark in any detail, but I would stress the importance of the dichotomy between 'transcendental' and 'transcendent' and note that, as Kant puts it, the word 'transcendental' serves merely as a backdrop, a frame or a horizon for what he calls experience. And that backdrop is the day-to-day life to which the sociologist can no longer remain indifferent. In a word, the transcendental method is a precondition for any understanding of the real.

A similar dichotomy can readily be found in sociology. In a sense, 'societal' refers to the essential categories that allow us to both understand and describe the banal situations of everyday life. The tragic, theatricalization, ritual and the imaginary are societal categories. The 'social', on the other hand, refers to a specific and accurately dated representation of life in society which tends to be abstracted from normal life because we insist on turning it into a prosthesis (the term can be used in a neutral and a-critical sense).[3] Whatever the truth of the matter, it is important to pay due attention to the fact that what I am calling the logic of form allows us to go beyond the intellect/sensible dichotomy, that *pons asinorum* of all theoretical reflection.

We have cited Simmel and Pareto, but it is also essential to refer, if only briefly, to Max Weber, who, in his own specific way, quite happily resorted to what I am calling 'formism'. We could find numerous examples in his work to illustrate how, in one way or another, he adopts a formist approach. We have only to look at the definition he gives of the expression 'the spirit of capitalism'; it is extremely subtle and is quite in keeping with the various elements of our analysis. If the spirit of capitalism does exist, 'it can only be an historical individual, i.e. a complex of elements associated in historical reality which we unite into a conceptual whole from the standpoint of their cultural significance' (Weber 1904–5: 47). The notion of a historical individual, like that of an ideal type, is no more than an empty set, a space which may be non-real and whose value is primarily heuristic. The essential characteristic of such a concept is that it is made up of 'individual parts' which can be observed in a given historical moment. Weber himself makes it clear that it is not a 'definitive concept'; it might not even be a 'conceptual formulation' (1904–5: 47).

This cautious approach is well adapted to social lability and it is not surprising that it should have produced a sociological study of the first order. One does indeed sense that this 'historical individual' is primarily a spokesman for all the individual parts that make up the social given. At the same time it provides a tenuous link between those various parts and thus makes it possible to paint a picture of an era. It reveals the architectonic of representations and practices that is both the cause and the effect of the circulation of commodities, speech and sex. It allows the parts to be integrated into configurations which are flexible enough to avoid the traps of rigid dogmatism and totalitarianism. Thus we very rarely encounter 'historical individuals' or 'ideal types' as such, but we can see how helpful they can be in a sociological investigation. Thanks to them, the minor events of everyday life, the humdrum saloon-bar conversations, the countless rituals that structure our days, all these elements – be they leisure activities or work – become pregnant with meaning without being inscribed in a pre-established finality. We can therefore say of the social fabric what Guardini used to say of ritual: it is *zwecklos aber sinnvoll*, meaningful but without purpose.

The one thing that these various modulations of 'form' have in common is that they emphasize the fact that the multiple situations of everyday life disappear as they occur, that we live them in the present tense. And it is important that this present tense, which is the field specific to sociology and which was for a long time concealed by Promethean ideology, should be restored to its rightful pre-eminence. Unless it wishes to become (or remain) a purely abstract representation, sociology must pay attention to the ethics of the instant that so deeply imbues the life of our societies in all their communicative or instrumental activities. What is more, and this is the implication of the above comments, 'formism' emphasizes appearances, spectacles, images etc., and all these realities tend to have been neglected by the Western tradition. Form both reveals our minuscule creations and gives them expression. It should also be pointed out that a sociology of the imaginary – and Gilbert Durand has outlined the main articulations of such a sociology – will certainly make it possible to pursue both these lines of investigation.

From an epistemological point of view, a sociology of the imaginary will be able to make sociological use of the insights of phenomenology. Thus the notion of the 'imaginal', as proposed by Corbin and Durand, should make it possible to observe in the here and now manifestations of the intimate bond between the intelligible and the perceptible (cf. Durand 1975: 12). It is appropriate to recall these basic truisms: just as life begins with limitations, or by being determined (cf. the Latin *determinatio*), so social existence exists only when it can be seen, when it takes on a form. *Theatrum mundi* is not an empty phrase. That its expression is multiform (political, economic, quotidian . . .) certainly legitimizes our sociological reflections on 'formism'.

Many authors sense in their own way that this is a contemporary problem. We can no longer interpret the world by using instruments which were once valid, but which now look rather outdated. The logic of the excluded middle and the subject–objet distinction, which were once basic to our sciences, are increasingly being called into question. In terms of our own concerns, we might say that paying attention to form in the way that I have suggested should permit the elaboration of a new anthropo-sociology which is both generous and open to the complexity of the social world. Edgar Morin, who with tenacity and erudition is attempting to lay the foundations for such a sociology in his work on methodology remarks (Morin 1977–80, vol. 1: 20): 'We need a cognitive principle which not only respects but reveals the mystery of things.' When he comes to define his method, he states that it is 'a swirling movement that moves from phenomenal experience to the paradigms that organize existence'. All the terms used in my analysis can be found here: 'experience' is another name for what I call empathy, and 'paradigm' can be understood as meaning a modulation of 'form'. Both can be tested and experienced in the chaotic 'swirl' of a social existence whose fertility and polysemy are far from having been exhausted.

It would seem that such an approach can attempt to reveal the social given whilst at the same time respecting it in all its complexity. That is why I contrast accommodating interpretations with over-rigid explanations. At all events, this constant movement between experience and paradigm, or between empathy and formism, clearly indicates that there is such a thing as the organization – I would prefer to speak of the organicity – of people and things, of nature and culture. Our task is simply to trace its contours. Notions are revelatory and they allow things to crystallize, but they also leave intact the fertile plurality of sociality. There is a very close connection between 'formism' and polytheism or, which is closer to our concerns, societal pluralism. And given that one-dimensional systems of reference are beginning to break up under the impact of social practices, it is important that the sociologist, who is indifferent – on this point – to misunderstandings and sarcasm alike, should more than ever be able to appreciate the extent to which this polytheism is both rooted in everyday life and active within it. The lucidity of those (and their numbers are increasing) who succeed in resisting the totalitarianism of normative world views should be devoted to that task.

# 5
# *The Analogical Method*

His mockery, which is based upon analogies and knowledge, is not without its pedantry and peevishness.

Pieyre de Mandiargues, *La Marge*

## 1 Interpretative proposals

We must now draw the conclusions from the critique of positivism
that we have outlined or, more accurately, bring out all that is
affirmative in that critique. Stressing the value of representations
(or ideology) and demonstrating the 'formism' of social life is no
mere *flatus vocis*. On the contrary, it requires us to put the emphasis
on methods that have, for a while, been left to one side. They
include analogy, metaphor and correspondence. Once again, I am
not suggesting that our analysis of these methods should be
exhaustive. Still less that they should be seen as the only methods
that can be used to understand social life. I am merely stressing
that they do have a role to play in sociology, and that they cannot
be dismissed as so-called supplements of soul like poetry, fiction
or mysticism. They are a way of getting away from methodological
practices that have become far too narrow and rigid. For my own
part, I would even argue that the adoption of these methods,
together with more classical analyses, will produce a much better
understanding of both the lability of the social lived experience
and its polysemic aspect.

More and more specialists in every domain are agreed that we need to find a way of approaching phenomena which, without constraining or reducing them, avoids complete indeterminacy. Metaphor and correspondence have obvious benefits to offer, and we are also beginning to appreciate their shortcomings; how to go beyond them remains an open question.

As I have already indicated, the interpretative attitude, of which Max Weber is the most consistent representative, certainly allows us to approach this question with confidence. It is not satisfied with a causalism that looks down at its object from on high, and nor does it accept a rather summary intuitionism. Some might say that the 'interpretative project' is a golden mean (Sironneau 1982: 30).

It is, perhaps, a dangerous watershed that connects all the experiences and situations, in the strong sense of that word, that make up the given world. This project certainly provides a basis for typology and comparativism, and their true fecundity has yet to be assessed. What is clear is that the introduction of the parameters we have just been talking about leads us to a relativism that is far from being the norm in the Western tradition. There is clearly a parallel to be drawn between the predominance of the concept in our civilization and its universalizing ambitions. And yet, despite its undeniable successes and achievements, our civilization has always tried to deny or destroy the assertion and the dynamism of difference. One might recall Spengler's dictum to the effect that claims to universal validity are always false inferences about the other.

In the long term, this attitude is inevitably harmful, and it turns against its proponents. One might, for instance, wonder whether the decline of the West may not be the price that has to be paid for our stubborn desire to want to know everything by reducing it to unity. When it has no more objects to classify, taxonomy begins to swallow its own tail. And, to pursue the biblical tradition's myth of the serpent who tempts poor mortals with the fruit of the tree of knowledge, we can advance the hypothesis that, once it has completed its trajectory, the concept-serpent turns into a vicious circle. I am not, I repeat – as disgruntled or ill-intentioned critics accuse me of doing – advocating intellectual irresponsibility. On the contrary, I am one of the many who are trying to demonstrate that many domains are still open to sociological investigation, provided that we approach them in an open and non-sectarian manner. I am not using these terms in any moral sense; I am simply attempting to describe an attitude of mind that is in keeping with the generosity and the will to life of social existence (see Lazega, Modak and Lalive d'Epinay, 1982).

Rather than trying at all cost to lay down laws, reveal purposes or elucidate 'why's' – and clerics of all times and all stripes have always had these normative fantasies – it is much more important to describe in phenomenological terms the shimmering and fragmented polysensuality of everyday existence, or to construct, in theoretical terms, formal frameworks that can serve as *conditions of possibility* for the polymorphism in question. There are many examples, both historical and trivial, of the monstrousness of life in society; it would be pretentious indeed to claim to be able to channel it, to subject it to rigorous and immutable laws. In a word, we must be too attentive to the richness of existential development and ask too much of interpretation to go on accepting the scientistic reductionism that flourished in the nineteenth century.

According to Spengler, mathematical laws allow us to understand dead forms; the way to understand living forms is to use analogies. Without wishing to claim that it is the only method of interpretation, *analogy* is a way of interpreting unstable phenomena by comparing them with similar situations or experiences. It does not, of course, prevent us from making mistakes. As I have already pointed out, the role of the concept is, by its very structure, to give a reassuring and supposedly comprehensive vision of the object of its apprehension. As with everything that a certain tradition has declared universal (universal spirit, universal history etc.), this is a local truth that has been generalized. This hypostatic process is a veritable magical ritual that individuals or groups use to build a somewhat fictional fortress to reassure themselves, just as children draw magic circles and just as animals use urine to mark their territories. The incantations are certainly understandable, and there is no question of condemning them, but nor should they be erected into absolute principles to which everything has to bow down.

It should in fact be recalled that fragility, errors and local truths are also part of the dynamics of cognition. This is increasingly recognized, and sometimes even recommended by those working in the 'hard sciences' as a way of breaking out of positivist closure. The first wave of scientism, which developed in the wake of the philosophy of the Enlightenment, naturally needed to adopt clear-cut positions, to discriminate and to distance itself from an essentially mystical or metaphysical world view. As in other periods of human evolution, there was a need to put a new emphasis on things that had been laid aside. I have already explained this mechanism. But the question is now being posed in different terms, and we have to be able to leave room for the imagination, for uncertainty and for bold thinking. This applies to all scientific research, whatever its object (see e.g. Feyerabend 1993, Morin 1980, Freund 1969 and the proceedings of the Cordova Colloquium on *Science et conscience*). These tentative developments in the hard sciences are all the more necessary in the social sciences.

The general consensus that emerges from conferences, debates, articles and books on the future of theory is that 'error can be a tonic experience' (Freund). We are moving further and further away from the great explanatory systems. Given its complexity, society is no longer amenable to a single determination, and perhaps the true scientific spirit is the spirit that 'allows itself to be refuted' (Morin). It is very easy to construct an abstract theoretical model or to supply an interpretative grid that can be applied to any phenomenon, but it comes as a surprise to realize that events always take place in the margins, that everyday life always asserts its presence, plays out its games, outwits us and tangentially resists analysis. In that sense, it really is scientific to advance hypotheses, to suggest lines of investigation, to make comparisons, or in a word to use societal polyphony to draw up a list of analogies that allow us to *interpret*. In that sense, we can endorse the criticisms Lévi-Strauss makes in the final chapter of *Tristes Tropiques* (1955: 531) of the reassuring rationalism that constructs an image of the world and society 'in which all difficulties can be solved by a cunning application of reason' and fails to 'realize that the world is no longer made up of the entities about which we are talking'.

That is indeed the problem. We are obviously not involved here in field-work, but we are trying to draw attention to the essential quality of social phenomena: their irreducibility to the injunctions of reason. Just as twelve-tone music was a reaction against classical regularity and romantic pathos, our research must be able to describe all the heterogeneous elements of the social lived experience, no matter how disparate they seem. They are all present *at the same time* in the social fabric, and we must be able to explain that fact. This method will define the specificity of a 'plural' sociology, as opposed to the various monisms that try to reduce everything to a single cause. It is in fact surprising to note that those who refer to our discipline's canonical authors usually ignore the texts and analyses that look at the fragmented and polyphonic world in which we live. Preference is usually given to emphasis on complete systems, structural constructs, certainties and apodictic proofs. The doubts, not to mention the antagonisms or discontinuities, are ignored. A curious intellectual mechanism!

I have already pointed out on a number of occasions that many great figures in the human sciences saw the originality of their work as stemming from a *coincidentia oppositorum*. This is not the place to draw up a list or to make an exhaustive analysis, but it is clear that Max Weber's 'paradox', Durkheim's concept of 'anomie', Pareto's residue/derivation dichotomy, Lévi-Strauss's nature–culture distinction and perhaps even Freud's condensation and displacement, are, as Gilbert Durand so rightly remarks (1979b: 221f), so many ways of recognizing the 'fruitful ambiguity' that lies behind all civilizational processes. Without going into detail, I would speculate that there is such a thing as an *oxymoronic structure*, and that can be found, with differing ingredients, in all societies and all civilizational spaces. No matter whether we look at primary gatherings, erotically based groups, parties, guilds, associations, or the most complex societies, we always find that what Lupasco and Beigbeder call the *contradictoriel* is at work. Unanimity – and it can be either recommended, forced upon or desired – is still with us, and political realism lies in the ability to recognize and manage conflict. The same applies at the level of the interpretation of societies. If we place too much emphasis on verification, we will fail to see our objects. We would do better to look at the antagonisms, to accept them and to understand how they function. The polytheism of values, which has been haughtily ignored by the French sociological tradition, quite simply means that we have to accept antagonism.

This oxymoronic structure did not escape the subtle mind of Ernst Bloch. The notion of 'non-contemporaneity', which he employs on various occasions, is in that sense instructive. According to Bloch it is an expression of the permanency of contradiction within social structurations. For Bloch it was of course something to be transcended, but the title of one of his essays – 'Non-contemporaneity and Obligation to its Dialectic' – suggests that the Marxist intellectual can transcend it only by working on himself. Be that as it may, Bloch's polemic against the relativism or empiriocriticism of Mach's school does allow us to specify *a contrario* the primary characteristics of the analogy or metaphor we will be discussing later. If we overlook his excessive language, which relates to the militancy of his undertaking, Bloch is criticizing the analogical method – or what he terms the theory of 'as if' – for its basic relativism, for the fact that it makes it impossible to arrive at some intangible Truth. The 'as if' always contains an element of doubt and Bloch wants thought to be useful, to be positive, if only in a critical way. Bloch naturally sees analogy as a by-product of bourgeois thought, or of 'bourgeois conceptual decline' (Bloch 1962: 258). What even Bloch's subtle Marxism cannot accept is the fact that doubt and fiction might be dynamic elements of knowledge. And for anyone who is not working within the framework of a 'must-be' logic, they correspond to the scepticism and relativism that underpin popular thought.

We can in fact agree that analogical thinking 'endlessly loosens things up in order not to have to act' (Bloch 1962: 263), but it has become almost a truism to admit that activism is by no means the only way to relate to others or one's environment. It is true that there is something indolent or contemplative about the meanderings of analogy. But do not intellectual meanderings correspond to existential meanderings? Even the history of the labour movement has left room for a libertarian 'Sublimism' (Poulot 1980) or for writings in praise of laziness (Lafargue 1883), albeit in its less canonical forms. A certain slogan from May 1968, which was completely misunderstood by the professional politicians and the managers of the revolution, was not without roots in what I have already termed the banal 'situationism' of everyday life: 'Never work.'

And it is true that this situationism does have something to do with the relativity of truth. Bloch's critique of the 'theory of the conformity of ideas to facts' (Bloch 1962: 258) can, conversely, be interpreted as referring to the individual's ability not to be confined to any particular status, to resist the injunction to have an identity, and to be alert, within the framework of sociality, to the mobility of the sensations and sensualism that characterize everyday life. Without going into any great detail here, whilst analogy can be condemned from a dogmatic point of view, it is clearly the most appropriate method for describing the disorganized will to life of societies.[1]

That said, it is clear that the 'as if' method has played a far from negligible role in analyses of social development. Leaving aside theoretical utopias, which, even if they were never achieved, did result in partial successes that have left their mark on human history, a whole intellectual current drew its inspiration from the analogical perspective at the beginning of the eighteenth century.

We need only think of Rousseau, who illustrates this current perfectly. A phrase in his *Discourse on the Origins of Inequality*

(Rousseau 1755 : 50–1) sums up the problem. In the philosopher's view, all possible research into society is based upon 'hypothetical and conditional arguments which are more likely to elucidate the nature of things than to reveal their true origins'.[2] This is a clear indication of the divorce between this form of research and causalist or metaphysical conceptions. Whether or not we achieve the desired result is largely irrelevant, but it is not irrelevant that thought should attempt to understand what is happening rather than its preconditions or effects. We might also note that those who stress teleology often have a tendency to control its direction or, if they cannot do that, to advise those who can. In short, Rousseau's 'hypothetical reasonings' are grounded in the *how* rather than the *why*. As is often the case, there is no reason to reject one in the name of the other. On the contrary, it would seem that hypothetical reasoning involves fewer unspoken illusions or fantasmatic projections. As a result, it pays more attention to the present. The relativism it induces is obviously not new, and historians of ideas who look beyond Western finalism have no difficulty in finding examples in the many cultures that do not situate themselves in relation to History and its linearity (whether or not its linearity is progressive or reactionary is relatively unimportant). Societies in which organicity has been lived and thought, in which myths have been valued, have always been analogical societies. And it was certainly the rural memories of the nature lover (the famous Rousseauism) that encouraged Rousseau to opt for an adventurous analogical method rather than the tranquillity of abstract thought.

Analogy is primarily a way of interpreting the present. Like a backdrop, it brings out things that would otherwise go unnoticed or be dismissed as insignificant.

It is in that sense that I understand Rousseau's reference (1755: 44) to a state 'which no longer exists, perhaps never did exist, and probably never will exist; and of which it is, nevertheless, necessary to have true ideas, in order to form a proper judgement of our present state.' This is quite in keeping with the 'as if' approach. A mythological or ideological reference or emphasis allows us to reveal what we live day to day. The paroxysmal situations I have analysed in connection with violence or orgies are good illustrations of what lie beneath it. This is a legitimate attitude and we have only to note the importance of fiction in the fabric of everyday life to realize that analogy has a major contibution to make to our investigations; the sociology of literature all too often overlooks the point. I have already pointed out elsewhere that we have to use the non-real to understand, and it is encouraging to hear a physicist and philosopher of the sciences admitting that 'We need a dream-world to discover the features of the real world' (Feyerabend 1993: 22). If today's sociology is to advance, it must heed this advice. Casting to the winds the caution that was once necessary, sociology must also be bold enough to adopt parameters ignored by the dominant positivism. Creative thinkers in all domains have done so. Whilst having no claims to being creative, sociologists – be they theorists, practitioners, empiricists or speculators – should be aware of the fact that they are also specialists in social representations and must therefore find a method that will allow them to be attuned to every vibration that runs through the social body. Because it allows us to establish parallels between societies that are far apart in time and space, analogy is a prime element in that method.

We can never understand a social aggregate solely in terms of its positivity. Freud's insights into the life of individuals should perhaps be extrapolated to groups. We would then be investigating accidents and events (what happens) rather than Freudian slips. Following in the footsteps of writers like Balandier and Morin, we would then be able to understand the dynamic of events by listening to a 'marginal discourse' which is, of course, an echo of a more distant discourse. In that sense, analogy is capable of giving a dynamic account of the 'anthropological structures of the Imaginary', which are now beginning to be seen as something more than superfluous supplements of the soul or insubstantial daydreams.

## 2 Resonances

I will attempt later to demonstrate in greater detail the important contribution analogy can make to an in-depth interpretation of sociality; unlike causalist reductionism, description actually can reveal the richness of the lived experience. For the moment, we can simply note that analogy is one modulation of the symbolic or imaginary dimension. As Sironneau remarks (1982: 94–5) in his analysis of 'demythologization', it is clear that analogy corresponds to a certain 'sacral image' of the world. It is also clear that the sacral image has been somewhat tarnished by modern and contemporary scientific developments. And yet a series of indices does seem to suggest (cf. Maffesoli 1979b; 1982), if not the return, at least the permanence of a cosmic correspondence whose effects have yet to be ascertained. In the meantime, we have to evaluate the importance of symbolic thought by adopting a transversal approach.

Just as we referred earlier to Bloch, we can begin by making reference to an extremely subtle author in order to see how non-rationalist thought has been devalued. I refer to Horkheimer who, in a discussion of Vico, analyses mythology as a 'primitive pre-form' (Horkheimer 1930). It is certainly a necessary pre-form, but it is still characteristic of primitive people and children. According to Horkheimer, the latter do not have the ability to form logical categories, but they do have imaginary universals or genres, ideal types or models which they use to explain everything. Their attitude allows them to become part of the natural and cosmic whole which, in repesentational terms, finds its privileged expression in analogies. Horkheimer later stresses that mythology is a distorted expression of reality based upon a lower degree of development. There is no point in dwelling on this linear vision, which is not, when seen in context, contemptuous but at worst condescending. It is, on the other hand, important to note that the relationship with the social and natural environment that charac-terizes so-called pre-logical thinking is very different to categorical reductionism. In short, 'anything goes', to cite Feyerabend's (1993: 19) trivial phrase. This attitude of mind is obviously very generous. Of course it can be disorganized and can induce methods that are difficult to accept, but ultimately it does reflect the incoherence of social life, which only an intellectual in a study or a technocrat in an office would try to reduce to a single factor. The use of analogy in a sociological investigation will therefore inevitably bring us closer to these primitive people, for whom magical thinking is not as outdated as we like to think. Particularly since, as many thinkers have admitted for a very long time, it is by no means certain that perceiving things in terms of ideal types is more 'primitive', in the pejorative sense of that term. It is even possible that, whilst it is less efficient in utilitarian terms, it may be better able to understand the organic texture that binds people to one another and to the natural world. The 'anything goes' principle suggests that, when it comes to interpreting societies, there are no leftovers, unless, like Pareto's residues, we give them the importance they merit.

Saying that anything goes, stressing the quality of non-categori-cal (that is, non-rationalist) thinking, or looking at symbolic partici-pation or analogy as forms of knowledge are in fact so many ways of stating once again that truth does not exist in itself, and that it is meaningful only in terms of a given social aggregate. This is the relativist attitude, and it means that the cognitive act is primarily focused on the society that serves as its support. In his reflections on 'savage' peoples and their wisdom, Claude Lévi-Strauss (1955: 154) has no hesitation about arguing the case for a 'search for correspondences'. He demonstrates that whilst this search is not 'a superior form of knowledge', it is 'at least the most fundamental and the only one common to all'. In comparison, 'scientific thought is merely the sharp point.' And it is clear that, if 'the sociologist can help towards the creation of this total and concrete humanism', he will do so by paying attention to all the wealth of this analogical thinking. Ethnology and anthropology have played an important role here, if only because they relativize the hegemonic claims of the Western way of thinking.[3]

It is clear that, if we do not accord it its rightful role, analogical thinking will make its presence felt in a perverse (*per-via*) manner. We have to be able to accept that the nineteenth-century myth of Progress, the great socialist dream of the turn of the century and even the representations that gave rise to the French Revolution, all functioned, whether we like it or not, on the basis of the sacred dimension, which a civilization can rarely do without. We see here the 'pseudo-morphosis' mechanism which turns an archaic form into a matrix for something that looks new. If we pay attention to this phenomenon, we may spare ourselves some disappointments and, more importantly, a good deal of terrorism. Once again, lucidity, which seems to be absent from our contemporary fantasies, allows us to qualify our inventions, our novelties and our technological discoveries, even when they seem to be highly original. Some research projects are both resolutely modern and capable of revealing residues and reminiscences of the dreams that have always haunted the human mind.[4] From an epistemological point of view, there is a lot to be gained from integrating them into our analyses as so many paradigms that add depth and substance to our various sociological research projects and theories.

In that respect, it is worth recalling a comment made by a spokesman for the Enlightenment: 'We always judge beings by *analogy* with ourselves. That is the source of men's natural tendency to personify even inanimate beings and to lend them a mode of existence similar to that which man feels within himself' (cited, Dontenville 1973: 9). Without attaching too much importance to the terminology, it is important to emphasize the role of the social animism that breathes life into everything around it. Be it God or Machine, it is always a *deus ex machina* which acts as a prosthesis for our existence and which, with varying degrees of consciousness, integrates us into a vast and complex network. The *Dionysian* fusion which, it seems to me, is now emerging is no more than a specific instance of the phenomenon. It is, however, important to stress that this basic animism has always haunted the human mind and even scientific thought. Fiction in all its forms is of course there to remind us of the importance of the imaginary; everyday life is also filled with an irrepressible element of fantasy. To say nothing of our scientific approach.

As Gilbert Durand remarks (1969: 62–3), 'Rationalisms and pragmatic approaches can never really cast aside their imaginary haloes . . . any rationalism, any system of reasons, brings with it its own fantasies.' Why make this point or why go back to it once again, if not to recall, at the risk of seeming repetitive, that we will never rid either individual or social structurations of their 'imaginal' element. We even have to admit that the history of ideas provides many examples of scientific thought going astray and appealing to mythical thinking to get it out of an impasse. A civilization in decline needs barbarians to regenerate it. As I have already noted, the strong argument of science needs the weakness (softness) of what it calls ideology if it is to make a new start.

Having rapidly outlined this situation and referring back to our earlier comments on magical thinking or non-categorical 'savage' thinking, we can now look at two or three scientific modulations of the 'animism' in question. Firstly, the notion of an *archetype*, as formulated by C. G. Jung. It has been both praised and damned. It is impossible to list all its critics and defenders and in the last analysis it is not important to do so. But if we look at it from a relativist point of view, note its tenderness and credit it with having a dynamic dimension – and it does seem to have that dimension in Jung's own writings – the notion of an archetype does explain the combination of reason and imagination which, whether we like it or not, structures our mental space. The dynamic archetype is at once a condition of possibility for and a backdrop to all the representations and actions that punctuate or justify our existential perambulations. And if we do so with an unprejudiced mind, it is easy to locate or bring together a large number of attitudes within the orbit of a small number of archetypal images. What is more, if we refer once more to Gilbert Durand, who provides (1969: 253, 72) a vigorous illustration in his masterpiece, the notion of an archetype is indeed relevant to the sociologist's concern with collectivity.

The characteristic feature of Jungian archetypes is that they take into consideration the great structures of the imaginary which, going beyond narrow individualism, concern and strike a chord in the human race as a whole. It is because of this characteristic that dynamic archetypes can polarize the multiple images that traverse our daily space. In a sense, they have an agglomerative function and provide a pivot for all the stereotypes the masses use to resist both political tyranny and the harrowing unpredictability of time and the forces of nature. At this point, knowledge merges with a certain *ars vivendi*. It is in fact clear that this way of interpreting existence cannot be reduced to 'laws' or orderly systems; it is more concerned with organic intuition, which is why the imaginal function plays such an important role within it. Whereas the principle of causality is based upon a fixed object, archetypes focus on shared visions and are fully involved in the lived experience and its verbal expressions.

It should of course be pointed out once again that this vision is not an abdication of intellectual responsibility. In that respect, the example of Max Weber is instructive. The present study owes a lot to the comparativism that structures his work. I, at least, do not think it an empty paradox to see his famous 'ideal type' as a scientific version of animism. A great deal has been written about this notion, but we need only look at Weber's own definitions. When, for instance, Weber remarks (1904–5: 98) that his observations on dogma will seem 'dull' to the non-specialist reader and 'hasty' to the theologian, he notes that:

> We can of course only proceed by presenting these religious ideas in the artificial simplicity of ideal types, as they could best but seldom be found in history. For just because of the impossibility of drawing sharp boundaries in historical reality we can only hope to understand their specific importance from *an investigation of them in their most consistent and logical forms.*

One could not hope for a better description of the specificity of analogical thinking: referring to typical forms without worrying about their existence, so as to bring out the essential features of the social fabric.

For my own part, I have emphasized elsewhere the heuristic value of paroxysmal forms (violence, the tragic, random events, orgies etc.) and it is clear that the method satisfies neither those who are too concerned about (with) actuality nor the grumblers who conceal their intellectual impotence behind a mask of scientificity. The 'ideal-type' method can in fact be extrapolated to many sociological investigations and it is coming into its own after a long period of neglect, now that cracks are beginning to appear in our catechistic certainties and truths. At times like this, a cognitive method really is a journey along a road; it follows the path of existence without surreptitiously claiming to be the lantern we need for our journey. Insofar as it is an animist form, an ideal type magnifies one or another feature of social structuration so as to reveal its efficacy. It allows a mythical identification with this or that figure, but ultimately it leaves intact the most banal and most intense aspects of daily life. Although they are not inscribed in some finality, the minor acts of normal life can find expression by sheltering behind ideal types which both justify and legitimize them.

The notion of 'archetypes' or 'ideal types', which I describe as 'animistic', brings us back to the fact that some social forms are invariants. Whatever we call them (Simmel's 'form', Freund's 'essence', Pareto's 'residues', Mach's 'model idea', Durand's 'schematic'), these constants provide the backdrop for many a sociological investigation; they allow us to reveal minuscule situations which would otherwise be concealed by dominant ideologies (religious representations, economic elaborations or political convictions) which owe their success to the power mechanisms they justify. What is more, and this is closely related to the above, the very fact that they have only an ideal existence means that these constants have a purely mediating function. Unlike conceptions based upon the primacy of ideas, theories or systems, the ideal-type perspective constantly subordinates ideas to facts. It implies a relativism or a scepticism which is primarily concerned with existential becoming and which is not obsessed with conceptual rigour. To be more accurate, this relativism brings into play the reasons and imaginaries that structure myths and social histories, either consecutively or concurrently. The constellations of images catalogued by Gilbert Durand, which are so many condensations of discourses and practices, are one example. In that sense, analogy is indeed a future-oriented intellectual method.

## 3  Collage and agglutination

Analogy looks to the future because it is capable of integrating elements that were excluded by the invasive positivism of the nineteenth century. And what is the sociologist being asked to do, if not to explain the wealth of a social given which is in a perpetual ferment? Rather than reducing it to the lowest common denominator, he should be interpreting, in the strict sense, the tangled web of passions and reason, feelings and calculation, day-dreams and actions that we call society. This is of course a somewhat stochastic view, but that does not make it unacceptable if we think of the unpredictable aspect of societal evolution. In that respect, analogy is eminently pertinent: it agglomerates, and traces dotted lines between situations that seem to be quite disparate. As with collage and other (dadaist and surrealist) artistic practices that have developed in recent decades, its aim is to bring together forms and contents which, whilst they are scattered, are still part of the world structure of a given period. Collage is, strictly speaking, a metaphor: it moves things to the same place and puts them together. This attitude obviously offers an alternative to the classical discrimination, divisions and breaks that are at work in Western theory and art. Collage mingles genres without worrying about their individual economies or logic.

From this point of view, and as I have already pointed out, nothing is alien to sociological investigation; its endless movement must take into account anything that is, at any given moment, a local expression of the discourse of the social. In that sense, we cannot establish a hierarchy between theoretical statements, romances for shopgirls, political manifestos or religious pronouncements. Each of these genres is a specific modulation of the overall discourse that a society pronounces about itself. Because it is comparative, the analogical method can provide a link between the multiple facets of a general representation. It might also be pointed out that the analogical link is not restricted to comparisons that can be established contemporaneously. Thanks to the contributions of history, ethnology and anthropology, it makes it possible to reveal all the invariant and changing elements in societies. It is this mode of thought that allowed a sociologist like Pareto to formulate his theory of 'residues' and 'derivations'. For my own part, as I have pointed out in my previous books, I take the view that the analogical link permits the transverse reading that allows us to interpret our times with the help of the deeds and chronicles of past societies. I am obviously not saying that this is the only possible method; I am simply describing a cautious approach designed to relativize the 'neophilia' that usually characterizes our age.

The possibility of grasping both the dynamics and the statics that are at work in any society is a clear indication of the vast field that awaits a non-reductionist investigation. It is also striking to note that, whenever an individual discipline takes on a new lease of life or frees itself from the fetters of sclerotic practices, it feels a need to break down the barriers that were erected – perhaps as a matter of necessity – to allow it to exist and to define its specificity. But just as a child or an adolescent finds its limits by testing out its parents, the originality we are seeking is somewhat strained and tends to fade quite rapidly. Other examples could be given, and I supplied some earlier. For our purposes, it is, however, enough to listen to a few authoritative voices which emphasize the importance of taking the broader view, of integrating unstable, fragile and non-real elements into the elaborations of the human sciences.

Georges Duby (1971: 11) suggests something similar for social history when he speaks of 'Science in the making'. He notes that as

> the history of economies was getting under way, some saw it as essential to complete the study of the material bases of ancient societies by studying their rituals, beliefs and myths, by studying every aspect of the collective psychology that determined individual behaviour and had as direct and necessary effect on the organization of human relations as the economic facts.

The suggestion is worth listening to, especially if we think of the productivity of this approach and of the research it has inspired. For our purposes, the important thing to remember is the need for accounts of what is conventionally known as the 'material' to converge with accounts of the collective consciousness, whose efficacy cannot be underestimated. This convergence, and the term is to be understood in its strong sense, implies a recognition (perhaps a forced recognition) of the agglutinative force that governs the social. As I have noted, the animism that structures our societies is by no means a thing of the past. The notion of 'animism' is obviously not to be understood in too strict a sense; our concern here is not with the history or sociology of religions. I am simply trying to use a metaphor to make it clear that it is difficult to divorce or separate one segment of human experience from another. The convergence I am describing is a way of becoming part of a larger ensemble. It may be another way of referring to the holism which clinical anthropology and, more recently, Louis Dumont have demonstrated to be the specificity of all life in society.

In similar vein, a scholarly account of irrationality in Greek thought (Dodds 1951) stresses the permanence of the magical thinking that binds us to the cosmic and societal *holos*. Such an analysis – when related to the transverse reading we have just mentioned – may allow the sociologist to interpret a whole series of attitudes and situations which, either as memories or in a more stereotypical way, continue to act or 'to be acted' in the course of everyday life. Thus, Nilsson's comment to the effect that primitive mentality is a fairly good description of the mental behaviour of most people today can, despite Dodd's reservations (1951: 8), be applied to social life as a whole, and even to technical and supposedly rational activities. Once the mechanism of rationalization and theorization – which, in modern and contemporary epistemology, functions as a categorical imperative – breaks down, we find ourselves dealing with a collective substratum which provides a basis for the passions, affects and blindness which, whether we like it or not, are also part of the actions of the social agents known as experts, technicians, bureaucrats, scientists and, of course, politicians. We could all apply this general comment to an infinite number of situations which, in both the public and the private domain, seem, despite their supposed justifications, to be marked with the seal of the irrational.

I am not suggesting that we require a normative description of such irrationality; we need only note that it is not easy to rid either individual or social structuration of their ties with the primitive world. Indeed, it is possible to take the view that what appears to be dysfunctional in terms of the royal road to Reason is in fact an index of the fact that we still have deep roots in a broader realm where passion and reason, nature and culture, gods and men, come together. In that respect, Dodds's analysis of Homer can be generalized to social life: 'Gods may appear at times in human form, men may at times share in the divine attribute of power, but in Homer there is nevertheless *no real blurring of the sharp line which separates humanity from deity*' (Dodds 1951: 10, emphasis added).[5] We will return to the problem of this rootedness, but it should be noted that the reference to the divine is quite Durkheimean. Dodds is clearly referring to a social aggregate that transcends every individual and which, at the same time, is bound up with the natural environment. This is the very essence of religion. As a result of this perspective, I have on a number of occasions felt it permissible to speak of an *immanent transcendence*.

This alternative way of relating to nature also opens up another important line of investigation. A separate study would be required for a full discussion of this question, but its importance for any reflection on epistemology must be noted. To adopt the terminology of the Frankfurt school, nature is no longer regarded as an object to be exploited (*Gegenstand*), but as a partner to be reckoned with (*Gegenspieler*). This inevitably has implications at the level of a society's self-representation. For our purposes, it is a matter of seeing how, in the context of the re-emergence of nature as partner, the notion of analogy takes on a new topicality. We have already cited Lévi-Strauss. The 'search for correspondences' that he observes amongst the peoples he studies and which, in his view, is still relevant to an interpretation of our era, is not unreminiscent of the rather more diffuse content of ecological movements, of the new value that is now attached to territory, to local issues and of the dialectic revival. Many works written from different points of view have looked at this state of affairs from a sociological angle. For my own part, I have attempted to underline its importance for an interpretation of everyday life (Maffesoli 1979b; 1982, chs 2 and 3). The question is as yet unresolved, and even investigations into the social meaning of technological developments cannot ignore it. Some will inevitably take the view that it is a phenomenon that is becoming more widespread, that it is becoming more diversified and nuanced and that its very existence calls into question the role of the sociologist.

We therefore have to assess, or at least indicate, the importance of these indicators from an epistemological point of view. It seems essential to go beyond the classic nature–culture dichotomy. Morin is exploring the issue in an exhaustive manner; to do justice to that intellectual adventure would require a further study. For the moment, I will simply refer to the suggestions put forward by Durand (1979b) who, following the example of the authors we have just cited, has clearly formulated the close connection that exists between culture and nature. He nicely defines it as an 'anthropological trajectory', which is intended to mark the path leading from the 'vital' to the 'cultural'. Such a comment may seem self-evident, if not perfectly banal, and yet if we look at it closely it has far-reaching intellectual implications. A new *ecology* – in the etymological sense of the word – is being outlined. In short, 'being-together' can no longer be studied in an abstract way; we must also take into account our relationship with the environment, with what I described earlier as 'nature as partner'. The characteristic feature of the anthropological trajectory is the dynamic paradox that there is such a thing as 'human nature, but it is a potential which exists in negative terms and which is realized only through the actualization of a specific culture' (Durand 1979: 25–6).[6] To take the definition further still, we might note that the realization of this power is to be understood in the strong sense. We can therefore no longer conceive of life in society in either an angelic (or idealist) way or a voluntarist way. We cannot, that is, prescribe what it must be and how it is to achieve this or that goal.

In the light of my research on violence, I would now add something that I have until now refrained from saying: it seems that the 'ecology' induced by the anthropological trajectory allows us to integrate the parameter of man as 'terrestial carnivore' into social analysis. That paradigm should subsequently provide a pertinent basis for an interpretation of the polytheism of values, the war between the gods (Weber), the ambivalence that psycho-analysis reveals so well (Freud's *Spaltung*), the *contradictoriel* of the logicians (Lupasco and Beigbeder) and the various antagonisms that structure the social. The mention of violence here is not a trivial matter: the transcendence of the nature–culture divide is not reassuring. Cruelty is at work there, as it is elsewhere. As I have demonstrated in my work on orgies, the figure of Dionysus that is emerging in our civilization is not entirely reassuring; various modulations of conflict and brutality are also involved. It has to be clearly understood that nature's return to the fore is not a peaceful process. The fact that this cruelty is integrated into a ritualized process may, however, make it less offensive. Be that as it may, the sterilized, frozen and moribund world that was based upon self-control (educational mechanisms) and mastery of the universe (exploitation of nature) is being replaced by a much more complex world based upon chance (the stochastic model), and death is an organic part of it.[7] It should not be forgotten that whilst Dionysus is a tree-god who is bound up with the notion of territory, he is also connected with the earth, where the buried dead represent the promise of new life. The return of nature also means the daily experience of death.

This dimension of the anthropological trajectory does involve separation; it involves compromise and integration and leads to what I call a conflictual harmony. This brings us back to the theme of *glutium mundi*, which meant so much to the alchemists, and which we can employ as a metaphor to interpret the many situations that are developing contemporaneously (religious sects, affinity groups, musical clubs, voluntary associations). Durand speaks (1969: 311) in this connection of a 'glischromorphous structure', as opposed to schizophrenic separation – which is a paroxysmal and pathological form of the mechanism of individualization and of the related vision of nature as an object to be exploited. The viscosity that typifies the 'glue of the world' brings us back to analogy. One of the effects of this new relationship with nature is that it obliges us to integrate rather than to discriminate. In that respect, analogy is a choice instrument. It means that the microcosm – social man – can be situated within a more or less benevolent macrocosm in which he wants to be involved. Astrology (in both its most sophisticated forms and as seen in popular magazines), wholefoods, the most recent forms of alternative psychology, the development of the arts of divination and the explosion of parapsychology are all indices of this 'viscosity'. *Glutinum mundi*. Whilst it neither despises them nor overestimates them, analogy can explain nature's evolution into culture. It makes it clear that what classical humanism saw as 'infra-human' is not in fact alien. Because it promotes an interpretative attitude, analogy opens up the way for the integration of intellectual reflection into societal organicity. In terms of our concerns here, we might say that the sociologists should no longer aspire to being schoolteachers who decide what is right and what is wrong; they should be content to draw attention to the polyphony of everyday life.

That is our central concern: the ability to recognize, despite all its vicissitudes, the wealth and fecundity of everyday life. We therefore have to agree to take down all the protective barricades erected by the so-called scientific attitude, which is more concerned with exploiting its capital than resolutely going down paths which are either poorly signposted or not signposted at all. Fortunately, the younger generation of sociologists are beginning to occupy domains which have until now been overlooked or despised, and are leaving the research bureaucrats and and institutions to play with their toys. Their boldness and their irreverence are the only things that count; ignoring dogmas, injunctions and 'keep out' signs, they are, to quote Georges Balandier (1971: 6), endorsing the 'demand for a general vision' that goes 'beyond the fragmentation induced by analysis'.

It is possible that metaphor and analogy can satisfy that demand. The suggestion at least deserves consideration. Rejecting both functionalism and critical thought – which is its corollary – and at the same time avoiding the traps of metasociological discourse, metaphor and analogy are rooted in a mythological substratum and draw our attention to the multitude of histories that structure all sociality.[8]

# 6

# *Physical and Social 'Correspondence'*

> How weightily thou speakest of all these mingled things, of
> veil and sickle and seed-corn; rightly too, since these things
> are related and are one in God, though to our eyes they are
> embroidered many-fold upon the veil.
>
> Thomas Mann, *Joseph and his Brothers*

It is time for an interlude. Let us think for a moment about Lévi-Strauss's search for correspondences. It would of course be easy to relegate it to the realm of poetry or day-dreaming, or to see it as an inconsequential little self-indulgence like hiring a dancing partner in idle moments. But it seems increasingly necessary to give it its rightful place if our sociology is not to be too incomplete.

Taking 'correspondences' into account means giving a new value to space, which has 'its own values'. Now that linear history is viewed with a certain suspicion, we are beginning once more to take the view that space can be the site of a real social investment. Until quite recently, everything to do with spatiality was the sign of an anachronistic or even reactionary perspective. Neither the educational process nor personal structuration escaped the law that made learning to use (or master) the dialectical tool a categorical imperative that it was difficult to avoid. For some, the issues at stake were quite clear: without a good historical vision of self and society one lapsed into schizophrenic excesses or into the all too common illness known as 'false consciousness'. As we know, this was not a minor illness. It goes without saying that, whilst there were a few cases of full-blown mental illness, the affliction was very widespread. Hence the role of the intellectual-doctor:

pointing out where history was really leading, popular common sense notwithstanding. This view, theorized in varying degrees, provided almost the sole basis for an intellectual method that for a hundred years ignored the countless significant attitudes – daily rituals, the anodine practices of living in a house, strolling, chatting, loving, scheming, etc. – that make up the greater part of the social fabric, and which were until recently refused admission into any serious sociology. Unless of course they were admitted only to be dismissed as alienation. It can on the other hand be recognized, or at least this is my hypothesis, that we are dealing here with a specific appropriation of existence which, whilst it may not be major, still merits attention.

It is true that the general thematic of 'correspondence', which brings together the various elements we have been discussing, has, since the French Revolution, been monopolized by a right-wing conception of politics. Until quite recently in the various regions of France, and no doubt elsewhere, references to local issues, dialects, the land and all it connoted were part of a well-defined political tradition. When I was young, the *Félibrige* [a Provençal literary school] made no secret of the the values it was defending or of where its political loyalties lay. As Slama's (1980) acute analysis clearly demonstrates, the fusion of self and world inspired many of the analyses made by Maurras, Péguy and Barrès. De Maistre too was in many respects one of those who pioneered the interpretation of nature as a 'vast communications system'. I would, however, point out that whilst we are dealing here with a right-wing ideology, it has to be admitted that its somewhat pagan overtones did disturb a Catholic establishment that was in other respects attracted to its 'organicist' vision.

That problem cannot be dealt with at length here, but it has to be mentioned, if only in order to point out that an ideological shift has taken place in recent decades. Increasingly, the values of rootedness and 'correspondence' are part of a left-wing ideology. This comment obviously requires some qualification, but it is clear that for the younger generation, ecological and regionalist movements are on the whole part of a 'left' culture. A more detailed study would even show that supposedly right-wing regionalist organizations or circles have, in the space of a few years, gone over to the opposite side. Ultimately, political connotations count for little; thanks to the mechanism of the saturation of values that is so dear to Sorokin, political connotations can vary and what was once the monopoly of one camp can become that of the enemy camp. It is, on the other hand, important to note that the 'correspondence' mechanism has major implications for the way we view the organization of society. To be more specific, it is clear that we cannot understand the problem of social alterity without referring to the problem of the environment, either overtly or more discreetly. In that sense, it is clear that the system that allows us to communicate with nature can no longer be ignored. Even if it does take a caricatural or even a commercial form, the correspondence between microcosm and macrocosm will find a way to express itself. Sexual ambiguities, the interest in astrology, the cult of the body, the obsession with the present and the fascination with death are all, in their various modulations, part of an organic vision which the contemporary belief in technology is powerless to eradicate. It may well be a pagan mysticism, but it seems to be undergoing a contemporary revival after a long period in which monotheist logic was dominant.

For our present purposes, this pagan correspondence has two primordial dimensions. On the one hand, to pursue the point just made, it is in technical terms an expression of the contemporary resurgence of the *interpretative approach*. It gives intuition and comparisons a role, takes account of the sensual dimension of social existence, and acknowledges the mythical force that mobilizes basic solidarity. In a word, it draws attention to the mystery of the unstable phenomena that integrate every individual into a cosmic or ecological whole. On the other hand, and this remains to be explored, the symbolist perspective outlined here – and it is to be understood in the strong sense – necessarily bring us to the multiple connections that make up everyday life. They too are modulations of correspondence. Correspondence is obviously not 'verbalized' as such, but it is possible to find it in all the everyday gestures and discourses that we tend to overlook or even discredit with the damning label of popular 'common sense'. The viewpoint I am describing does of course contain an element of vitalism. That is, however, an unqualified judgement because, as I have had occasion to say more than once, cruelty too is part of social organicity. If this world view has to be given a name, it would be more appropriate to describe it as 'tragic'.

We can analyse the relationship between the mechanism of correspondence and solidarity by looking at the implications of the saturation of the 'progressive' and 'individualist' values that were so typical of Western bourgeoisism. It should be recalled that in traditional societies, the force presiding over various social aggregates – and which, *pace* Durkheim, I propose to call 'organic solidarity' – is defined primarily in spatial terms. The naturally 'extended' family is defined by a territory. La Roy Ladurie's analyses (1975) of the 'domus' and Glotz's work on ancient Greece (1904) clearly demonstrate the close connection that existed between communities and their environment.[1] The assertion of individuality was a gradual process. If we read Clisthenes the Athenian, for example, we find that in Greece the new emphasis on rationalism gradually came to emphasize contractual associations (the division of land into *demes*), at the expense of classical or family ties.

Although the development whose premises we are describing is increasingly marked, it is not dominant in any absolute sense. The sociality/space relation still exists at a subterranean level. I am of course exaggerating to some extent, but it is important to underline its survival if we are to understand its contemporary revival. Sociologists are agreed that rural values still survive, even in industrialized countries. For more than a century we have of course been seeing an exodus from the countryside as a result of industrial development, but kinship, mythical loyalties to home-lands, the purchase of second homes, and even the minor theme 'getting back to nature', either communally or individually, are all ways of establishing a 'correspondence' with a piece of land that still has an imaginary pull. It is the same with the working classes or, more generally, the urban population: their appropriation of space has often been overlooked, as have the phenomenon of kitsch (Moles, Dorflès), various urban rituals (travel, markets, pubs), all the secondary spaces that are being created on the borders between city and suburbs,[2] and – and why not – the increase in allotments. These are all ways of 'corresponding' with a cosmic environment, whatever its dimensions.

To turn to eyewitness accounts, in the novel, memoirs and even ethnology, we are seeing the development of a 'literature of nostalgia' which reminds us of our roots and the life-styles of the 'good old days'. This is not the place to make a critical analysis of this trend. For the moment, we need only note that it is enjoying considerable success. It plays an important role in the revival of local feasts, folklore, popular festivals and the rebirth of old customs and costumes. Such manifestations are obviously not devoid of commercial motives – that is self-evident – but at a deeper level we have to ask why they enjoy such success on the margins of a mass consumer society (we can ignore arguments about the chronic imbecility of the masses). It seems to me that they are a highly ambiguous expression of a desire to live *symbolically* a relationship with a shared territory. The common denominator in all the situations listed above can be seen as an index of what Lévy-Bruhl calls 'participation'. It could mean the excitement of a festival or of trade, the occupation of a territory, a feeling of belonging to the land, merging into an urban crowd, discussing a handful of vegetables from an allotment or comparing ways to use recycled tyres. These are all ways of avoiding isolation, escaping the limits of one's own body, becoming part of a collective body or, in short, sharing a wider space. Its expression varies from one period to the next, but basic sociality requires a shared space, and it always transcends abstract politics and apparent isolation.

It is even probable that societal equilibrium, which is a prime object for sociological investigation, rests primarily upon two elements which are at once heterogeneous and complementary: space and time, nature and history. Although the point can only be made in cavalier or simplistic terms here, it seems that balanced societies are societies which are able to live, in 'contradictory' fashion, the inherently dynamic and static dimensions of the given world. It is in that sense that 'correspondence' is relevant to our discipline: it allows us to change registers, to switch accents, and therefore to paint an extemely full picture of the social aggregates we are trying to describe. The above examples are a good illustration of the intersection of actions and affects that makes up the greater part of the minuscule attitudes that are the foundations of everyday life. Space may well be a closed field of economic and/ or political forces, but it is also the creation of minor investments which establish an extremely vocal network.

I am thinking here of Piaget's phrase 'reciprocal genesis' (Piaget 1950: vol. 1: 36–7), which allows us to analyse how social life takes shape in a constant interaction between active passion and the environment. This is not a one-way traffic. Piaget's analysis shows that the 'material' aspect of the environment is primordial. It both adapts the passions – passion being the prime human characteristic – and adapts to them. It is this interaction that produces the 'unstable equilibrium', which is not unreminiscent of Goethe's *beweglicher Ordnung*, that I have mentioned elsewhere (Maffesoli 1982: 69). It is precisely because it keeps us in touch with this process that 'correspondence' is a relevant analytic tool. Because it ignores fictional divisions, it allows us to interpret the system as a whole. We will have to come back to this point, but it is likely that so-called systems theory reflects similar concerns. Poetic correspondence, which has been out of favour for some time, can thus become a model for a more open and more generous scientific practice which is in keeping with the characteristic polysemy of sociality.

The peculiarity of this unstable equilibrium is that it explains the partial and tenuous adjustment, and the combination of unpredictability and certainty that, in the last analysis, make up our social perambulations. The various communities that make up societies exist in a state of *coenaesthesia*. That is what 'makes them tick'. There are breakdowns, failures and accidents; natural and political tyranny are certainly present. Violence and carnage are often part of everyday life. And yet, society survives, much to our astonishment. In a word, it adapts and reaches accommodations, and in a sense, that is the key to the mystery which explains its vitality 'in the face of everything'. This adaptation is obviously not a matter of will-power and it is not even a conscious process. And yet it happens, even after the most terrible blows of fate. What is the source of this equilibrium?

It should also be noted that this equilibrium is subject to eclipses and that its efficacy can vary. To adopt a Spenglerian stance, we might say that it suffers the repercussions of the transition from culture to civilization. When 'culture' is dominant, its vigorous constitution allows it to integrate antagonism, heterogeneity and conflicts between values. When, however, 'civilization' takes over, its anaemic structure tends to make it reject anything that departs from a monovalent schema. Being closer to foundational values, culture has nothing to fear because its pluralism is the source of its strength. The same cannot be said of civilization, which has less confidence in its mobilizing representations. Be that as it may, historians have observed that the weakening of a society is often related to a decrease in antagonistic tensions and to the rise of one value. Societal actions and passions are based upon a living paradox. The answer to our question about equilibrium is this: it is possible to use heterogeneity for social structuration. Just as we can agree that that the physical world is the product of the tension between the various molecules that make it up, so it is increasingly recognized that antagonistic values are the very things that ensure the survival of a society.

In order to explore this thematic we must, of course, refer to Max Weber, who has been either ignored or distorted by moralists of all stripes, but one also is put in mind of Pareto, who saw a close link between heterogeneity and equilibrium. The theory of equilibrium is certainly central to his sociology, and anyone who is familiar with his brilliant little *Il mito virtuista e la letteratura immorale* (Pareto 1914) will know that it is because it is polytheistic that an equilibrium of opposites can play its role. We need only refer to Busino's pertinent and erudite study (1968) of Pareto's sociology to realize how important the notion of equilibrium is to our project:

> The theory of equilibrium is based on the notion of the interdependency of factors at a given historical moment and on the constancy of laws of equilibrium existing independently of the history of particular societies. Society can be likened to a mechanical system of interacting forces; forces constituted by a hidden force: residues.[3]

Whilst a detailed discussion of Pareto's 'residues' would require a separate study, we must emphasize the role of interdependence and of the constancy of the laws of equilibrium. The former are determined by the latter. Busino subsequently demonstrates that the creation of an equilibrium no more means homogenization than stability means immobility.

A digression on equilibrium was necessary to provide a 'rational' explanation of the correspondence mechanism. We can now see that the search for links between microcosm and macrocosm is a modulation of a general conflictual harmony based upon the invariance of types (ideal types) which, although they do not exist as such, do inform social behaviour. The task of sociologists – and their dynamic role – is to reveal the specificity of contemporary expressions. By revealing the social roots of a specific expression, he can also explain how it provides a basis for the 'sympathy' which quite literally cements together the various aggregates (relations between lovers, group relations, parties, associations, nations etc.) with which we are so familiar. Correspondence therefore allows us to understand both the real stability of social aggregates, and the multiplicity of actions and affects that bring them to life. Just as a culture medium is, despite its relative tranquillity, swarming with interactions and all sorts of fevers, many different currents flow through societies; they merge and diverge, but there is nothing very logical about their movements. If we observe the life of a neighbourhood, we begin to get a good idea of the importance of these interactions, of the theatricality that is involved, of the multicoloured appearances that offer themselves to our gaze, of the objective chance of meetings and the mini-dramas and major tragedies to which they give rise. We see the birth of passions, and the labour that supplies the backdrop. All this is a clear illustration of the slender but solid threads that structure the social fabric.[4] It is also a reminder of the need to understand how every element in that fabric acts upon every other element. Once again, a symbolic correspondence – just like the love of nature that turns scents and sounds into a set of spatial markers – means that complementarity and pluralism are effective tools for the collective appropriation of a space.

Once we get away from a narrowly causalist vision, cease trying to explain social life in terms of a single determinant (or overdeterminant), and no longer argue in terms of inevitable catastrophes or other linear perspectives, we begin to notice correspondences that poets and mystics perceive intuitively. And we certainly come back to the 'holistic' analysis which, curiously enough, sociologists constantly seem to avoid, even when they claim to be doing the opposite. Because it rejects the psychologistic and economistic schemata that are the causes and effects of individualism, correspondence focuses any attempt at interpretation on a moving whole, on Piaget's 'unstable equilibrium'. To cite Goldmann (1967: 1000) it therefore 'tends to create an increasingly broad domain of the surrounding social and physical world'. This last remark is particularly pertinent, and clearly demonstrates that, now that the social cards are being dealt in a different way, we have to start playing a different epistemological game. We cannot go on using old tools in our attempt to analyse the emergence of these new/ old environmentalist values. It is in that sense that the notion of correspondence is the nodal point where the three dimensions that structure any society – relations with natural alterity, relations with social alterity, and our understanding of both – intersect. These relations can somewhat crudely be subsumed beneath the terms ecology, sociality and gnoseology. We must reject the reductive approach, and think these three elements and their intersection simultaneously. Following Durand and Morin, we must demonstrate the constant interaction that structures both the culturalization of nature and the naturalization of culture.

This interaction allows us to shed a new light on the organic solidarity that is fundamental to many social aggregates, and it is another way of describing the *coincidentia oppositorum* of the three elements (ecology, sociality and gnoseology) that we have just mentioned. If correspondence is – and to this extent it remains true to its poetic origins – primarily a way of sounding our relationship with the physical environment, it can provide an explanation for the bonds that structure the social environment. The physical environment is in a sense the matrix of which those bonds are born and in which they develop. It is because we live together – or are forced to live together – in a given environment that we have to develop it. This is a relativist vision, but it seems necessary to adopt it from the outset if we are not to lapse into a banal unanimism that could become very abstract. We can therefore attempt to interpret solidarity in terms of compromise.

Historians of religion, and especially historians of popular religion, have often noted the syncretism that characterizes cultural representations and practices. It is, for instance, well known that the gradual expansion of Christianity's audience from the time of Constantine onwards resulted in a loss of doctrinal purity. As it spread, it absorbed local beliefs. It baptized gods, exceptional individuals (heroes, witches and saints) and took over various shrines and sanctuaries. Theriomorphic myths did not escape its imperialism, and were quietly integrated into the Christian bestiary. It was thanks only to their adoption, and the contamination it implies, that Christianity succeeded in influencing a way of life. The process is not confined to Christianity. From Alexander the Great to communist ideology and the Muslim epic, human history clearly demonstrates that syncretism is one form of the compromise which, overtly or otherwise, provides the basis for all societies, be they long-lived or short-lived. It is 'as if' a symbiotic mechanism – and symbiotic is to be understood in the etymological sense – allowed people with different beliefs to live together. The mechanism has rarely been described by intellectuals, as it is the most reliable indicator of the popular relativism that so offends the holders of intellectual power. It is, however, instructive because it stresses a *primum vivere* that ignores all obstacles.

What is more, this societal 'symbiosis' clearly shows that any lasting sociality is directly linked to adaptation to the 'ecology' of a given territory. In his remarkable work on French mythology, Dontenville (1973: 7f) uses a host of specific examples to demonstrate that different beliefs can coexist to the degree that they all accept the natural forces that are venerated in their locality. We can extrapolate from this and say that the degree to which foreigners and migrants are accepted is directly proportional to their ability to adapt to the physical environment that influences the rites, usages and customs and life-styles of the social life of a given locality. Even incomplete studies clearly demonstrate that the townspeople who have in recent years succeeded in putting

down roots in the French countryside are those who have succeeded in establishing a symbiotic relationship with the natural
environment. Similarly, current research on Graissessac, a mining
village in the Cévennes, shows how successive waves of immi-
grants (Italian, Spanish, Polish and Portuguese) have amalgamated
to create a specific way of life based partly on the attraction–repulsion of the mine as a natural force, and partly on their
adaptation to the very special environment of the harsh mountains
of the Cévennes.[5] It is striking to see how, in the space of a few
decades, their customs, their relationship with their work and the
meaning of their festivals have become quite specific, and have
been strongly determined by the physical environment. The community that is emerging from this process of adaptation is certainly
unusual and, whilst it is not a model, it is a pertinent reminder
that similar examples of sociality are more common than one might
think.

No matter whether it uses traditional mythologies or contemporary societal theories of 'roots', the symbiosis in question is based
upon a natural and social correspondence which, whilst it is
impossible to establish any priorities, founds the fact of 'being-
together'.

We can of course refer to Durkheim and his analysis of totemism.
In paradigmatic terms, it may still be of contemporary relevance.
It is by no means certain that increasing rationalization has put an
end to magical thinking. To pursue my hypothesis still further, it
is possible that we are witnessing a re-enchantment of the world.
It is as though – and the same thing has has been observed in other
historical periods – the system of representations were concurrently
using two modes of expansion, each with its own sophisticated
logic. A rigorous analysis cannot ignore either mode, especially as
the dividing line between the two is far from clear. We must not
be afraid of saying again that the rationalist outlook has been (and
is being) fully explored; magical thinking is, in our day, the poor
relation. And that is clearly wrong, if we think of the multiplicity
of everyday facts that are quite incomprehensible if we do not refer
to magical thinking.

In the light of the above, it is clear that the 'bond of mystical
sympathy' which, according to Durkheim (1912: 149), 'unites each
individual to those beings, whether living or not, which are
associated with him', is still relevant to an analysis of the basic
sociality that finds expression in the life of urban neighbourhoods,
supposedly dehumanized housing estates, villages that are coming

back to life, or suburbs whose individuality is certainly worthy of our attention. The correspondence expressed there is not the same as that of the primitive tribes described by Durkheim; but we do find in affection for a stone, the bustle of the market, discussions over a drink or a game of bingo, in the collective battle with the weather, or in the intersection of ritual journeys, 'a solid system, all of whose parts are united and vibrate sympathetically' (Durkheim 1912: 150). It is impossible to say that solidarity once existed, and no longer exists; it is, rather, a matter of discovering its contemporary *modulations*. We have only to pay a modicum of attention to everyday life, its body language and its humdrum discourses, to find a correspondence whose profundity is, as is often the case, hidden on the surface.

Judicious observers, whatever their function (sociologists, journalists, travellers etc.) are all capable of describing the mechanisms behind mystical identification with an object or an element in a bestiary.[6] Such identification, regardless of its object, brings us back to the community it founds and/or strengthens. There are countless festive rituals, sporting gatherings, and collective events; each of them is a reminder of what I have described elsewhere (Maffesoli 1982) as the 'body in expansion'. It can only be understood in relation to a physical environment, be it 'nature', a town or a neighbourhood, or in other words a space, with all the emotional resonance that term implies. Correspondence is therefore both a societal reality and a mode of investigation; it is a way that allows us to interpret both Greek polytheism and the totemism of Australian tribes. And why not the polydimensional values that are beginning to trouble our own society? Each of the above examples is of course specific, but they all express a relationship with the cosmos, seen as a whole in which everything is all of a piece. It is possible that there is nothing new about the complex system of the contemporary world; if we wish to explore its meanders, it might not be inappropriate to look at traditional hermetism, for whilst there is no one-to-one comparison between Bruno's 'memory systems' (see Yates's remarkable study (1966)) and our 'contemporary information technology', it can be argued that both are ways of dealing with the problem of how to communicate with the social and natural environment. Recognizing and employing combinations means, *volens nolens*, accepting the pre-eminence of the the idea of interdependence, of connection and therefore of a oneness which, unlike a reductive Unity, functions with a plurality of interacting elements.

This, then, is what is at stake. Correspondence allow us to take into consideration the whole of the social dynamic, and gives an in-depth vision of what I have called a real 'culture medium'. Metaphors aside, this is something that cannot be rejected by those who remain loyal to the rationalist and critical tradition. The field of investigation is becoming broader and calls for a collective endeavour, to the extent that that is possible. We thus come back to Gramsci's beloved notion of an 'organic intellectual', even though the context might not be the same; we are dealing with the 'invention' of representations as well as with the societal will to life. Representations are not the abstract products of the will; they emerge, obviously in specific ways, from the practices, passions, affects, common sense and the various communities – large and small – that make up societies. By adopting this ambitious approach, and ignoring the *imperium* of linear or progressive perspectives, we can combine traditional visions and resolutely modern concerns. A coincidence of opposites if ever there was one! But where sociology is concerned, it is clear that a combination of the two should allow us to give the societal fact its full dignity. There are in fact no minor objects in social existence. Every element, whatever it may be, has an effect on every other element. In their various ways, politicians, journalists and advertising and communications specialists have long understood this. It would be regrettable if intellectuals could not come to terms with its effects.

A rapid reference to systems analysis is perhaps appropriate here (for a more detailed discussion see Barel 1973). It is possible that systems analysis represents, at least in part, an attempt to describe, in rationalist terms, a pluricausal conjuncture. Systems theory takes the view that any given set is open to various energies and causes. A set is self-regulating, dynamic and coherent, and, in the best-case scenario, it can absorb elements as disparate as religious, aesthetic, moral, political and economic representations. We can also accept that the analysis of systems explains both the static and the dynamic element in societies. Having no particular competence in the matter, I can only suggest that many sociologists might find 'systems theory' an acceptable way of looking at the problem of organic solidarity, which is not based upon separation, discrimination or mechanical functionalism, and which can differentially absorb contributions from every aspect of the physical and social world into an endless interaction or correspondence.

It must, however, be pointed out that, unlike approaches which, with varying degrees of sophistication or subtlety, are based upon causality, the defining characteristic of the organic dimension is its ability to absorb paradoxical viewpoints. It takes account of the random events that punctuate life in society; it accepts both its incoherence, and the fact that the passions have an important role to play. There is no need to dwell on the point; it merely has to be noted because paradox relates, as I have noted on several occasions, to the tragic dimension, which becomes more pronounced as the 'I' gradually gives way to the 'we'. Individualism and the social State can provide a dramatic solution to the problems that arise, but they always do so in reductive terms (enslaving nature, sterilizing existence, reducing alterity). What I call sociality accepts the same problems as a destiny. When there is no longer one essential pivot (the individual, the State), and when the polytheism of values and roles comes to the fore, paradox reigns supreme. And correspondence may be a very good way to manage and interpret paradox.

# 7
# *Ever Renewed Life*

Divinity is at work in the living, but not in death; it exists in what is developing and changing, but not in what has developed and become frozen. As it strives towards the divine, reason must therefore have dealings only with what is developing, with the living.

Goethe, letter to Eckermann

## 1 Cyclical thought

Paradox, the resurgence of the tragic, and the above comments on correspondence and the organicity of things are primarily a reminder that whilst civilizations are mortal, they definitely go through highly differentiated phases. Whereas the drama of bourgeoisism – from the Hegelian dialectic to the class struggle and to light comedy – is basically active, the tragic is basically somewhat asthenic, at least in terms of what might be called the projective (*pro-jectum*) dimension. It is not that, as some would have us believe, disgust or lassitude are dominant, but rather that a certain relativism has been introduced. And because it has a rather clearer vision of the 'return of the same', that relativism concentrates its attention on the present and on related values (see Maffesoli 1979b). It is important to stress this point, as our interpretation may depend upon it. If we take the temporal triad of past, present and future, the emphasis that is placed on one or another element will reappear in all the acts and representations that structure a given society (or societies). And we can observe that an emphasis on the present goes hand in hand with an emphasis on mythology, which, under various names and in many different ways, is one of the preoccupations of modern consciousness. With the prophetic gift that his work so often exemplifies, Proust describes his interlocking narrative as representing an 'Einsteinized' time which, as has often been pointed out, is close to being a myth. What is certain is that the evocative power of records of the past stems from the fact that they allow us to perceive and interpret the *hic et nunc* more clearly. This is what is at stake in mythical time and, as Durand reminds us (1979b: 286), one of its characteristics is that it takes us out of 'the one-dimensionality of blind history, and places us in a discontinuous universe'. This is very close to the 'Einsteinization' of time and the cyclical return of the same, just as there are many bridges between myth and the present. Examples include the minuscule and ritualized situations that clearly demonstrate that a tension or extension towards the future is much less important than the potential intensity of repetition.

Given that our reflections on sociological method lead us to the conclusion that 'life is constantly renewed', we have to look, if only for a moment at the cyclical vision, which so often has a bad press. In the present context, we can only suggest that it is a line of research for a specific study of the tragic view of the social. It must, however, be noted that it marks the intersection between a large set relating to correspondence, the environment, nature, local issues, etc., and a set encompassing the multiple elements of everyday life, hedonism, scepticism, or, in a word, everything that puts a value on lived experience. The basic assumption behind it is of course that social life must be studied for what it is, and not in terms of what it ought to be. We have to recognize that there is, for better or worse, such a thing as the acceptance (and perhaps the affirmation) of existence. Nietzsche was the great bard of this thematic, which clerics (intellectuals) find so unacceptable. They constantly attempt to decipher it, decode it and find the truth that lies behind supposedly false appearances. We therefore have to stop being suspicious and attune ourselves to banality. According to the cyclical view, no matter whether we attribute it to a deity or to nature, it is clear that *posui in visceribus hominis sapientiam* is a basic principle that explains the stubborn survival of life in society.

Such an assumption might of course lead to an overevaluation of the nebulous entity known as 'the people'.[1] That hypostatic entity, assuming that it exists, does have one virtue in that it can be contrasted with the reality principle of life in society and can therefore be deflated, if need be. The same cannot be said of the intellectual pretentiousness which, because it constructs systems on the basis of abstract concepts, can function perfectly well in a vacuum. Like Weber's ideal type, the former attitude has the virtue of being able to reveal a whole series of phenomena that are inscribed in our day-to-day theatricality, and which are at best despised for that very reason. Western iconoclasm, with its mon-ovalent rationalism and loathing of images, is incapable of retain-ing an impression of anything it cannot integrate into its system. And yet the play of the imaginary is the clearest expression of sociality's cyclical scepticism. Nothing in sociality is uniform, linear or explicable in terms of a univocal concept. On the contrary, it is a realm of profusion, redundancy and repetition. One has only to think of the doublets, or the slightly different versions of the heterogeneous lessons in which myths find expression. Myths use a truly cyclical technique. The importance of repetition in hum-drum descriptions or in everyday conversations is also strikingly important. This almost obsessional repetition is clearly a way of both acknowledging and denying the passage of time. In that sense, cyclical repetition is an effective defence. Similarly, the development of the comic strip – particularly the work of artists like Reiser, Brétecher and especially Lauzier (see Pennacchioni 1982) – is a remarkable index of a type of narrative that cannot be confined within linearity.

The most noticeable feature of mythological doublets, repetitive conversations and the redundant derision of comic strips is their ability, perhaps despite themselves or at least without explicitly wanting to do so, to make an implicit critique of dogmatic discourses and to state that, to a large degree, social man never changes and that the same always returns. They can be playful, religious or grating, but they are a repository for the agnostic anomie which contends, in the face of both theological power and its secular expression (the State), that nothing new ever happens in human history. Mythical stories, vignettes and graffiti – which are all 'minor' expressions of thought – remind us, without attaching too much importance to the fact, that the one thing that merits our attention is the present, which is always with us and always self-identical. Leaving others to worry about hell or the nuclear apocalypse, they remind us, thanks to their incoherence and repetitions, that the only things that matter are good stories and images that disappear before our very eyes. Their inclusion in collections or albums does of course give them a semblance of unity, but their real value is their ability to crystallize a beautiful moment, to describe a situation or to paint a fleeting vision. In that sense, they are part of an 'ethics of the moment' which shows little concern for heavenly paradises or radiant futures, but which in some obscure fashion insists on living *all the same* existence crippled with vicissitudes which is, despite or because of that, still captivating.

It may seem futile to dwell on the minor discourses that emerge from an obscurely cyclical vision, and it is clear that they are not the only elements at work in social life, but it is probable that their contribution will considerably broaden the spectrum of sociological interpretation.

One element that clearly brings out the importance of cyclical relativism to the collective consciousness is the popular attitude towards politics. Once again, there is a lot to be learned from saloon-bar talk, and it would take a specific research project to analyse all the degrees of suspicion with which political activity is viewed. It would be more accurate to say that an interest is taken in political activity to the extent that it is an art with its own rules. In Mediterranean countries, for example, a political speech must, like *bel canto*, be moving; it must arouse passions and solicit affects. Rationality is a different matter. There is no need to to appeal to anyone's convictions. It is especially entertaining to observe these phenomena at election-time. It is certainly amusing to record the conversations that take place after a party political broadcast, and to listen to comments on debates between leading personalities, but it enrages the increasingly rare individuals who believe in rationally based political programmes. The way all political parties are being invaded by 'public-relations' specialists is in that sense instructive. European election campaigns do not, of course, yet look like American-style parades, though they are becoming similar. And we should have no illusions about the care politicians take over their images, or about the growing importance of the public-relations experts who create those images: the goal is to stage a spectacle that appeals to the heart rather than the intellect. Entertainers are not taken in by this; during major electoral campaigns they withdraw from the scene to rehearse for their next tour.

Politics openly admits to being a spectacle because that is the way the masses see politics. Despite all the election manifestos and promises, and the drives to recruit supporters and members, no one has any illusions about the realities of power, or about the harsh necessities of exercising power. Only militants believe that candidates should keep their promises; if the voters are convinced of anything, it is that they are not required to do so. Sociological inertia ensures that we vote because we have got into the habit of doing so, and we usually vote for the same political side, but – with the exception of a few rare historical moments – we vote without any great confidence as to what is to be expected as a result of voting. In that sense, the political show is indeed part of the *theatrum mundi*. It is one of those good stories that provide a break and interrupt the all-pervading tedium of social life. There have been many investigations, some more serious than others, into this 'voluntary servitude'. The explanation may lie in the insatiable curiosity of children: let's make believe, and see if it changes anything. Given that we cannot go on 'playing schools' or 'playing mummy and daddy', we 'play elections'. In saying that I am not trying to say that this is wrong. What right do we have to pass judgement on an attitude, especially a playful attitude? I am simply stressing how much our social mentality (also known as mass opinion) owes to the cyclical view that 'there is nothing new under the sun'. Ultimately, political oppression is always the same, and people are, in an almost conscious way, well aware of the fact. Princes may come and go (and it is preferable for them to go), but their actions are always abstract and when they claim to be speaking and acting in the name of the most deprived, they always demand submission or conformity to a norm. Could it be different? There is too great a divorce between the viewpoint of politicians who look down from on high and the impulses behind basic sociality.

One could go on making such common-sense comments, which are a good indication of the 'mood' of everyday life, and they can be compared to more sophisticated considerations. It is always interesting to compare an ideology's (in this case the ideology of the return of the same) popular expressions and its more sophisticated modulations. From a Weberian point of view it is clear that, where the human sciences are concerned, the recognition that antinomic value-systems exist in different societies, or even within the same society – which is captured in the expression 'the war between the gods' – results, if not in an absolute 'value-free neutrality', at least in a certain scepticism about the very concept of Truth. In a paradoxical (or in other words dynamic) way, Weber attempts both to think rigorously and to generalize, and to recognize the capriciousness and the ephemeral nature of human passions. It is clear that many of his analyses are based upon what

I call popular relativism. The antinomy of values can never be resolved, and ultimately it is their antinomy that allows societies to survive. Basically, and to put it rather crudely, so long as the gods wage war on one another, humans can live in peace.

A similar perspective can be found in Pareto's sociology. Just as Lévi-Strauss observes that 'man has always thought as well as he does now', the sociologist from Lucerne was convinced that 'man is always the same'. The conviction is expressed in cursory fashion in his *Treatise on General Sociology* (1923). Many of Pareto's analyses are imbued with scepticism. If one looks at his life and work, one might conclude that his scepticism reflects all the disappointments of a blighted career. Having been an ambitious engineer in Florence, a conscientious economist and then a somewhat disillusioned professor of sociology, Pareto realized that action is futile because the history of human societies is dominated by eternal return and repetition. It may be a mere point of detail, but unlike his exegete Busino (1968 : 51), I would not describe Pareto as a 'pessimist'; it is, perhaps, more accurate to say that he was imbued with the tragic feeling of existence. Being a good observer of the political activity of his day, he was well aware that its claims to be rationally based were a pure fiction, and he was determined to follow through the implications of his argument. That is why I am saying, in the framework of the present analysis, that his outlook has a lot in common with the popular scepticism we were discussing earlier.[2] In the political realm, not to mention all the other human activities which do not make explicit claims to being political, reason is no more than a 'derivation', a legitimation which masks the incoherence, vagaries and individual interests of passion. One is inevitably reminded of the Machiavelli of the *Storia*, who did so much to reveal all the ambiguity and ambivalence of human actions. We do not have to change a great deal; if we simply alter the names of the protagonists and the parties, we have an analysis that can be applied to every era in which the political dimension is dominant.

It is clear that the political game is a privileged arena for the observation of the cyclical return of the same: observations can be made over long periods, but also over the period of years or even months that follow an important election. The same process can be seen to be at work in many societal attitudes. When the future is dominant, the collective consciousness looks as a whole to the future; when the present comes to the fore, we see the resurgence of a cyclical vision. Why? Perhaps because of the mechanism of saturation, which has been well described by Sorokin. Values, like everything else, become worn out and tired. Whatever the truth of the matter and, given that we cannot answer the question 'why', we can perhaps look at the 'how' and all that it implies. If we cannot do that, we will understand nothing about societal evolution. The myths and the imaginal function that return in force in the entertainment field (and which, in recent years, have focused around figures like Elvis Presley, Marilyn Monroe and Claude François), in republican institutions (the Panthéon ceremony, Versailles, the 14 July etc.) and in public festivities (the many fêtes organized by local politicians and the public authorities), are all expressions of both the saturation of a linear concept of time and of the desire to recuperate the *hic et nunc* that haunts everyday life. Now, the best way to understand the present is to compare it with the great moments of the past. Proust's metaphor of Einsteinized time is a good example. Cyclical life reminds us of the temporality of passion, which is more powerful than any rationalist construct. It is perfectly legitimate to want to reform or revolutionize this state of affairs, but first of all we have to recognize it for what it is, for the cyclical rhythm of its various rituals introduces us to a new epistemology which is still in its infancy.

Perhaps this is what Pareto meant by the logico-experimental method he held so dear. When stripped of its positivist veneer, it emphasizes the factual and the present that solicit us. It forces our understanding to make the endless 'transition between formism to empathy' that I described earlier. We have to have the intellectual open-mindedness to leave our studies and to hang around in bars or wander the streets. We may well laugh, pull a face or shrug our shoulders, but that is the way to come to terms with the breadth, intensity and variations of a living, breathing society. Our object is not a dead body. Its life can be either monotonous or eventful. It may be unfulfilled, or it may be full of joys. But our object is alive, and that is something that the intellectual eunuchs, technocrats and lounge lizards will never understand. Rather than applying the same old methods, which may well have stood the test of time but which no longer have anything to say about anything, we must resolutely enter into what Nicholas of Cusa called the spiral of knowledge. In his day, medieval dogmatism was running out of steam, and a new world was coming into being. It is not impossible that something similar is happening today.

Rather than rejecting or denying the existence of all these paradoxes, antinomies and antagonisms, perhaps we should accept them for what they are. Our *considerations* will obviously not have the certainty (or the rigidity) of theoretical or divine Truth, but their jerkiness will be in keeping with their labile object. Perhaps we will then be able to 'transform vicious circles into virtuous cycles', as Morin (1977–80, vol. 1: 19–20) puts it.[3] To the extent that *virtù* is, as Machiavelli, Guiccardini and other thinkers of the *quattrocentro* teach us, the cement that structures all sociality. A new epistemology is meaningful only if it allows us to think about everyday life in a totally non-conformist way. In that sense, it is helpful to recall the etymology of the term 'encyclopedism': *agkiklois paidea*, meaning 'a cyclical process of learning'. That is precisely what is at stake here: paying attention to the lived experience, the efficacy of cycles and the renewal of knowledge are closely bound up with one another. It is not that we have to construct a closed system or a literally totalitarian mode of thought; it is more a matter of taking stock of the breaks, events, minuscule day-to-day acts, or in a word the swirling movement of existence that it is so difficult to reduce or confine by means of rigid knowledge. Morin, who, despite much sarcasm, is at the forefront here, describes (1977–80, vol. 1: 19–20) the coming revolution in thought in terms of 'a swirling movement that shifts from the phenomenological experience to the paradigms that organize that experience'. It would be difficult to improve on this formulation: intellectuals all too often forget that the road to knowledge is also a walk through life. It would be a mistake to think that the 'existence' in question means narrow individualism or subjectivism. I have, I think, already demonstrated that, as we come under the influence of the Dionysian paradigm, we are moving towards a communal fusion that is well described by the metaphor of a cluster of bodies supported by a 'territory'. Cyclical thought stresses the transcendence of individualist reductionism, and plunges us into the endless movement of the cosmos and relations with the other. Far from capitalizing commodities, bodies and theories, it introduces us to the joyous expenditure of a conjuncture that might be called thought incarnate.

## 2  Style fragmented

When we are confronted with a cyclical evolution and its interpretation, our traditional points of reference naturally vanish. There is no finality and no determinate meaning in the circularity of things;

meaning is not to be found here or there: it is everywhere. Discourses (from works of erudition to thrillers), actions and situations are not goal-oriented. They are valid in themselves and are exhausted as soon as they appear. This makes the sociologist's task very difficult. There is no concealing the fact that undertaking the 'encyclopedic task' (as defined earlier) is like walking a tightrope. Research programmes which are constantly being called upon to supply justifications and verifications become fragile. Finding a solution to this state of affairs is out of the question – it is impossible. We would do better to go on seeing it as a problem and to remember that, as Rilke puts it, it is by living it as a problem that we find the solution without being aware of it.

The admission that there is a mystery has nothing to do with with some vaguely existentialist stance; if we go back to its etymological meaning, a mystery is something that creates a bond between initiates. Rather than attempting to solve it, let us accept the paradox: the simplicity of existence has as its corollary the difficulty of its expression, but that difficulty is one of the things that cements our being-together. This paradox has to be taken into account in any sociological investigation. Our task is to speak of existence's 'hot' movement in a language which is, whatever we try to do about it, essentially cold. We have to explain social lability in curiously static terms. There is a discrepancy between our language and reality. If we take this aporia into account we can elaborate a sociology which respects the given world and which does not pontificate like some boring schoolteacher who forever says what things 'should be'. Our critique of positivism implies that we have to recognize the importance of ideology, take note of the efficacy of form, analogies and metaphor, and observe the return of a cyclical world view. We will then be in a position to understand the plural aspect of existence. What is more important, we will be forced to grant a certain pre-eminence to the popular common sense which, despite the cost and the pain it often gives us, remains our discipline's *ultima ratio* and its essential point of reference, if it is not to lapse into complete abstraction. We only 'discover' things that already exist.

Many people have said that their ideas 'were in everyone's head'. Gide, for instance, used to say that the only reason he wrote was 'to be reread'. This is simply another way of saying that reading is a way of 'recognizing' what we already know. Perhaps the sociological method should integrate what has until now been a purely fictional or poetic parameter. That would not mean renouncing our intellectual ambitions. On the contrary, if we adopt that parameter rigorously and persevere without boasting or becoming paranoid, we will be able to participate in the actualization of our times, in the strict sense of the term. Every era has to discover itself, and this is a way of participating in our era's self-discovery. Any observer of the educational process knows that adult experience has only a relative importance for children; they have to invent their own way of life. The same is true of theory and, especially in our day, of sociology. Together with other modes of expression, it must describe the present that is our destiny; it must help to blaze a trail or at least update the signposts that mark it.

It follows from what we have just said that this 'setting out down the road', this method (*meta odos*), does not have to create a new language or a new grammar. At most, its vocation is to 'give a purer meaning to the words of the tribe'. In that way, the gap between language and reality can be reduced. The daily gestures (discourse and action) of sociality have a 'style'. We simply have to pay attention to it. Sociality's style is, naturally, sometimes jerky. It consists of dialogues and of notions which are not necessarily logically connected. We find in it the scents and sounds typical of any form of life that has not been imposed from the outside. We are, in a word, dealing with the theatricality that makes up the fabric of everyday life. As the hero of Pieyre de Mandiargues's *La Marge* says, love of a town's market is 'proportional to love of life'. Markets are the setting for pathetic, grotesque, comic and dramatic situations which are often a condensation of the existential content of a whole day or some other period of time. As we can see from this example, the 'style' of banality is a stimulus, not to judging, criticizing or pronouncing about our objects of knowledge, but to interpreting and expressing. Is that any less glorious? Not necessarily, but it is certainly more difficult, because we cannot content ourselves with our usual abstract verbosity. The verifications asked of us lie in part in our ability to describe social phenomena as adequately as possible.

The suspicious thinking that develops out of Marxism, Freudianism and/or scientistic positivism obviously has difficulty in accepting such a phenomenology. It would rather assume that actions and discourses have a hidden meaning; they are always assumed to be structurally defective. This approach widens the gap between language and reality, when it does not create it. Any discipline obviously needs a specific vocabulary, a vocabulary being to the intellectual what a tool is to a workman, or what a set of rules is to an administrator. There is no question of denying that legitimate use can be made of specific languages. But nor can we accept uncritically what is known as jargon. Jargon often masks a series of tautologies or, worse still, a set of truisms which, if it were not for the way they are dressed up, would have no right to be officially rated as 'scientific'. A further instance of the same attitude is provided by the stilted language we sometimes find ourselves listening to. It was invented with clerical initiates in mind; their 'discoveries' are so trivial that, without it, they would be unable to discuss their specialisms or look each other in the eye without bursting into laughter. I am not suggesting that we should turn our noses up at them. No one is innocent in this matter, and it would be a brave person indeed who dared to cast the first stone, but it is essential to take lucid note of this eminently intellectual failing. And at time when there is a revival of inerest in epistemology, and in a period when the field of sociological investigation is expanding without any fear of *ukases*, we have to revise our modes of exposition too. Clarity is not synonymous with frivolity, and an 'essayism' with a noble ancestry may well be a pertinent way to capture the upsets that so often characterize life in society.

In an essay on the Académie Française, Ernest Renan (1921: 341) notes that one of its goals was 'to purge the language of the scoria introduced by the *pedantry of academe and the Bar*: it tried to teach people to write like well-spoken people.' His comment could be extended to the point I am making, which is intended to be a reminder that organic reflection is preferable to abstract ratiocination. We require a form of thought that can describe its own place and time, and enable others to do the same. No matter what we call it, academe always claims to speak on behalf of others, and always claims to be elaborating a theory *a perennis*. In its fantasy of perfection, it has difficulty in getting to grips with social upheavals and events. To hell with scholasticism, its solemnity and its injunctions. The 'style' of everyday life has a rambling side to it which is worthy of our attention; these are elements that cannot be synthesized, and which call for a 'contradictory description'.

Max Weber was one of the first representatives of our discipline to use the comparative method and to demonstrate its utility in his study of macro-sociological forms. Not being constrained by the scientistic scruples of Weber's day, we can apply the same comparativism to what I term the style of everyday life. Once we use different theories or comments in an attempt to elucidate a phenomenon, we avoid imposing an intellectual model, but we can also get to grips with the plurality of social words. And we should therefore not be afraid of eclecticism. I have demonstrated elsewhere that nothing is important in itself because everything is important. That is the lesson we learn from various rituals. When we analyse a category or describe a phenomenon, we should therefore not be afraid to introduce a plurality of authors. The fact that they disagree guarantees that our approach will be polydimensional. What is more, far from making very naive (but quite understandable) claims to being original, this perspective is based upon classical or traditional analyses, and therefore demonstrates that there is nothing very new under the sun in the human sciences. As folk wisdom tells us, making use of whatever comes to hand is not an index of inconsistent capriciousness, but of a flexibility that can adapt to the various avatars which punctuate natural and social existence.

It should also be recalled that flexibility is a characteristic of all creative thought. The history of ideas demonstrates more than adequately that every great theory is, in the phase which institutes it, structured on the basis of a dialogue or confrontation with the ideas of the past, which can be either enemies or allies. Its institutionalization is a gradual process (and one that does not always take place), and usually results in a deadly dogmatism. True to his methodology and his convictions, Gilbert Durand rightly asks (1979b: 202): 'Is Science anything but constant eclecticism?' Hypotheses are formed, are compared and are rejected. They either cease to be pertinent or develop fully, depending upon the circumstances and the situation, though chance too has a role to play. Those working in the exact sciences agree that 'coherent pluralism' (Bachelard) is productive, and there are even stronger grounds for arguing that it has a role to play in the interpretation of social phenomena. Just as a myth is a metalinguistic or metahistorical 'crossroads' (Corbin, Durand, Lévi-Strauss), everyday style is an intersection between actions and words which, if it is to be described, requires a multiplicity of signposts that allows them to be situated as accurately as possible. These of course merely create the conditions of possibility for a more exhaustive approach, but it is thanks to their diversity that we can situate a given social space in relation to others and in relation to its environment.

This topology has nothing to do with the classic appearance/essence dichotomy, or with the dialectic that supposedly reconciles the two. Every element in the description is significant; it allows us to create a totality, an ambiance, in the true sense of the term, that influences our recognition of the whole. As in *Gestalt* theories, the perception of the whole comes first. It may well be muddled, but the term has no pejorative overtones; it is not an initial stage that has to be transcended if we are to arrive at true clarity. To be more accurate, chaos and clarity are intimately bound up with one another. Once again, we come back to 'correspondence', which explains why we either 'have a feeling for' or reject a place, a situation or a community and, therefore, the actions that are connected with it.

It is precisely because it is part of a coherent pluralism and can adequately describe a given ambiance that the approach outlined here – a modulation of what is known as the 'sociology of knowledge' (see Maquet 1949) – is based upon a variety of theories and perspectives. It does not respect divisions between specialities, and it introduces genres (fiction and poetry) that are normally reserved for leisure moments. It does so with a certain insolence which is not necessarily calculated; it simply reflects the fact that social objects laugh at academic barriers. There is an element of provocation involved, but as the word's etymology (*pro-vocare*: 'to call forth') reminds us, that is because sociality, which is what we are concerned with here, urges us ever onwards and forces us to break out of the reassuring circles of fragmented knowledge. It takes us back to the holism that was the starting point for the great sociological investigations made at the beginning of the century.

There is of course a danger that all this will turn to farce, or result in a construct that is built any old way. Given that we cannot always avoid this, perhaps we should confront it, or – why not? – accept it. Something resembling life can sometimes slip through a loosely-knit fabric.[4] By badgering learned analyses, by using and abusing notations from heterogeneous fields and contexts, we may be able to introduce mobile elements that allow us to visualize things that are hidden or dismissed as insignificant by stricter standards of proof. Existential polysemy will not tolerate reductive logic. If we do not reject conflicting intellectual contributions, and play one off against another, we will obtain a more impressionistic but fuller picture of the social whole. We know that the life of societies is based upon a multiplicity of disagreements and antag-onisms which, when placed end to end, produce a coenaesthesia that is a constant source of wonder. It is therefore only natural that, when we attempt to describe it, we should use an approach which is equally heterogeneous and paradoxical. We have to gamble on the possibility that, by doing so, we will be able to arrive at, if not a system, at least a contrasted and balanced fresco.

The above comments do not imply that erudition is useless. Nor do they deny the need for specialist sociological research: the sociology of work, economic sociology and quantitative sociology (to cite only a few examples) all have a place, but it is essential to breathe new life into a general sociology which, as Gurvitch (1967: 153) points out, can provide a new and precise framework for more limited and detailed analyses. My own view is that general sociology has less to do with a search for 'hidden meanings' than with the interpretation of societal 'affirmation'. Whereas erudite specialists focus their attention on specific problems, the approach we are outlining here is singularly ecumenical. The literary genre known as the *Menippean* is a good example of what I mean. Menippean satire has a polemical force: 'It is constructed like a landscape of quotations. It comprises every genre: the short story, letters, discourse, poetry and prose' (Kristeva 1970: 68). It is also interesting to note that, whereas the bourgeois world developed and regulated unitary genres, the Menippean has something in common with the modern novel, Joyce being a prime example. For our purposes, constructs that use a number of different genres are a good metaphor for the intellectual attitude that records every-thing that the experience of life puts before its eyes. To the extent that it is a condensation phenomenon, it might be compared with the tumultuous situations (celebratory meals, various gatherings, urban micro-events, ritual violence or day-to-day violence etc.) which condense modes of expression that are normally dispersed throughout life. In these situations – which, because they are paroxysmal, tell us something about the underside of daily life – we find different combinations of dialogue, invective, songs, cries, stereotypes etc., or in other words the verbalizations that normally punctuate social communication.

To refer again to the Menippean, separation is a thing of the past; life in all its polysemy is a form of theatre. There could not be a better expression of the ambitions of interpretative sociology, especially as we are not attempting to apply a pre-established theoretical schema; the use of a mixture of genres helps to relativize intellectual paranoia. We cease to be demiurgic intellectuals who 'produce' theoretical objects; we begin, in a sense, to be 'acted upon' by a series of ideas which are active within the social body at a given moment. The use of heterogeneous references is also a way of indicating clearly the saturation and cyclical return of social representations, whilst at the same time stressing the primacy of the mechanisms of sociability that allow them to exist. By identifying some of the pivots around which social practices and representations revolve, we can explain both the invariance and the wave-like aspect of the elements that structure existence. This combination of statics and dynamics goes by a variety of different names, and plays an important role in what is conventionally known as popular wisdom. It also provides a basis for a scepticism which, because it believes in nothing, is quite convinced that everything is possible.[5]

# 8
# *The Epistemology of Everyday Life*

The gift of second sight ... It had always seemed to him
that Herminien used, and would in future use, this constant
ability to analyse casually and distractedly. Perhaps his ties
with life lacked strength, as although he took a penetrating
interest in many things, his interest always wandered.

Julien Gracq, *Au Château d'Argol*

## 1 Societal experience and sociological formalization

'Un petit cours de sens-communologie' ('A short course in
common-sensology'). That is how Schopenhauer (1819: p. xxvii)
describes, in French, his *The World as Will and Idea*, which was his
response to what he saw as the dominant rantings of his day.
Whilst I am well aware of being immodest when I say it, I have
been attempting something similar throughout these pages. They
are the result of solitary reflection, impassioned polemics, diatribes
with students and colleagues and even – why hide the fact? –
insubstantial day-dreams, and their ambition is to recall that,
unlike other sciences, sociology owes a great deal to a life without
qualities, to the run of the mill, and to a daily existence that is
made up of anecdotes and tragedy.

Economic problems are of course still of great importance, and it
is not easy to forget geopolitics or the crucial importance of
education, bureaucracy and technological developments. All that
has, however, been well 'covered' by sociology. Sociology must
therefore recognize that it has a duty to put down roots in a daily

experience which is *not so much a content as a way of establishing a perspective*. The manager of a major industrial company has admitted that the conflicts that plagued his firm had more to do with day-to-day life than ideology.[1] His lucidity ought to cause some concern to 'intellectual workers' who are all too often so obsessed with their concepts and critiques that they forget that the social flow often obeys a logic which is not logical. If we try too hard to keep our distance, we tend to forget what gives intellectual work its legitimacy. In his *Discorsi*, Máchiavelli draws a distinction between what is thought in the palace and what is thought in the market-place. If we define the latter in the broadest possible terms (sites of economic, political, but also symbolic power) it is clear that the distinction is still pertinent. It is certainly an anthropological constant. The question I propose to ask is this: can we still understand what is thought in the market-place?

There is in fact such a thing as day-to-day empirical 'knowledge', and we cannot do without it. All these practical skills, verbal skills and life-skills, with all their multiple and diverse implications, constitute a given, and phenomenology rightly reveals just how rich they are. Now if there is one essential problem, one real *experimentum crucis*, for positivisms (neo-Marxism, functionalism, conservatism), it is the elaboration of a criterion that can, on the one hand, ground the *de facto/de jure* distinction in reason and, on the other hand, legitimize the supremacy of the latter. Given the quasi-monovalency of rationalism, it is perhaps necessary to emphasize the originality of our empirical knowledge. That is what I have been trying to do throughout this book, and, as we will see, many intellectuals who are in no sense irrationalists will support my views. It has been said that Kuhn's (1962) rebellion against the pretensions of positivism demonstrates that sociology has much more in common with common sense than geometry (R. H. Brown 1980: 72). We have to weigh the full implications of that remark. The most important point made by Kuhn is that the shift from one scientific 'paradigm' to another is a response to sedimented 'anomalies' that are overlooked by the dominant mode of thought. The history of the sciences is a testimony to the accuracy of his observation.

Where social life is concerned, it is quite obvious that everyday existence consists largely of anomalies, or so-called anomalies. Or, more accurately, that as a result of several centuries of moral domestication and normalization, many attitudes and situations have gradually come to be classified under the 'anomaly' rubric.

Hence the paradox, which is well known in its political or even juridical form: the minority 'excludes' the majority. This can lead to the social structuration described by Orwell in *1984*, where the real actions of ministries are antiphrastically described as what they are not. Be they humorous (Fort 1949; see also Brodu 1982) or scientific (Auclair 1982), 'human-interest stories' tell us a great deal about social reality, and bring out both the extent and the importance of the anomalous. 'Monstrosity', defined in its etymological sense, is a fact of everyday life. Only beautiful souls and moralists deny the fact. For the purposes of our reflections on epistemology, we need only point out that a science that shuns contact with everything that the dominant rationalism regards as disturbing or monstrous is in danger of becoming a 'one-armed octopus'. We find here the theoretical justification for the recent interest in the humdrum, the normal and the everyday: what is rejected often, like a subterranean centrality, provides a solid basis for the whole of sociology. Like the *mundus*, the cesspit that constituted the visible world according to the Romans, sociality is determined primarily by what Pareto called 'residues'. The term is, of course, to be understood in all its various senses.

Excessive concentration on *society* and the purely rational, intentional or economic elements that constitute it, leads us to overlook *sociality*, which is in a sense a *communalized empathy*. *Erlebnis* and *Einfühlung*, which in the German tradition relate primarily to the individual domain, can also be understood in a collective sense. Sociology cannot go on ignoring the fact that the values associated with vitalism are *also* at work in the constituent elements of the social game. If we recall that, we can, unlike certain sociologists with their over-manichaean analysis,[2] avoid the traps of disembodied scientific research without thereby lapsing into the platitudes of what Boudon calls the 'intellectual *tout Paris*'. It should not be forgotten that, before it locked itself away in the name of some conceptual purity in a solitude which, like any ghetto results in either flight (usually into advertising) or a slow decrepitude, the academic world did in its heyday play its part in the elaboration of the discourse of its day. Being a veritable 'collective intellectual' bound by organic ties to the society as a whole, it had a multidimensional – scientific, aesthetic, ethical and political – vision of its cognitive project. In short, it served an interpretative function: explaining the whole of social existence. Now that the positivist interlude is coming to an end, and apologias for discrimination and separation along with it, we can once more begin to look at social life in holistic terms.[3]

This is a difficult task. We have to walk a tightrope, without the safety-net that was gradually put in place by two hundred years of rationalist caution. Holism is a specific methodology designed to bring us into intimate contact with the meanders of social existence. Many, of course, take the view that it is simply a collection of repetitions, *petitio principii* and unverifiable assertions. And yet I have every confidence in an approach which is beginning to bear fruit, inspire research projects, stimulate original thinking and orientate social actions and modes of being.

Without claiming to be exhaustive (and here we would do well to recall the caution of Max Weber, who called his methodological reflections 'essays'), we can describe the close links that exist between the interpretative attitude and experience. At the beginning of this book, we dwelt at length on the fascination (and perhaps the infatuation) that the 'inhuman sciences' exercised over the human sciences, and especially sociology in its formative period. We might recall, if only briefly, that for Popper the scientific value of a theory depends upon 'its power to rule out, or exclude, the occurrence of some possible events – to prohibit, or forbid, the occurrence of these events' (Popper 1992: 41; cf. Popper 1934: 34–9). He refers to this as 'the problem of demarcation'. We may well disagree strongly with Popper over this point. To be more accurate, we might note that he is speaking of criteria for science, and that sociology is scarcely scientific. As has been said again and again, in sociology 'anything goes'. Anything can be a method, a way of setting out on the journey. In that sense, experience, whatever it may be, has a cognitive potential. Demarcation may be a notion specific to politics, ethics or a certain form of science; in no way can it define knowledge.

This rather enigmatic remark is intended mainly to determine, *a contrario*, the buffer that allows sociology to exist as a method. It is striking how many extremely sophisticated analyses admit to being unable to account for their objects of analysis. Although this mood is ill-defined, it is quite widespread and contributes not a little to the contempt in which our discipline is generally held. We will have to come back to this point in more detail, but it is clear that the revival of the so-called 'life-stories method is, when it does not fall back into the scientistic rut, a response to the feeling of impotence that Bertaux expresses (1979: 18) so lucidly: 'The truth is that sociologists do not know very much about the societies in which they live.' The admission is somewhat banal, coming from an intellectual, but it becomes disturbing when it applies to sociologists who, with their well-known complacency and presumptuousness, claim to be able to tell the truth about society. Either by using jargon or by dressing up truisms in mathematical or statistical guise, sociological research reports and works on theory endlessly complicate their analyses in order to conceal their impotence. In that respect, it is worth recalling a line from Goethe's *Faust* (1808: lines 671–2): 'You were to be the key / But cannot lift the bolts, however shrewd your words.'

When we try to be too scientific, we lapse into a Byzantinism that is only distantly related to the social existence we are supposed to be describing. It does, on the other hand, act as an 'Open Sesame' that gives access to the many restricted and sectarian intellectual cliques that flourish in our capital cities. Be that as it may, in terms of our present concerns, it is important to describe an attitude of mind that can avoid fantasies of exhaustivity and at the same time supply elements for an in-depth interpretation of sociability. For, and this really is the paradox, in our attempts to be too complete, we fail to see the essential point; by being too discriminatory, we suppress the meaningful with all the blind efficiency of a bulldozer that crushes everything in its path.

It has to be said that this efficacy is legitimized by the great trend towards rationalization and intellectualization which Max Weber analyses so well. A careful reading of Weber allows us to observe, however, that social rationalization by no means implies the generalized rationalization of everyday existence. The comments I make in an earlier work (Maffesoli 1979a) notwithstanding, participant observation, reading the various media, listening with suspended attention to saloon-bar conversations, and the intrusion of minor news items, does force us to note that, as Weber (1913) remarks, in general individuals become more and more distanced from the rational basis of the techniques and rational rules that concern them practically. He adds that, on the whole, their basis is usually more hidden from them than the meaning of the magical techniques used by a witch-doctor is hidden from savages.

Although it by no means challenges it, this resistance increases as technological progress develops, and it means that we have to adapt both our instrumentation and our epistemological ambitions accordingly. Existence has its clandestine side, and we can never perceive it in macroscopic terms. The quantitative documents at our disposal do little to explain it. To extrapolate from a remark made by Weber, we thought that the disenchantment of the world that resulted from developments in science and technology also affected the subjective life, mass phenomena and political and everyday life. It is time to admit that this is not the case. The gods, their myths and their rituals have changed their names and their forms, but they are still hard at work in both sociality and the environment. This clandestinity, which I have already termed a subterranean centrality, finds its expression in perfectly banal situations that might be likened to Freudian slips. Unlike Freudian slips, however, they are valid in their own right. It is because they fail to take them seriously that distinguished politicians, business-men, adminstrators and journalists find that, in many domains, they are quite disorientated by the turn taken by the events they are supposedly directing or at least controlling.

The cognitive aspect of experience forces us to pay attention to events and phenomena, to everything that is inscribed in the moment and the present. I have already used the great categories of duplicity, theatricality, the tragic and ritual (Maffesoli 1979b) to explain this. I would now like to stress that they can have a considerable sensory, or even sensual, charge. In his book on Montaigne, Starobinski (1982: 2) states that 'phenomenism' and its various modulations are 'the familiar results of sceptical doubt'. It is true that sceptical doubt is an extremely widespread societal form which outweighs our apparent faith in various moral, reli-gious or political values. 'Situationism' and popular doubt are closely linked. We also find a similar combination in the theoretical attitude: phenomenism and scepticism. Sceptical doubt is obviously not a panacea, but it can certainly alleviate the intellec-tual paranoia which, after two hundred years of good and loyal service, has opened up an extremely wide gulf between the social base and its representations.

Without wishing to lapse into mechanicism or simplistic materialism, it is clear that we are dealing with a process of reversibility, of retroaction between the mastery of time and space that typified bourgeoisism, and theory's rational project (*projectum*), which was so well suited to both functionalism and critical thought. The optimal condition for such an approach is, to quote Marx, '*post festum* knowledge'. To remain within the same register, it might be more appropriate to speak of *post mortem* knowledge.[4] If, on the other hand, we focus on the realm of experience, we observe things *in statu nascendi*, with all the well-known difficulties, uncertainties and incompleteness that implies. We have to admit that many social experiments, alternative life-styles, the collapse of many dogmatisms, a certain existential tolerance – and we can all give concrete examples – all suggest that we should take a cautious, if not sceptical, view of established certainties, and that we should be bold enough to think about the present without accepting too many liabilities.

Talk of an epistemological 'break', or even of 'critical distance', is therefore pointless. I am suggesting that we should interpret the popular view of the present (as expressed in redundancy and theatricality) by looking at intellectual *variations* which prove nothing and say a lot. A few years ago, I proposed the notion of 'monstration', as opposed to the classical *demonstration*. Whereas demonstrations look for unity, the goal of a 'monstration' is to record plurals (plurals are by definition 'monstrous'). Hence the need for redundancy, variation and reflection which, like waves dashing against a rock, return, perhaps repetitively, to similar but non-identical subjects and fashions. That is how the texture of everyday life is woven.

In his ongoing work on methodology, Morin has attempted to apply the intellectual principles I am describing to an object that lent itself well to this kind of analysis: the totalitarian structure of the USSR. Whilst I do not agree with Morin's suggestion that the task of the intellectual is to train politicians, I do agree that 'Cartesian reason and the reason of utilitarianism inevitably dissolve or reject the monstrosity of the real, which seems quite unreasonable to them' (Morin 1983: 23; see also Morin 1977–80 and 1979). The nature of the USSR was obviously a paroxysmal example, but similar remarks also apply to the life without qualities that we see in our neighbourhoods and cities.

It is only natural that politicians should attempt to adapt reality to their conceptions of reality. As they think in terms of programmes, they naturally reject, and often resist, anything that does not fit in with their concepts. The administrators or top civil servants who serve and protect the public 'know' what society is and what it should be; they can thus deny the existence of anything that does not fit in with their schemata. They do not have to think twice about it. It is, on the other hand, dangerous for scientists to model their behaviour on that of bureaucrats. And that is what has been happening for more than a hundred years. Max Weber's famous distinction between the Scientist and the Politician is not a mere *flatus vocis*. It makes an essential point that tends to be forgotten. This is not, of course, a matter of passing moral judgement, but a way of pointing out that what is legitimate on the part of a politician or a bureaucrat is dangerous on the part of an intellectual. We can reject or deny things in order to act more effectively, at least in the short term; doing so when we are trying to interpret is much more debatable. In interpretation, what 'is' takes priority over 'what should be'. Hence the non-responsibility of the intellectual: his task is not to *answer to others* or to *answer others*, but to listen to others. This is the eternal relationship with alterity which, throughout the ages, has found expression in religion, politics and bureaucracy, and which has always been differentiated. Some (churches, parties, the techno-structure: Promethean categories) manage relations with the other, and others (mystics, poets, thinkers: Dionysian categories) speak of its mysteries. It might not be a very good idea to confuse the two categories.

We have to be very vigilant about this, as the mechanism of reduction has a natural appeal for intellectuals. It has been shown that, when it uses the unity of the thinking subject to introduce some order into the variety and confusion of the world, the philosophy of consciousness simply becomes a substitute for the 'objective ontological unity' that characterized the world of medieval Christianity. Both are ways of reducing polysemy. It is easy to demonstrate that monotheism and monothetism obey the same logic. Just as God is One, the world becomes Unity, and can be explained by One thinking subject. This provides the basis for what I call the suspicious thinking that discredits or marginalizes anything that escapes unity. Karl Mannheim states (1936: 59) the problem with great clarity: 'the experiences of everyday life are no longer accepted at face-value, but are thought through in all their implications and are traced back to their presuppositions.' Indeed. For monothetism, the situations, experiences, attitudes and discourses of everyday life have no validity in themselves, and have to be related to something external, to something belonging to a realm that transcends them. This is a reductive mode of thought which both refuses to see everyday monsters and fears them.

Our daily existence is fragmentary and polysemic. It is made up of light and shadows and is, as is increasingly recognized, the product of a *homo* who is both *sapiens* and *demens*. Unless we wish to miniaturize it (see Belassi 1983), so as to contemplate it or master it, channel or asepticize it (and these fantasies are constants in the human sciences), we have to accept that all its constituent elements are part of an architectonic which may well be hierarchical, but which cannot do without any of its elements, no matter how minor. This brings us back to the mystical or poetic theory of correspondence that we discussed earlier. It may have an important contribution to make, because it allows us to make it clear that fiction does not have a monopoly on situations in which there is a correspondence between people and things, and, on the other hand, to show that, despite the claims of our dominant iconoclastic rationalism, images do have an attraction that is inevitably socialized. Causality no longer applies; we enter into the cycle of repetition and ritual that is so important in everyday life. In the play of theatricality, forms combine as metaphors, and a chain of metaphors is more important than any one metaphor.[5] This sequence of metamorphoses should not of course be interpreted in a linear-historical way, but in a sinusoidal way, as though it were a dotted line consisting of *'rapti'* and latencies which can still stand any test. That is my image of sociality. As the mystic put it: 'God uses curved lines to write straight.'

This cycle is imperfect (compared with the self-confident directionality of linearism), but it is therefore very much alive, and it demands a theory that constantly doubts itself. One of the basic rules of scientific method is a perpetual willingness to be proved wrong. The hard sciences are obviously based upon that attitude. Curiously enough, the same cannot be said of the human or social sciences, which work with a series of reifications. The only aspect of the demand for truth they retain is the tendency towards dogmatism and the fantasy of excommunication. And yet it has often been said that, if there is one domain in which flexibility is necessary, it is the domain of the social, whose essential characteristic is its lability. I must stress once again that this is not a matter of progress, but of the re-emergence of problems which had been temporarily overlooked or marginalized. I have already pointed out that there are no 'Americas' in the human sciences; we never discover new worlds, but it has to be remembered that the prime quality of a specific piece of work is that it can and must reveal new and previously overlooked aspects. As Max Weber (1928: 138) notes: 'Every scientific "fulfilment" raises new "questions"; it *asks* to be "surpassed" and outdated. Whoever wishes to serve science has to resign himself to this fact.' Such a common-sense remark – the kind of remark one might hear a couple of times in the course of a scientific career, and which, sometimes, can even be made during a research project – should lead us to regard as, at best, puerile the claims to exhaustiveness and intangibility that all too often typify the monologues we hear in our disciplines. An interpretative schema is valid for a given period of time, and sometimes for a given place. It can also serve as a point of reference. It can be used in a historical perspective, and the acuity of its insights may give it an intrinsic value. But attempts to extrapolate from a schema always lead to dogmatism, and often to the legitimation of the harshest tyrannies. As Marx said of the bourgeoisie's view of history, it is a mistake – and quite pointless – to say that 'until now (until me), we have had science; now, there is no further need for it': the *ultima verba* has been pronounced.

We have still, of course, to make the connection, recognize the correspondence and establish comparisons between our various thematic or historical approaches, but that can be done without privileging any one of them. We are free to use them, and free not to use them. This is an aesthetic or nominalist attitude which *de facto* gives more importance to situations and realities than to theories. To go back to a notion which is beginning to acquire a certain legitimacy in sociology (R. H. Brown 1977), we should use concepts as though they were so many metaphors that allow us to *experience* life and facts in all their concreteness. Metaphors can point to, emphasize or bring out characteristic features of social life without constraining them. The only elements we need to retain of the various theories that attempt to explain life in society are the metaphors. Metaphors are the quiet moments in a theoretical approach, and they may bring it closer to its objects. I am thinking of Francis Ponge's joke about literature: 'it is not made with concepts, but with "conceptacles", by analogy with the receptacle of a flower.' I wonder whether the same might not be true of sociology. Unlike those who regard the relativization of the concept as something scandalous, I maintain that we would do better to employ 'conceptacles' – the things I analyse when I speak of the terms 'notion', 'metaphor' and 'category' – that are capable of 'receiving' life rather than reducing it. When we look at either classical or contemporary works, be they works of erudition or more occasional pieces, we should concentrate on the exceptional moments (or should we be speaking of moments of lassitude?) when the conceptual fabric is loose enough to allow us a glimpse of the social reality that supports it, the moments when the societal fact coincides with the sociological fact. We should concentrate on these moments because they cannot fail to illuminate the picture we are painting. It so happens that all analyses work in this way, even when they do not admit to doing so: great authors have their epigones on the 'left' and the 'right', not to mention their heretics and their schismatics, and their distant cousins and vague intellectual allies. They all come to terms with the master's concepts, and rework them for their own purposes. Which only goes to show that absolute fidelity to a concept is, by the very nature of things, an impossibility. The expression *traduttore traditore* also applies to anyone who attempts to operationalize a system.

It is important to stress this point, as it allows us to demonstrate that, whatever we may feel about it, revisions are always necessary. Concepts too are unstable. The above comments on the diachronic point of view can also be applied to the synchronic dimension. A single situation must be looked at from a variety of viewpoints. And, like it or not, this multiplicity is a *de facto* refutation of eternal concepts and of explanations 'in the final instance'. A minimum degree of lucidity obliges us accept that, as Mannheim (1936: 92) puts it: 'Our definition of concepts depends upon our position and point of view which, in turn, is influenced by a good many unconscious steps in our thinking.' We would therefore do better to accept the particularism of a given body of thought, and therefore its products, if only because they can later be enriched by being compared with other perspectives. Yet if we limit definitions in this way, we discover only 'the approximate truth' (Mannheim 1936: 75). All this may seem self-evident, but its implications are rarely spelled out.

It implies, for instance – and as can never be said too often, the primacy of societal existence. Defining social existence as such is not our task; that comes within the remit of philosophical theory. It is, however, important to stress that, once the economic component has been identified and analysed, we have a residue. The same can be said of the political aspect, the organizational aspect, and of analyses which focus on work, leisure or consumption. It is the residue, as defined by Pareto, that is problematical for the sociologist of everyday life. To that extent, we are dealing with a goal or, to use the vocabulary of phenomenology, an intentionality, rather than a content. The residual existence we can observe by looking through various social categories is always a factor in sociality. This, quite simply, is what is meant by 'coexistence'. The intensity of being-together finds its clearest expression in the interstices of official life, in the moments or spaces that are appropriated in which I call a 'minuscule' way or, as Moles (1982, and forthcoming) puts it, 'in a contraband way'. We will have to come back to this point, but it is clear that sociality itself, various forms of solidarity, conflicts and *détentes*, and in a word the passion that is so important in social structuration, all involve things that are usually ignored. Many would see 'residues as factors in sociality' as a frivolous research topic. They are difficult to quantify, and are therefore unworthy of the attentions of 'intellectual workers'.

And it is true that the two aspects I am emphasizing – residues and being-together – do not easily lend themselves to conceptual rigidity. That is why we have to elaborate new investigative methods. I have explained elsewhere (Maffesoli 1979b) that the social will to life is not verbalized in any one particular way, just as technical and social skills are not expressed through rigid and intangible laws. To take a familiar categorization, the determinism and interaction at work in social life – and I would add that they are continually imbricated – cannot be confined within a normative schema. Empirical knowledge constantly escapes rational constructs, and thumbs its nose at them. Phenomenological sociology inevitably comes to the same conclusion. As Schutz puts it (1960: 73): 'Our knowledge in daily life is not without hypotheses, inductions and productions, but they all have the character of the approximate and the typical. The ideal of everyday knowledge is not certainty, nor even probability in a mathematical sense, but just likelihood.' It is clear that this 'typical' and 'likely' mode of knowledge brings us into fairly close contact with existential chaos, the rhapsody of popular discourse and the multicoloured spectacle of our cities.

Let me make it quite clear that I am not making an apology for irrationalism – which is in fact the invariable result of dogmatism – but simply outlining *a theory of knowledge which accepts that the structural incompleteness of sociality implies intellectual incompleteness.* We can therefore use a plurality of approaches of all kinds to elaborate as accurate a description as possible of a given moment and space. A reflexive patchwork is not the worst way to interpret a specific society; the free spirits who attempt to break down disciplinary barriers and definitions are all agreed that fluid analysis, multiple references and sources of information are the best way of looking at the vital flow we are trying to interpret. In his essay on '"Objectivity" in Social Science and Social Policy', Max Weber (1904: 51) makes a distinction between 'what should be' (*Seinsollende*) and 'what is' (*Seinde*) and demonstrates (1904: 56) that it is:

naive to believe, although there are many specialists who even now occasionally do, that it is possible to establish and demonstrate as scientifically valid 'a principle' for practical science from which the norms for the solution of practical problems can be unambiguously derived.

The comment that this is 'naive' is symptomatic of the way Weber is constantly torn between rationalism and relativism. The nonsense that characterizes all life in society means that we have to adopt a low profile, determine potentials, describe the forms taken by multiple relational situations, and explore missed opportunities and shattered dreams; in short we have to apply to *the divinity known as sociality* the same apophatic theology as was applied to God in the Middle Ages. We can only speak of it *a contrario* or tangentially. We must say as little as possible about it. We must adopt a cautious attitude which begins by purging the mind of its absolutist fantasies by declaring them invalid, in the full knowledge that our natural instincts will always make us go slightly further than we wished to go. Given that a propensity to extrapolate is in a sense a natural failing on the part of the human mind, relativist caution can never be exaggerated.

Julien Freund, France's great Weber specialist, confirms this interpretation in his introduction to *The City* (Weber 1921), in which he displays his usual didactic clarity. In his view, Weber constantly pleads the case for adopting a variety of approaches to the same phenomenon, and does not regard any one approach as being superior to the others. It is in Freund's view futile to look for universal explanations based upon more or less arbitrary generalizations (Freund 1982: 16). This is indeed the lesson that is to be learned from interpretative comparativism. Ultimately, an approximative truth is potentially more 'scientific' than an apparently exhaustive approach, because the latter tends to view other approaches in terms of either affinity or conflict. As a result, an approximate truth will, *volens nolens*, construct an architectonic that is much closer to social reality than one produced by the haughty isolation of a perfect system that leaves nothing undefined. The city, as described by Weber, Simmel and the Machiavelli of the *Storia* – their common source of inspiration – is in that respect an instructive metaphor. It is a disparate, *contradictorial* (Lupasco) set, and yet it is all of a piece. Light and shadow, places of ill-repute and monumental works, work and pleasure are arranged in a complex construction which permanently rules out grotesque and grandiloquent reactions, no matter what assumptions they are based on.

Whilst it may seem self-evident, it must be pointed out, if only as a possible line of further research, that the logic of the 'must-be' which underpins the conceptual or systematic approach is primarily *moralistic*. I think that there is a distinction to be made between the ethic that binds together the social body itself, that cements and preserves a coenaesthetic equilibrium (I have spoken (Maffesoli 1982) in this connection of an 'ethical immoralism'), and any morality that is imposed from the outside. Its imposition is eminently praiseworthy, as the goal is to make the masses happy even if they do not wish to be happy. Which explains why clerics and intellectuals are, no matter what they call themselves, hopelessly moralistic. Perhaps because men who are perpetually 'cuckolded' by history – to either their satisfaction or their irritation, depending on how the prince treats them – are under the illusion that they can influence reality. Yet what could be more contingent than ethics? Like Montaigne and Pascal before him, Max Weber makes the point on numerous occasions: on the one hand, the anomic and the canonical have different values in different times and places; on the other, even within a given society or a given era, developments and changes take place within the ethical order. It may be banal to say so, but it is still useful, as it reveals the structural fragility of constructs that claim to be imperative necessities in their own right. That they have their validity goes without saying; as we have already said, they are all essential to a pluralistic approach. When, on the other hand, one or more of them begins to see itself as the *ne plus ultra* of theory, there is a real threat because, in one way or another, it will try to establish a hegemony (through institutions, academic bodies, commissions, publishing or the media). That problem is beyond the scope of the present study, but we can note that, because of an overriding structural effect, the logic of the 'should-be' results in the hypostasization of theoretical products, as opposed to the social substratum.

Common sense puts it eloquently: the road to hell is paved with good intentions. Creating bespoke worlds is dangerous, and has serious implications. Bureaucracy, State violence, terrorism and the techno-structure, to cite only a few contemporary problems, all developed in the tutelary shadow of critical or institutional modes of thought which dreamed of worlds 'as they should be' rather than observing existing worlds. As a result, those modes of thought inevitably legitimize apparatuses in which there is an increasingly wide gap between the 'instituting' and the 'instituted', or between society and basic sociality.

It should be recalled that, unlike ethical and utilitarian modes of thought, which are exclusive, Weber's position is both pluralistic and aware of the contingency of social customs, and it implies a tragic vision. Situations in social life do not, in other words, have any purpose, or rather the fact that they acquire a purpose does not prevent them from being ephemeral. Weber obviously does not pursue this logic to its final conclusion, as does his friend and fellow admirer of Nietzsche, the sociologist George Simmel. Indeed, according to Simmel, if we wish to judge an event we cease orientating ourselves with reference to a final goal that is placed outside the event and which supposedly gives that event its meaning (see the essays in Simmel 1980). According to this view, anything that happens has a right to be taken into consideration *because* it happens. This does not imply that it is impossible to think about events; it does imply that thought must recognize the profundity of the factual. Hence the bitter grandeur of the tragic sense of existence. The sociologist can now follow the path that leads from what I call formism to empathy, or from experience to phenomenology. This is a further instance of the ideal-type method. It is clear that, ultimately, relativism provides the matrix for both empiricism and phenomenology.[6]

Conceptualism finds it difficult to accept experiential knowledge, but it is just as difficult to reject it in the sociological realm, and it finds its theoretical conditions of possibility in relativism or pluralism. The revival of ethnomethodology, the first stammerings of participant sociology, experiments in action-research, and the development of life stories are all a response, if not always an explicit response, to a disillusionment with all the various sociotheoretical purposes and to a recognition of the importance of popular wisdom. Unlike scholastic visions, which have always existed and which still have a good future in front of them, the type of research I am outlining is intended to demonstrate that, to quote Mannheim (1936: 63), thought 'is not confined to books alone, but gets its chief meaning from the experience of everyday life', or from 'the shifting values of the everyday world'. This is of course an approach which, much to Bloch's apparent regret, works on the double-entry bookkeeping principle: it recognizes the legitimacy of both logic and experience. There are, however, periods in which normative constructs can no longer mobilize minds, and moments when the perfection of the radiant future fails to detract from the allure of the facticity and imperfection of the existing world. And as this life-instinct does not imply the abdication of intellectual responsibility, it is possible in the midst of ordinary life to find significant structures which have a value of their own. If we turn away from the institutional sociologies that still, for the moment, dominate our universities, we find what might be clumsily described as a desire for empirical knowledge amongst the young sociologists who study supposedly minor or frivolous objects. The social sciences cannot in fact fence themselves in with a deadly excess of scruples. They study a social realm which is both a 'given' (we will come back to this point) and something that is alive. Explaining both these aspects is indeed a major challenge which should inspire those who are so intellectually demanding as to want to break the fetters of conformist thought.

In an essay on Augustin Thierry, Renan (1921) discusses different ways of writing history and, without denying the industry of what he calls 'the Benedictine school', meaning the methodical and somewhat laborious extraction of historical raw material, demonstrates that understanding 'the confused tangle of passions and interests' that characterizes the life of cities and peoples requires not only erudition and lucidity, but also originality and passion. 'The extended meaning of things can be grasped only by understanding *the present*, and the present's willingness to give up its secrets is proportional to the level of what we stake upon it' (Renan 1921: 111, 117).

It is indeed the understanding of the present that forces us to relativize, if not jettison, all those theoretical presuppositions that corresponded to a stage in which the *individual and the economy* (personal and social) were the main pivots of social structuration. Those pivots allowed various reductive processes to operate, notably by eliminating the polysemy and monstrousness of experience. It so happens that the heterogeneity of social life in all its dimensions is now becoming a major contemporary issue. Nothing – neither sexual identity, psychological characteristics, productive functions nor social determination – is willing to remain quietly within the frameworks elaborated by general theories. It is quite obvious that this existential disorder has its effects on scientific propositions and research. In my view, this brings us back to experientation, which is, let us remember, the basis of all scientific work. In a discussion of what he calls the 'Novalis complex', Bachelard stresses that there is a link between erotic friction and a friction lighter. In his view, love may have been 'the first scientific hypothesis about the objective production of fire' (Bachelard 1938: 34). The comments – and they are made by a man who was a great theoretician of both the exact sciences and the imaginary – are a clear indication that production as a whole, and theoretical production in general, is closely bound up with everyday life.

It is because there is something at stake in everyday life that it becomes an object for the understanding. I have already used the image of Dionysus to indicate that we are, in my view, reverting to a more physical relationship with the social world and the natural environment. The divorce induced by objectivity is giving way to the intuition of experience. The terminology is of course somewhat crude, but it is clear that, to cite Durand (1980: 47), we are moving towards 'experiential communication', to the extent that 'a fundamental compassion' – defined in the true sense of the term – lies at the root of any Science that aspires to being human'. To take only the most obvious examples, astrology, macrobiotic food, ecological movements, alternative medicines (see Lalli 1983: 165), the importance of nature, regional loyalties and the stress on 'locality' all show that the 'keep your distance' stance, which was once common to epistemologies and social practices alike, is giving way to a more 'participatory' mode of being. The individual and/ or collective body is beginning to experience the world, and to experiment with it.

In order to describe the change that is taking place, a change whose effects will be felt in the decades to come, we can turn to Alfred Schutz's notion of 'familiarity': the world accepted for what it is, 'as taken for granted', the world as something pre-given (Schutz 1953: 13, 228). These expressions clearly indicate the emergence of a relationship with the world which is quite different from that with which we are familiar from the criticism or activism of bourgeoisism. A few years ago I therefore suggested (Maffesoli 1979a: 47, 145, 149, 207, 286) that we should use the expression 'the social given'. I did so in order to stress that we can have a relationship with the world that is not based upon mastery (conceptual, economic or political), but upon tolerance, or, to be more specific, on the intuitive perception of an obvious and unavoidable truth. As the author of a good introduction to interpretative sociology puts it: 'The pre-given world is the physical world and the social world accepted as indubitable'(Williame 1973: 36). The comment is banal, but it certainly has far-reaching implications as it recognizes that experience is a primal reality which thought can illustrate, but not reduce.

In order to characterize, if only briefly, a relationship with the world that is based upon an intuitive experience, we can adopt the distinction made by the art historian Wilhelm Worringer. In the course of a very detailed analysis of pictorial and sculptural works, he establishes a dichotomy that overlaps with the distinctions we have been making. According to Worringer, some periods are dominated by what he terms *abstraction* whilst others are characterized primarily by *Einfühlung*. Without going into any great detail, 'abstraction' is based upon a distanced view of the phenomena of the outside world. According to Worringer (1916: 15), it expresses 'an immense physical dread of space' and leads the mind to purify itself of everything natural or, one might say, familiar. *Einfühlung* or what I am calling 'empathy', in contrast, is an intuitive communication with the world and relates to a cosmic feeling. It therefore 'inclines toward the higher truth of organic life, that is toward naturalism in the higher sense' (Worringer 1916: 13). We are dealing here with a pantheism based upon the great trust that exists between humans and the various elements of the given world: sensualism, vitalism, and naturalism. The same polarity sometimes tends to dominate both everyday life and art. This is an organic attitude which emphasizes participation, as opposed to separation; it is a way of feeling oneself within things (*Sich-in-den-Dingen-fühlen*). This form is a particularly enlightening way of interpreting many of the situations we can observe in our own time. And it is quite obvious that a discriminating and reductive rationalism is much less well-placed to account for them. Sociology too must be permeated by the *Einfühlung* that is beginning to affect the whole of the social body. More specifically, it is very childish to erect conceptual barriers against the vital flux of a social existence which is in perpetual motion.

## 2 Pluralism and empathy

A historical example given by Max Weber sheds particular light on our concerns. He uses an analysis of Luther's notion of *Beruf* to demonstrate a qualitative change in the Western tradition. Something new is emerging. With the Reformation, a new relationship with the world and with things begins to take shape. I will not make a commentary on Weber's analysis. I will, however, cite one remark: 'His acceptance of purity of doctrine as the one infallible criterion ... was in itself sufficient to check the development of new points of view in ethical matters' (Weber 1904–5: 85).[7] I am not suggesting that we generalize on this basis, but it is clear that, being preoccupied with the elaboration of his doctrine and anxious to preserve its rigour, Luther failed to understand the social movement that was developing around Thomas Munzer at this time. The term 'ethical' is being used in its strongest sense here: alternative ways of life were not absolutely impossible, given the turmoil of the moment, but the institutionalization of a specific doctrine was profoundly incompatible ('in itself') with the social life that was finding expression in countless peasant and urban rebellions. In Luther's view, the uncontrolled action of the *Schwärmer* threatened to tarnish the image of a doctrine that was becoming respectable. Weber's example is a powerful demonstration of how a theory that takes the view that it exists 'in itself' can forget the movement of which it was born, or even turn against it.

From the Peasants War to the Bolshevik Revolution, not to mention the French Revolution of course, 'correct' theory has always been subordinate to mass movements and the shared experiences of the masses. I have already (Maffesoli 1979a) shown that shared experience is, insofar as it is a prime mover, the real motor behind human histories, especially if we think of the day-to-day ordinary activity which, as can never be repeated too often, makes up the greater part of the social fabric. It should not be forgotten that the experience we have been talking about at such length is the corollary to the lived experience, which, at least for the sociologist, can only be studied from a social point of view.

Before we go on to deal directly with the question of the importance to be accorded to sociality, a word must be said about a problem which is closely related to that of experience, namely polytheism. In various ways, we know that sensualism, the importance of the imaginary, a conception of time marked by the present and by the tragic, and intellectual relativism, all emphasize the plural aspects of social life and the pluralism of approaches to those aspects. In more modern terms, we could say that one-dimensional thought cannot interpret the polydimensionality of lived experience. It is necessary to point out that this is an *epistemological issue* because many 'beautiful souls' claim, with varying degrees of perfidiousness, that it is merely a political issue.[8]

The political dimension is merely one of many elements in social life, and whilst it may once have played a prime role, especially in the first half of the twentieth century, that is no longer the case today. There are periods in which a society (or a set of societies) functions with reference to one dominant value, but these things are cyclical, and there are other periods in which different and contradictory values appear to be in permanent competition with one another. Each of these aspects represents a specific force. It is clear that there are active, triumphal moments which require a unitary ideology or a body of doctrine that is directly efficacious: in intellectual terms they privilege concepts. Thus, according to Marx, the 'weapon of criticism' anticipates 'the criticism of weapons'. We also find in history more lusty or passive periods which place less emphasis on expansion, and more on intensity, where restrictions of space bring greater depth of relationships. At such times, it is possible for a plurality of values to function.

To go back to the distinction made by Worringer, we have established an antinomy between abstraction and *Einfühlung*. Although these categories are exclusive they frequently overlap. A superficial monotheism often conceals eminently pantheistic practices and modes of thought, popular Catholicism being a prime example. Similarly, coherently and indivisible monotheistic tendencies often continue to exist in polytheistic periods. We can therefore assume that in the hedonistic decades to come, the economic form will still be of considerable importance, even though it will no longer be hegemonic. What is certain is that if we look at everyday life, we can see a revival of both religious syncretism and polytheistic values. An intuitive relationship with nature tends to facilitate their emergence and the intellectual debate simply cannot go on ignoring it (Worringer 1916).[9] This is what is known as an epistemological issue. It is quite obvious that this perspective belongs to the tradition of scepticism, which has many branches in any society. To be more specific, and to refer to our own discipline, it is part of a tradition that is forcefully illustrated by Max Weber. For Weber, it was essential to admit clearly that social existence is based upon an endless struggle between different systems of values. The war between the gods, as described in Greek mythology, can help to illustrate, if not explain, the antinomy of values. Every member of the Pantheon is, so to speak, a crystallization of characteristics, a set of attitudes, practices and desires that are lived and represented in everyday existence. Attitudes and feelings become polarized and the conflictual tension between them is the basis for all social structuration. In many of his writings Weber returns to the notion of a polytheism of values, which is in a way a leitmotiv in his work. There is, however, one particular text (Weber 1928: 147–8) which describes this sensibility in admirable fashion, and which deserves to be cited *in extenso*:

> If anything, we realize again today that something can be sacred not only in spite of its not being beautiful, but rather because and in so far as it is not beautiful. You will find this documented in the fifty-third chapter of Isaiah and in the twenty-first Psalm. And since Nietzsche, we realize that something can be beautiful, not only in spite of the respect in which it is not good, but rather in that very respect. You will find this expressed earlier in the *Fleurs du mal*, as Baudelaire named his volume of poems. It is commonplace to observe that something may be true although it is not beautiful and not holy and not good. Indeed it may be true in precisely those aspects. But these are surely only the most elementary causes of the struggle that the gods of the various orders and values are engaged in.

The deep scepticism and simultaneous love of life that emerge from these lines imply that many honest convictions imbued with fine feelings are fit only for anthologies of hypocrisy. It is because it constitutes this struggle between the gods and between values that Weber can assert on the same page (1928: 147): 'If one proceeds from pure experience, one arrives at polytheism.'

Life is the product of heterogeneity and of the tension between different systems. It is not surprising that this vital heterogeneity should give rise to a number of different interpretations (see Durand 1980: 66).[10] It must, however, be accepted that an intellectual sensibility that stresses life and experience (to which I would add the humdrum and the run-of-the-mill) will place more emphasis on the plurality of reasons and sensations. There is a link between experience and comparativism: both are at once a cause and an effect of the *societal pluralism* that is in so many ways increasingly characteristic of the life of society. It is tedious to have to say it again, but, no matter where we turn, active collectivities and groups (sports clubs, musical clubs, sexual groups, associations, networks, tribalism) are coming to the fore. An emphasis on vital experience is inducing sociality.

It is a commonplace in discussions of everyday life to say that this implies introversion and ideological introspection, if not a lack of social will, and that it is a sign of the civilizational fatigue that characterizes all periods of decadence. In my view, this way of looking at everyday life owes a great deal, wittingly or otherwise, to the critique inaugurated by Henri Lefebvre (1958–81), who sees everyday life as a manifestation of false consciousness, and who argues that existence as it is can only be a symptom of what it should be. On the contrary, I would argue, against the assertions made by certain of my colleagues and friends,[11] that the sociology of everyday life can be a way of interpreting what I call 'the societal in action', or in other words sociality. This has nothing to do with some hypothetical return of the subject. On the other hand, it does seem to me that experience and relativism which, as I have said, seem to be undergoing a new lease of life, relate to collective actions and collective feelings. At a very basic level, we have only to remind ourselves that, if we pay attention to everyday life, we give a new emphasis to the ordinary gestures that make up the life of our streets and markets, and structure a life without qualities which is all too often regarded as insignificant, but which is in fact the 'residue' (Pareto) around which social exchange, defined in the broad sense, is articulated. Analysis clearly demonstrates that these gestures are the result of being-together. They are both its cause and its effect; they go beyond both the metaphysical category of subjectivity and the politico-socio-economic category of the individual. Does it have to be pointed out yet again that one of the characteristics of Worringer's *Einfühlung* (Worringer 1916; cf. Maffesoli 1982: 12) is the need for a loss of self (*Selbstentäusserung*), and that a loss of individuality is always a precondition for entry into what I call a fusional realm. Losing one's own body within the collective body, either metaphorically or literally, seems to be the characteristic feature of the emotional or affective *community* that is beginning to replace our purely utilitarian 'society'. In that respect, the symbolic (*sumbolon*) transcends pure rationality.

We see in the cyclical evolution of social, political and religious forms a succession of individual/rational and societal/affective structurations, even though it is impossible to explain why one replaces the other in terms of single cause. These are, of course, categories whose sole purpose is the establishment of a perspective. They can, in other words, be used to elucidate situations, practices, representations and fictions that would otherwise be incomprehensible. Thus we can argue that in our own day the societal (or, at a more trivial level, the group) takes precedence over the individual. It is also possible that this change of emphasis justifies my claim that sociology is the ideology of our period. Indeed, and here we can once again hide behind Weber (1913), from a sociological point of view, identity is never anything more than a relative and fluid state of affairs. It is clear that, unlike philosophy, psychology or even economics, sociology is less concerned with the individual, or with contractual and rational collections of individuals, than with the masses as such, and with their specific characteristics.

The sequence mentioned earlier can be observed throughout human history. And it is now accepted that periods of so-called decadence (or renaissance, depending on one's point of view) are marked by an emphasis on societal (group) structurations. Thus the emblematic figure of Dionysus gives rise to what Weber calls 'emotional cults', as opposed to the atomization characteristic of bourgeois or aristocratic dominance. Here we see the ideal type of the people (Weber's concept of the *'popolo'*), or the masses who periodically return to the fore. At this point, some terminological clarification is required: 'the people' is an ill-defined mass reality, which can be characterized in terms of softness, non-action and non-logic, whereas 'the proletariat' corresponds to an identity (the Marxist tradition's 'historical subject') with a task to perform. And because that task is rational, it is inscribed within the meaning of history.

It so happens that this emphasis has certain methodological implications. It implies what I term the establishment of a perspective. Because, on the one hand, we are dealing with increasing numbers of affinity groups or restricted groups, and because, on the other, those groups require us to adopt a specific mode of approach which has little in common with theories which attempt to analyse the rational intentionalities, logical activities or interaction of autonomous individuals acting in unison and with a common purpose in mind. It must be recognized that the epistemological basis for the emergent sociology of the eighteenth century and especially the nineteenth century was provided by social atomism. It attempted to understand complex groups of all kinds in individualistic terms. Similarly, those individuals who did belong to groups were necessarily and unavoidably studied in institutional terms (family, work, parties, trade unions, churches, States). Although this schematism was not without its efficacy, one wonders whether the 'primal group' might not be the real foundation for any social life. The *Grundkörper*, or the matrix for individual modes of being, in a sense provides the themes for an affective community, as opposed to a rational society. Franco Ferrarotti uses this shift of perspective to argue the case for the relevance of the biographical method (see the excellent synthesis in Ferrarotti 1983: 62–5). It is clear that this hypothesis is more likely than the various institutional or critical approaches to be able to explain the survival of the archaic values of neighbourliness, solidarity, and restricted groups, or in other words the 'agglutinative' structure (cf. ch. 5.3 above) that has succeeded in resisting the rationalization of the world.

Many of the aporia posed by the individual–society relationship, which is a veritable *pons asinorum* for sociologists, appear to have been, if not resolved, at least demonstrated to be inconsistent. Relations with alterity, or phenomenological sociology's 'thou-orientation', are not, it would seem, an epiphenomenal product of a humanist ideology or something that can be dismissed as unimportant, but the essential structuration of society. It might be argued that this is a truism, but how are we to explain the fact that this sociality is never (or rarely) part of the conceptual apparatus of those who produce social theories? To the extent that the sociology of everyday life is not so much an object as a transverse reading of the various moments that structure a society, it can be shown that what I term sociality is an essential category, at least in the contemporary social situation in which we find ourselves. Taking his inspiration from the entire phenomenological tradition, Schutz has, with great pertinence, established a link between *experience* and *alterity*, notably through his analysis of what he calls 'thou-orientation' (*Du-Einstellung*). It is this experience of the other – of his lived experience in terms of my lived experience – that provides a basis for the interpretation of the different 'worlds' that make up a given period. To adopt Schutz's terminology, the world of contemporaries (*Mitwelt*), the world of predecessors (*Vorwelt*) and the world of partners (*Umwelt*) together make up the world of lived experience, which is the cause and the effect of all societal situations.[12]

For the 'formist' perspective I am using, this 'orientation towards the other' is of course a pure form. Being the substratum of being-together, it influences its observable forms. According to my analysis, it is what Schutz calls *Erlebnisnähe*, or proximity on the basis of lived experience, that constitutes determinant groups. A determinant group might, depending on the degree of proximity, be the 'we' into which we merge, a union we join for ideological reasons or because we need protection; it could be a productive collectivity, or an association established with a rational goal in mind. Specific research will reveal their various individual characteristics, but we must begin by stressing their *conditions of possibility*, or in other words the impulse to be with others. Pareto called it a residue, and it is indeed a basic structure which, no matter what we call it, appears in all social action. Everyone who stresses the concrete or experiential aspect of the given world also stresses the foundational role of the 'co-existence of other human beings' (Mannheim 1936: 53). It goes without saying that coexistence can take the form of mere sociability, intensely erotic relations and conflictual turmoil. Social sympathy (Max Scheler) or what I call empathy is a more or less intuitive expression of an experience that is lived collectively. The triad of 'experience', 'collective' and 'lived' may have far-reaching implications for any methodological renewal in sociology, especially if, as we have already said, it is based upon a biographical approach or, more specifically still, primary groups (Ferrarotti).

It must, however, be noted that the analysis of sociality outlined above will not be comprehensible unless we agree to challenge certain of the key concepts of classical sociology. Those concepts were introduced by Durkheim, and they are the untouchable foundations of our discipline. I refer to everything pertaining to the *organic* and the *mechanical*. To take up a suggestion I made some years ago, I think that we can quite simply invert the terms of the argument: recent work by anthropologists and historians would seem to indicate that the functional organicity of an *organized whole* is one of the major characteristics of traditional societies, whereas the dominant feature of economistic and atomistic societies is a calculated attitude towards relationships which may have something to do with the 'mechanical'. We can even say that organic solidarity is possible to the extent that individual personalities disappear and are absorbed into the collective organism, whereas mechanical solidarity depends upon decisions made in 'good faith' by typical personalities. We can thus invert the terms of the definition given by Durkheim (1928). It would seem that it was the 'unconscious' nature of traditional organicity that offended Durkheim's rationalism (Maffesoli 1979a: 210n. See also the work of Dumont).

This is the starting point for all my comments on sociality: we have to rethink the theme of the *organic*. It explains the survival of archaic forms and situations, the 're-enchantment of the world' that we are currently witnessing, a certain sensualism and, above all, the new emphasis on 'the local'. Technological advances have no power to block this process; they may even be promoting it.

It is not surprising that a certain interpretation of the French school of sociology, influenced to some degree by functionalism but fundamentally mechanistic, finds this revised perspective unacceptable. It seems to me, however, that revisions have to be made if we are to understand a 'subterranean centrality', which we can no longer afford to ignore. Politicians, shrewd administrators and lucid economists are all concerned about the status of the 'black economy' in this period of crisis; we are talking about a whole 'black society'. If changing our intellectual habits allows us to understand it, it will have been worth it.

We must therefore look for provisional or relativist definitions that are bound up with experience, and which can go along with existence rather than imprison it. In one way or another, many philosophers and sociologists stress the fact that human actions are predicated upon a pre-understanding of the environment. This is the great theme of popular wisdom or common sense: social coenaesthesia, which we can acknowledge to be a structural element in the equilibrium we inevitably find in the life of societies. Although it is trivialized in saloon-bar discussions and in idle chatter, this wisdom is still of invaluable assistance in our encounters with destiny and the passage of time, in affective or 'sympathetic' liaisons, and in our relationship with death. These are of course general categories, but they are constantly diluted in the minuscule creations of everyday life. That is why sociologists should attach great importance to this common sense when they elaborate their theories. Schutz insists that there is a constant relationship or interaction between individuals' 'stock of knowledge at hand' and intellectual constructs. In his view, 'The thought objects constructed by the social scientist, in order to gasp this social reality, have to be founded upon the thought objects constructed by the common-sense thinking of men living their daily life within their social world' (Schutz 1953: 59). If, as I have suggested, we accept the hypothesis of the organicity of social life, intellectual constructs must be organically related to their substratum. The term 'organic intellectual' (no pun intended) should not be applied to the political realm, as it has usually been since Gramsci. It should be applied to the realm of sociality. The collective lived experience of the world that is corresponds to the intellectual experience, which merely underlines one or another of its features, compares it with others, illustrates it or uses it as a metaphor. This, in a word, is the ideal-type attitude, which can take both diachronic and synchronic forms. This is the common-sensology I discussed at the start of this chapter. Yet fear of 'spontaneous sociology', which is a convenient excuse for intellectuals, most of whom come from the bourgeoisie, has so influenced our discipline that we still have to stress the specific efficacy of basic sociality. I would add that the most important feature of a sociology of everyday life, which is beginning to acquire a certain respectability in many countries, is precisely that it draws attention to that fact.

In a remarkable article which both draws theoretical conclusions from empirical research and establishes a programme for future work, Lalive d'Epinay rightly notes (1983a: 82; cf. 1983b) that the 'viewpoint of the *vulgus*', which comes into play when we look at the everyday, can be regarded as a *'methodological lever'* which forces us to apply differential and complementary analyses. The works of the author and his team are an excellent example.

The viewpoint of the *vulgus* may help us, finally, to specify the relationship we are trying to establish between experience and sociality. It seems to me that the routine–event dichotomy (Lalive), Balandier's repetition–event dichotomy, or the parallel Javeau establishes between 'the everyday' and 'sub-events', all imply that the link between the social and history is eternal. In this paradigm, all that matters is what is remembered, namely the great historical moments, the political signifiers and the grand narratives that are assumed to represent a given period. In his 'Theses on the Philosophy of History', Walter Benjamin suggests (1969a: 257) that the historian should 'brush history against the grain' and empath-ize with the oppressed, the mediocre or in other words anyone who is involved in normal life. The ambition of a sociology of everyday life and, more generally, of a revitalized epistemology, is to understand the history of the oppressed, which historiography has not seen fit to record.

If that is the case, the dichotomies we have just mentioned are no longer pertinent. History, with its various correlates (and especially the subject as actor), is less important than human histories of all kinds, no matter how insignificant they may be. But, as I have already pointed out, their 'insignificance' is the repository of sociality, its defence against powers, which for their part are interested in the meaningful (in the sense of having a purpose?). If we take the view that nothing is *Important*, insignificance implies that *everything* has its importance. To put it metaphorically, we might say that whilst VIPs do exist, there is no such thing as a situation with VIP status. The term *'situation'* is of course Goff-man's, but it is worth pointing out that it was also an emblematic term used by a small avant-garde group in the 1960s, namely the situationists, whose theory has had a profound influence on intellectual developments in recent decades.[13]

From their point of view, the everyday, or in other words anything that escapes the tyranny of power, can be the object of a real investment. The lived situation, no matter how minuscule it may be, short-circuits false dichotomies; it exhibits and verbalizes its profound ambivalence, it is here and there; but at the same time, its sense of ambivalence allows it to recognize that life can still be lived. It was the situationists who said that 'our ideas are inside everyone's head'. This is common sense if ever I heard it, but it is an incitement to listen rather than to pass judgement. It is this basic curiosity that allows us to understand that anything goes, that nothing should be overlooked, and that we cannot establish hierachies. Thanks to a curious semantic shift, 'event' or 'what happens' once meant 'an occurrence of some importance'. The approach I am outlining here is an attempt to get back to the original meaning of the term.

If we recognize the humdrum element in the societal fabric, we can give a new value to its natural space: the community, the crowd, the being-together, the disorganized and multicoloured collective life that is the prime metaphor for the *complexity* confronting the sociologist.

The re-emergence of the everyday therefore does not involve a narrow concentration on the individual subject. It signals the very opposite, namely sociality. How we approach the latter remains, naturally, to be determined.

The lived world that is the concern of an interpretative sociology takes precedence over theoretical representations, does not refer to anything outside itself, and is based upon a collective experience. It can be summed up in three programmatic words: *common sense, the present, empathy*. The essential characteristic of these three levels is their communality. Even so, and even though it may seem somewhat paradoxical, the best way to grasp this sense of the collective is to use tools that make due allowance for subjectivity, or at least for the formalization of subjectivity that the phenomenological perspective terms *typicality*. We can agree on the fact that art is an inextricable combination of the subjective and the objective; subjectivity is crystallized in an objective form which inevitably strikes a chord in other subjectivities. It is this movement, which gives specific periods their dynamism, that gives art its vitality. If we look at human histories, we find that great creative moments result from a constant interaction between these two structures. When, on the other hand, either the objective or the subjective is dominant, we find either a deadly institutionalization or an equally disturbing individualistic decadence.

In my discussion of the Mafia, or rather of the 'mafia attitude' as a metaphor for sociality and its autonomy, I make a distinction between the individualist paradigm (individual, State) and the societal paradigm (person, communication). The personality of each individual and the vitality of the whole are inversely proportional to the development of individualism (Maffesoli 1982: 87–90; 1979a: 210). If we bear in mind the term's Etruscan etymology, 'person' clearly refers to a *type*; thanks to this 'theatrical mask', we are able to take part in a play and become an element in it. Types which are delineated in this way produce what I term an *immanent transcendence*, meaning that a combination of a substratum and its transcendence. What is more, whilst an individual must be 'one' and have one function, a person can exist in the plural (*'je est un autre'*), and can play every role in succession. On the basis of these two perspectives – transcendence within a community and pluralism – we can attempt to use 'type', 'subjectivity' and 'intersubjectivity' as operational categories. The result will of course be no more than a framework or, as Simmel would put it, a 'form', but empirical research is already beginning to flesh out these proposals.

Without going into the subject in concrete terms, mention should be made of the biographical or 'social life-story' method. In this perspective, either the 'restricted group' (Ferrarotti) or the narrator as subjective unity (Catani) gives a summary account of everything that makes up his or her social or natural environment, immediate or otherwise. Like a histological section, that account will reveal all the salient characteristics of a given moment. That is my understanding of what Catani (1982) calls the 'assumption of the I' into a broader category.[14]

As the defenders of both biographical methods and the phenomenological approach always point out, the relationship between the observer, who is himself biographically 'in situation', and the narrator(s), is ambiguous. That parameter must also be taken into account. We can, however, see how it allows us to compare two microcosms, and that it can generate a sympathetic situation that is conducive to the interpretation of empathy.

In this situation, the observer is obviously not as detached as the positivist scientist. He is not necessarily a full participant, but we can say that he is in correspondence with, understands or feels certain of the values he is analysing. It is even possible that this is a 'sociology of the depths' (Durand) which is based in part upon empathy. The metaphor is illuminating. *Pace* Walter Benjamin's 'Theses on History', we do not, however, necessarily empathize with the oppressed. Or at least, something that is true of history may not necessarily apply when our subject is very much alive. Although it is not possible to say so with any certainty, those who use this method in the social sciences may tend to 'collude'. They are involved in what has been called a 'romantic sociology'. As they snuffle around the social, they scent, in either tiny or massive doses, something they already possess. In what can be seen as the central chapter of his remarkable book on the biographical method, Ferrarotti (1983) speaks of 'biography as interaction'. It is in fact because it is assumed to be able to explain *Erlebnis* that it too must be an experience.

The interaction that takes place in an interview, and which should be the object of a separate study, is, however, an excellent illustration of the fact that we can 'understand the social by looking at the irreducible specificity' of a person or a group of persons who are interacting (Ferrarotti 1983).[15] Such an epistemological stance makes a radical break with classical scientific practices which, following the Aristotelian tradition, argue that Science deals only with generalities. Like Ferrarotti (1983: 51, 55, 63), we might say that every individual is 'an individualized synthesis' of society. The biographical method therefore allows us to find the philosopher's stone that so many intellectuals have been seeking since the nineteenth century: *a concrete universal*. As in the original (and holistic) sociological project, the goal is knowledge of the whole, but it can be attained by studying nodules like personae and interaction. It should of course be pointed out that this implies a vision which, according to Oscar Lewis, must be panoramic. According to Lewis, the celebrated pioneer of the biographical method (1962), different versions of the same event told by different members of the same family make it possible to introduce nuances, to relativize things and to arrive at the broadest possible vision; to extrapolate, they can be likened to different approaches to a single social fact. Once again, we can see that interpretative sociology is inevitably and resolutely *comparativist*. It also gives us a notion, *typicality*, which well expresses the conjunction of universal and particular. The term, which is employed less frequently than Weber's 'ideal type', is in a sense at the interface between the two dimensions we are concerned with in our discussion of epistemology: on the one hand, it means that everyday practice is organized around a small number of major polarities, and, on the other, it indicates that those polarities can be understood on the basis of a small number of structural constructs. Observation, biography and life-stories allow us to identify typicalities which in themselves involve us in a descriptive process. This is why a person and the systems of interaction in which that person is situated are in a sense crystallizations. If we simply study them for what they are, we have the key to the societal given. It is well known that Mauss theorized the theme of how habits come to constitute the life of societies. In similar vein, Schutz speaks (1953: 277–94) of a 'stock of knowledge at hand'. That knowledge – habits, coded situations, rituals, popular wisdom and cultures, common sense – is organized by collective experience into 'types' which can be explained in terms of various forms of 'typicality'.[16]

I said earlier that it might be paradoxical to attempt to use the notion of 'person' to talk about sociality; this is in fact because a 'person' is a condensed form of a lived experience, and we know how important that can be. When the gnostics spoke of the intimate connection between microcosm and macrocosm, they shared the same intuition. As we know, rationalism and positivism, which have left such a mark on sociology, cut themselves off from the warm and disorderly side of existence as a result of their concern for rigour. This means that, to adopt the terminology of an article that prefigured the present book (Maffesoli 1981a), there is a gulf between the 'sociological fact' and the 'societal fact' that supports it. By going back to individual experience, to the mechanisms of interaction, and to the circulation of feelings, we can at least narrow, if not fill in, that gulf. Life-story situations and biographical approaches can certainly reveal the 'indigenous knowledge' or 'sociological deposits of untold wealth' that Bertaux (1980) finds in human experience, and which we can also see in what phenomenology calls 'symbolic constructs'.[17] The revolution in looking that I am proposing will allow us to recognize the full cognitive value of the run-of-the-mill experience of everyday life. Subjectivity, which can provide us with a 'methodological lever', is not to be understood as meaning a sentimental exacerbation of an autonomous and solitary ego. On the contrary, it is no more than a typical element within a complex structure; but, when viewed from different angles, that typical element proves to reveal something about a broader whole. The sociological implications of research into the structures of the imaginary (Durand), the reappropriation of the mythical dimension of social existence, and the new attention being given to experience and life, are all based upon a subjectivity that understands itself in a quasi-intentional way and, as I have already demonstrated with respect to everyday life, exists coenaesthetically within a differentially structured organic order. To go back to a convinced 'objectivist', namely Durkheim, it is always instructive to read his asides and footnotes. When, for instance, he discusses the notion of the soul, he writes (1912: 269–70 n. 1):

> But we know today that the unity of the person is . . . made up of parts and that it . . . is capable of dividing and decomposing. Yet the notion of personality does not vanish because of the fact that we no longer think of it as a metaphysical and indivisible atom. It is the same with the popular conceptions of personality . . . They show that men have always felt that the human personality does not have that absolute unity attributed to it by certain metaphysicians.

Here we have the ingredients for our analysis: the plural nature of the personality and common sense. There is nothing arbitrary about the connection between the two. The plural nature of the personality is the source of the strength of what Durkheim calls 'the soul of the collectivity' and 'the collective patrimony', and of what I, throughout these pages, have been calling sociality. This also justifies the use of typicality in a non-exclusive way. The existence of pluralism within the human personality and the correspondence between that pluralism and what I term the social given means that we can organize our research around techniques which include subjective parameters. This also allows us to rethink the interesting notion of '*habitus*'. It has a long history, which it would be interesting to formalize. For the moment, we can very briefly recall some stages in its history, beginning of course with Aquinas. Many educated representatives of our discipline have been struck by this philosophico-religious reference, which involves an allusion to Aristotle as well as Aquinas.[18] Not having any great competence in the matter, I will simply recall the main articulations of Aquinas's analysis, which will be found in paragraph 49 of the chapter devoted to Virtue (which I cite after Desclée de Brouwer's 1953 translation of the *Summa Theologica*). The primary meaning of *habitus* is trivial but rich: it describes the 'fit' 'between the man who has a garment, and his garment' [*inter habentem indumentum et indumentum quod habetur, est habitus medius*]. There is, however, nothing 'factual' about this fit, which is essential to existence: 'Having studied acts and passions, we must

now study the *principles* of human action: (1) intrinsic principles
... The intrinsic principle is power and *habitus.'* [*Post actus et
passiones, considerandum est de principis humanorum actuum. Et primo,
de principiis intrinsecis ... Principium instrinsecum est potentia et
habitus.*] *Habitus* is therefore a quality, in the true sense of the term,
which realizes (or negotiates) a relationship with the world; it is in
a sense grafted on to 'power', the matrix for the social will-to-life
which allows us to adapt (cf. Maffesoli 1979a, ch. 1). The same idea
reappears in Goethe during the nineteenth century and in Spengler
at the beginning of the twentieth. Using an example drawn from
botany, Spengler explains that the *habitus* of an organic group also
includes a certain *life* expectancy and a certain developmental
*tempo.* This *habitus,* which helps us to interpret human thought and
action in time and space, has always, according to Spengler, been
the origin of the *concept of style,* which finds concrete expression in
types of dress, government, communication and everyday movements. This is a good definition of a cultural *habitus,* which is
something of considerable interest to a sociologist. As we have
already noted, we find something similar in Schutz's 'stock of
knowledge at hand'. We also find it in the reference made by
Mauss at roughly the same time to 'the techniques of the body' in
a famous text which is both well known and curiously overlooked:
'Hence I have had this notion of the social structure of the *"habitus"*
for many years. Please note that I use the Latin word ... [French]
*habitus.* The word translates infinitely better than *"habitude"* (habit
or custom) the *"exis"* the acquired ability and *"faculty"* of Aristotle'
(Mauss 1979: 101). It need scarcely be pointed out that the notion
of *habitus,* as popularized by Pierre Bourdieu, has now become part
of our intellectual *doxa.*

This short historical digression will have been worthwhile if it
allows us to understand that the link between typicality and
subjectivity has nothing to do with the logic of individuation but
relates, rather, to an organic, global or architectonic order in which
the various elements of the whole fit together. The notion of *habitus*
does a lot to explain this non-conscious arrangement. It opens up
immense possibilities, and the new emphasis on the body, spectacle, eating, rites, sexuality, fashion, posture, or in a word the
complexion of the social, gives it a great contemporary relevance.
At the risk of seeming repetitive, it has to be said once more that
everything we might refer to as the microscopic, as opposed to the
great generalizing agencies, obliges us radically to revise our
epistemology. The effects of this revision, which was announced

by Simmel, can be seen in many contemporary research projects. Everything that has been said of fashion – which is at once a personal statement and the most social statement of all – can also be said of all human situations (Belassi 1983; Perrot 1981). This implies that we can see in all these situations a crystallization or condensation of all the characteristics of sociality.

It is this crystallization that grounds typicality in reason. Unlike polite talk of introversion and exaggerated individualism, the epistemological perspective we are outlining here allows us to understand that what is involved is the constant interaction between intersubjectivity and intrasubjectivity. Dilthey sums up this relationship, which provides the theoretical basis for community, as a 'biographical experience' which is a condensation of the *Zeitgeist* of a given period, which finds expression in all social situations. The biographical experience, from Schutz to contemporary life stories, implies a new sociological approach. Subjectivity is no longer a handicap or a flaw to be eliminated; it is, rather, a springboard to a more complete vision of societal existence. If we accept it for what it is, the *subjective* can be a means of understanding the *intersubjective*, or in other words the increasingly common concern with (or reality of) alterity or communication.[19]

Let us leave things unresolved. A great deal of theoretical and empirical research is being carried out along similar lines, and will inevitably overturn our established certainties. I will, however, point out, again with reference to the work of Gilbert Durand, that typification goes hand in hand with a reactualization of myth, and that all this implies an initiatory procedure rather than a triumphal reductionism (Durand 1982: 206). Neither history nor the autonomous ego count for a great deal. In this vast *theatrum mundi* we simply play roles that seem to be dictated by destiny. Similarly, thought unveils reality rather than creating it. We have come a long way from the pretentiousness of conceptualism, but we are still dealing with a real intellectual issue, though it is one which is more global, less frenzied and, as I said in the introduction, metanoiac. In this perspective we should remember the story, which is meant to be suggestive rather than categorical, about the Japanese archers who hit their targets because they concentrate on themselves.[20] They are past masters in the art of self-abnegation; in that sense, they are spokesmen for a societal order in which they are more than elements. That is what is at stake in the new conjuncture of action and knowledge, and of knowledge and sociality.

Thought – snake
    'In the tree, the breeze cradles
    The viper I am wearing . . .
    I may be a beast, but I am an intelligent beast
    Whose venom, though vile,
    Is far worse than the wise man's hemlock!'

Paul Valéry, *Ebauche d'un serpent*

# *Notes*

## Perspectives

1 For the term *'societal given'* and the similarity with Schutz's 'pre-given', see p. 150.
2 As the ever-logical Tacussel puts it (1982: 253, cf. 331, 359): 'Quite apart from introducing modifications into a way of life, the metanoiac process always indicates a conflict between two epistemologies.'

## Introduction

1 A good application of this distinction in the field of art will be found in Worringer (1916).
2 Mention should perhaps be made of the debate around the crisis in the sciences that was opened by Husserl and then taken up by by Popper, Habermas and Gadamer. Perhaps it should be analysed at great length, but quite apart from the fact that these reflections are now well known, they are too dependent upon German 'critical thought'. There is no denying its importance, but it may not be able to account for the specificity of the social lived experience and especially its characteristically cognitive dimension. Occasional reference will be made here to Popper or Habermas, but it should not be forgotten that they are still too close to the very thing they are criticizing. Even so, their work provides an irreplaceable source of inspiration and therefore merits careful study. See Popper (1934), Habermas (1968) and Gadamer (1960).
3 On Windelband and Rickert, see Habermas (1968).
4 See Lefebvre (1958–81). On time budgets, see Busch (1975). Cf. the analysis and bibliography provided by Javeau (1983b).

5 The term 'romanticism' has recently (1985) been adopted by Alain Touraine.

6 I do not agree with Freund's suggestion that we use the term 'formal sociology', partly for reasons of euphony and partly because I have already used 'formism' in a number of articles. Freund's introduction to Simmel (Freund 1981) is in other respects admirable, and analyses the notion of form at some length.

7 The similarity between formism and biology is dealt with by Durand (1985), to whom I owe this information.

8 The following can be usefully consulted: Durand (1969: 25), Puech (1978: 4). Cf. Watzlawick (1978: 7) and, of course, Lupasco (1947) and Beigbeder (1972).

9 Cf. Ferrarotti's (1983: 29) critique of quantification.

10 On the theme of pluralization, see also Boudon (1979).

11 Cf. Sorokin, and Maquet (1949). Cf. also the 'line of sight' discussed by Javeau (1983a: 22).

12 Cf. the reference to stereoscopy in R. H. Brown (1977: 66).

13 In his preface to Simmel, Freund (1981) criticizes him as 'a dilettante, a brilliant essayist'.

14 On the creation of interstices as a means of promoting thought, see Maffesoli (1976: 13).

15 In addition to the work of Clastre and Berthoud, see Goldmann (1967).

16 On this form of pluralism, cf. Lévi-Strauss's (1983: 24) comments: 'All true creation implies a certain deafness to the appeal of other values.'

17 On rumours and the importance of rumours as a means of discrediting intellectuals, cf. Poulat's comments (1977: 38f) on Bénigni, and his careerism, scepticism and warped and unscrupulous intelligence: 'No one can stop the rumour mill once it has been set in motion. It would be fascinating to analyse it in sociological terms. It does not necessarily need any real basis: all it needs is a theme, a milieu that is ready to listen, and a victim or a hero. And then it can proliferate. First, there is talk of morals, and then talk of money...' One should naturally also consult Morin (1969), Shibutani (1966) and *Sociétés*, 0 (1984), 40–4.

## Chapter 1 The Fascination of Positivism

1 Ideology is to be understood here as meaning simply a corpus of ideas; no value-judgement as to its truth or falsity is intended.

2 On Pelagianism and the idea of Progress, see Moulin's erudite article (Moulin 1981).

## Chapter 2   The Experience of Relativism

1 It will be recalled that this is the second translation of Durkheim's Latin thesis, which was entitled *Quid secondatus politicae scientiae instituendae contulerit*. Cf. 'What is rational is precisely what exists *most often* in reality. Thus his [Montesquieu's] ideal logic is *to some extent* situated in the empirical world. But there are exceptions which introduce an element of ambiguity into his concept of law' (Durkheim 1892: 54; emphasis added).
2 The expression is from Nicholas of Cusa's famous treatise. On this author, see Gandillac (1942) and Steenberghe (1974).
3 See also Baeta Neves Flores (1978; 1984).
4 For an analysis of this notion of Lupasco's, see Durand (1979b: 68).

## Chapter 4   Towards a Sociological 'Formism'

1 The reader is referred to the documented analyses provided by Perniola (1980).
2 Ever since a famous German car manufacturer put it so concisely (*Mercedes ein Begriff*), the creative departments of advertising agencies have been looking for the concept that can best characterize the products they are trying to promote. The brutality of this utilitarian practice is a good illustration of the essential characteristics of the conceptual approach.
3 Its apotheosis can be dated to the nineteenth century, a period in which sociality was being channelled, set to work and controlled. On these definitions and their developments see Maffesoli (1982).

## Chapter 5   The Analogical Method

1 It is interesting to note that popular resistance can also take the form of the 'as if' attitude. We act 'as if', but that does not prevent us from keeping our distance from the various powers that succeed one another on the political stage. This duplicity, which is verbalized in varying degrees, is also a cognitive act, and it is therefore of interest to the sociologist. I deal with with this question in ch. 7 of my *La Conquête du présent* (Maffesoli 1979b).
2 Cf. Sorel's (1908) critique of this position.
3 Balandier has for years been trying to demonstrate the importance of grounding sociology in practical and theoretical anthropological

experience. See e.g. Balandier (1983a). A similarly relativist view will be found in Spengler (1922–3).

4 Cf. A. Moles's paper read to the Centre de Recherche sur l'Imaginaire (Paris) on 'Les Mythes dynamiques'.

5 Cf. Lucien Lévy-Bruhl's view that there is in the human mind, and regardless of its intellectual development, an ineradicable element of primitive mentality.

6 Cf. Durand's definition of the anthropological trajectory (1979: 38): 'the constant exchange that exists at the level of the imaginary between subjective pulsions and objective assimilations and intimations emanating from the cosmic and social environment'.

7 The reader is referred to the work of L. V. Thomas (1976, 1980, 1982, 1983), who develops this perspective with great competence.

8 See Coster's excellent work on analogy in the human sciences (1978). Unfortunately, I was not able to consult it before writing this chapter.

## Chapter 6   Physical and Social 'Correspondence'

1 For a contemporary analysis of the resurgence of local values see Bourdin (1983: 220).

2 See e.g. Sansot, Strohl, Torgue Verdillon (1979) and the work of the Groupe de Recherche sur l'Imaginaire Social (Grenoble) on the suburbs.

3 It is impossible to overemphasize the originality and meticulous nature of Busino's attempt to promote the work of Pareto. See in particular his prefaces to a number of volumes of the Droz edition of the works of Pareto and the articles in the *Revue Européenne d'Histoire des Sciences Sociales: 'Cahiers Vilfredo Pareto'*.

4 I suggest some lines of investigation elsewhere (Maffesoli 1979a). See also Girard and Mazol (1980) and the work of the Centre d'Etude sur l'Actuel et le Quotidien.

5 Certain pages of Goethe's *Wilhelm Meister* capture this relationship between the mine and the environment. So too do the final pages of Zola's *Germinal*, which describe Etienne's departure from Montsou (Zola 1885: 422): 'And beneath his feet, the deep blows, the obstinate blows of the pick, continued. His mates were all there; he heard them following him at every step. Was that not Maheude beneath the beetroots, with that back and hoarse respiration accompanying the rumble of the ventilator. To left, to right, further on, he seemed to recognize others beneath the wheatfields, the hedges, the young trees. Now the April sun, in the open sky, was shining in his glory, and warming the pregnant earth. From its fertile flanks life was leaping out, buds were bursting into green leaves, and the fields were

quivering with the growth of the grass . . . Again and again, more and more distinctly, the mates were hammering.'

6 See e.g. Dupuy's description of the Palio in Siena (*Libération*, 13, 14 and 15 August 1982). He compares the ceremony, which is not at all picturesque, to the Eucharist. I have referred elsewhere to the similar 'fusional' fiestas that take place in the small towns of Sicily and to the wine festivals of the Campagna Romana, which are still orgiastic. It is quite inappropriate to speak of archaic survivals; these are polymorphous extensions of a social form.

## Chapter 7   Ever Renewed Life

1 I will discuss the notion of the 'people' or the 'pleb' in a future work.
2 Cf. expressions such as *'plus ça change, plus c'est la même chose'*.
3 It is no accident that this project can be compared with the work of Durand (1969, p. 321f).
4 Over the last few years, I have found to my surprise that my analyses of bureaucracy, violence, everyday life and 'orgies' are well received by the social workers to whom I give lectures. And yet they, like everyone else, are children of the twin sources of contemporary ideology: Freudianism and Marxism. To my surprise, their response to my lack of modesty and and occasional irony was a calm self-assurance: for them, my incoherent 'monstrations' echoed the practices and situations with which they were confronted on a day-to-day basis. That, to me, is the most solid verification. My work of interpretative sociology, owes a lot to the many discussions I enjoyed with them. My sincere thanks to all those who recognize themselves in this description.
5 On style as a 'category of knowledge', see P. Brown (1983) and Paul Veyne's preface to the French translation of that volume (*Génèse de l'antiquité tardive*, Paris: Gallimard, 1983). The same idea can be found in Simmel.

## Chapter 8   The Epistemology of Everyday Life

1 Interview with the chairman and managing director of Renault, *Libération*, 19 July 1983.
2 See for instance Boudon's pertinent but one-sided analysis (1975: 88).
3 On the rationalization of existence, see Maffesoli (1979a, chs 3 and 4).
4 The use of euphemisms does little to capture his intellectual vampirism, which is a constant reality.

5 I have demonstrated elsewhere the importance of theatricality and rituals in social life. With his usual brilliance, Baudrillard (1983) develops similar ideas on metamorphosis.

6 Bloch (1962) makes a similar comparison, but for him it represents, of course, a hateful intellectual position.

7 On the Peasants War, see Bloch (1960). On the Luther–Münzer debate and the accusations of 'stolen, unexperienced, apish mimicry', see Mannheim (1936: 193n).

8 Cf. e.g., at the opposite ends of the confessional spectrum, the old religious fantasy *redivivus* of controlling the scientific Word and its political expression, Vincent (1983) and Six (1983). In Vincent's case, it might be a mistake to attach too much importance to what is, ultimately, more an attempt to settle old scores than an intellectual exchange. I will, however, permit myself two comments on what is conventionally known as the 'new right', one polemical and the other more general.

There was a time when, having freed themselves from the domination of priests of all denominations, free-thinkers found themselves at odds with 'red priests' and their politico-theoretical dogmatism. Nowadays, the priests tend to be pinkish rather than red (see Morin's (1984) discussion of similar themes), but they still set themselves up as watchdogs. They are incorrigible militant-believers. It takes a clever man to know the way, and yet they know the difference between good and evil, science and ideology, good authors and bad, and of course good and bad political choices. The most cunning even know what Sociology is.

This would not be dangerous coming from people who, given that they cannot do so through occupational therapy, have to sublimate their resentment of their *taedium vitae*, were it not that they are so pretentious as to claim to be able to elucidate the actions of various authorities (political, technocratic, academic, trade-union) which are still influenced by simplifications of retired theoreticians. They want to return to active service, to serve at all cost, but they forget that if intellectuals want to be dogs (cynics), they should bite authority (all authority) and if they want to be a guard, they should guard sociality, which is not reducible to the social, to say nothing of the political (I explain this at length in the first chapter of Maffesoli 1979a).

Because they are obsessed with conceptual reductionism or formal arguments, they fail to understand that *a certain* sociology (which may be verifiable) can content itself with an allusive way of describing the uneven, disorganized and non-logical aspect of the life of societies; this attitude is less concerned with defining 'what things should be' than with providing food for thought. But that implies a popular or populist sensibility that is sadly lacking in our pontificating petty-bourgeois intellectuals who, having never exercised power, have always wanted to make the people happy. This is particularly obvious in the article in question: the different parts of the analysis are like the elements of Freud's joke about the kettle; their function is to deny the existence of situations that offend their politico-ethico-scientific convictions. And their convictions are at once weak, under threat and therefore peremptory. As for being 'verifiable', no one working in this protected environment is likely to be in a position to grasp the monstrous aspect of what I call the subterranean centrality. The empathy discussed in this book implies an ability to find (and to frequent) places where we see an 'ethical immoralism' that is quite alien to the beautiful souls who criticize me. Just imagine – and smile at the thought – their reactions. I mean of course their intellectual reactions. To take up the 'anonymous enunciation' they reproach me for, and which I would attribute to the 'man without qualities', I recall, given that this note is addressed to men of the church, that it was 'normal for Protestants to regard themselves as following a sophisticated religion, as opposed to Catholicism, which they deemed to be popular' (Retz 1984: 1276). To generalize, we might jokingly draw a parallel with the human sciences. It is quite obvious that describing social heterogeneity requires 'a delicacy which is not . . . to be expected of a pedant from Geneva' (Retz 1984: 159).

A parallel is frequently drawn between polytheism and the intellectual tendency known as the 'new right'. There is no basis for this smear tactic, though this means that we should not deny the quality of its contributions in this and other areas. At the same time, it is a matter for regret that this movement goes on using a journalistic label that can only damage it, if only because it invalidates its arguments from the outset. I feel quite at liberty to say this in that I feel myself to be altogether alien to its cultural tradition, and in that I disagree profoundly with this movement, particularly over its Promethean ideology, the importance it gives to political forms and its diagnosis of the strength of sociality.

9  Cf. the excellent essay by Miller (1979: 69), and, of course, Augé (1982) and my own studies on the polytheism of values (Maffesoli 1979b; 1982).

10  A similar notion will be found in Lévi-Strauss (1983: 17–18).

11  Examples would include Javeau (1982b), although a later article by the same author (Javeau 1983a) suggests a shift of perspective. On the new focus on the individual subject, see Balandier (1983b), Touraine (1981), Moulin (1981) and of course Sennet (1977). See also (Lefebvre 1958–81, vol. 3).

12  Cf. the analysis made by Williame (1973: 78, 81, 85) and the summary given by Javeau (1983a: 25–8).

13  The group had nothing in common with leftism, but was close to the 'workers' council' tradition and *Link-radikalismus*. The Situationist

Internationale published a journal (usually known as *SI*) which was republished by Van Gennep, Amsterdam, in 1970.

It has to be said that, having been one of the targets, sociology has displayed a curious ability to forget the situationists. Cf. 'Aux poubelles de l'histoire' in *SI* 12 ('969) on the notorious plagiarism commited by Henri Lefebvre.

14 The following should also be consulted: *Cahiers internationaux de sociologie*, 69 (1980); *Revue de l'Institut de sociologie* 1–2 (1980) and *Revue suisse de sociologie*, 1 (1983). It was while I was completing this book that I first read Ferrarotti (1984); ch. 6 is devoted to 'the person'. Cf. Mauss's comments on 'A Category of the Human Mind, the Notion of Person, the Notion of Self' (Mauss 1979: 57–94) and Matta (1983).

15 As well as a major essay on theory, the book contains (pp. 100–43) an extremely useful 'bibliographical guide'.

16 As Javeau has remarked in various articles and lectures, it is important to recognize that Schutz is the father of the concept, which has been subject to a number of inelegant borrowings.

17 For a very rigorous analysis of the symbolic, see Crespi (1983a).

18 I am thinking of conversations with and communications from Motta in Recife, Lalive d'Epinay in Geneva, Ledrut in Toulouse and Rist in Geneva.

19 Cf. Habermas's reference to Dilthey (Habermas 1968: 180). Cf. Spengler's argument that the 'gigantic' history of Chinese or ancient culture is, morphologically, an exact equivalent to the 'little' history of individual men. Cf. the very similar formulation, which derives from Schutz, in Noschis (1982: 49): 'Typicality allows us to get beneath the surface of things, or in other words to move from the subjectivity of biographically determined experience to the abstraction of intersubjective elements.

20 Cf. Vattimo and Rovatti (1983) and, for the Japanese anecdote, Slama (1980).

# Bibliography

Adorno, Theodor (1951), *Minima Moralia: Reflections from a Damaged Life*, tr. E. F. N. Jephcott, London: Verso, 1978.
—— (1966), *Negative Dialectics*, tr. E. B. Ashton, London: Routledge, 1973.
Aquinas, Thomas, *Somme théologique*, Paris: Desclée de Brouwer, 1953.
Auclair, G. (1973), *Le Même, l'autre*, Paris: Gallimard.
—— (1982), *Le Mana quotidien*, Paris: Anthropos, 2nd edn.
Augé, M. (1982), *Génie du paganisme*, Paris: Gallimard.
Bachelard, Gaston (1938), *Psychanalyse du feu*, Paris: PUF.
Baeta Neves Flores, L. F. (1978), *O Combate dos soldatos de Christo na terra das Papaggios*, Rio de Janeiro: Forense Universitaria.
—— (1984), *Imaginaçao social jesuitica e instituiçao pedagogicas Maranahno e GranPara*, UF Rio de Janeiro: Museu Nacional.
Balandier, Georges (1971), *Sens et puissance*, Paris: PUF.
—— (1972), *Gurvitch, sa vie, son oeuvre*, Paris: PUF.
—— (1980), *Pouvoir sur scène*, Paris: Balland.
—— (1981), 'La Sociologie aujourd'hui', *Cahiers internationaux de sociologie*, 71.
—— (1983a), 'Qu'est-ce que le quotidien?', *Cahiers internationaux de sociologie*, June.
—— (1983b), 'Essai d'indentification du quotidien' *Cahiers internationaux de sociologie*, 74.
Balazs, Etienne (1968), *La Bureaucratie céleste: recherche sur l'économie et la société de la Chine traditionelle*, Paris: Gallimard.
Barel, Y. (1973), *Prospective et analyse de systèmes*, Paris: La Documentation française.
—— (1983), *La Reproduction sociale*, Paris: Anthropos.
Baudrillard, Jean (1983), *Les Stratégies fatales*, Paris: Grasset.
Beigbeder, M. (1972), *Contradiction et nouvel entendement*, Paris: Bordas.
Belassi, P. (1983), 'Iconographie de la vie quotidienne', *Cahiers internationaux de sociologie*, 74.

Benjamin, Walter (1928), *One-Way Street and Other Writings*, tr. Edmund Jephcott and Kingsley Shorter, London: New Left Books, 1979.

—— (1966), *Briefe, vol. 2*, Frankfurt am Main: Suhrkampf.

—— (1969a), *Illuminations*, tr. Harry Zohn, New York: Schocken.

—— (1969b), *Charles Baudelaire: A Lyric Poet in the Era of High Capitalism*, tr. Harry Zohn; London: Verso, 1976.

Bergson, Henri (1955), *La Pensée et le mouvant*, Paris: PUF, 3rd edn.

Bertaux, D. (1979), 'Ecrire la sociologie', *Information sur les sciences sociales*.

—— (1980), 'L'Approche biographique', *Cahiers internationaux de sociologie*, 69.

Bethoud, G. (1972), *Plaidoyeur pour l'autre*, Geneva: Droz.

Bloch, Ernst (1960), *Thomas Munzer als Theolog der Revolution*, Berlin: Aufbau Verlag.

—— (1962), *Heritage of our Times*, tr. Neville and Stephen Plaice, Cambridge: Polity, 1991.

Bosserman, P. (1981), 'G. Gurvitch et les durkheimiens en France, avant et après la seconde Guerre Mondiale', *Cahiers internationaux de sociologie*, 71.

Boudon, R. (1979), *Effets pervers et ordre social*, Paris: PUF.

Bouglé, C. (1904), *La Démocratie devant la science*, Paris: Alcan.

Bourdin, A. (1983), *Le Patrimoine inventé*, Paris: PUF.

Bourricaud, F. (1981), 'Contre le prophétisme en sociologie', *Cahiers internationaux de sociologie*, 71.

Brodu, J. L. (1982), *Charles Fort, précurseur excentrique du domaine anomalique*, Université de Paris VII: UER Charles V.

Brown, Peter (1978), *The Making of Late Antiquity*, Cambridge, Mass.: Harvard University Press.

Brown, R. H. (1977), 'Métaphore et méthode: de la logique et de la découverte en sociologie', *Cahiers internationaux de sociologie*, 62.

—— (1980), 'Ordre et révolution dans les formes normales du discours et de la conduite', *Cahiers internationaux de sociologie*, 68.

Busch, M. C. (1975), *La Sociologie du temps libre*, Paris and The Hague: Mouton.

Busino, G. (1968), *Introduction à une histoire de la sociologie de V. Pareto*, Geneva: Droz.

—— (1983), *Pareto, Croce, le socialisme et la sociologie*, Geneva: Droz.

Catani, M. (1982), *Tante Suzanne: une histoire de la vie sociologique*, Paris: Librairie des Méridiens.

Clastres, P. (1974), *La Société contre l'Etat*, Paris: Minuit.

Coster, M. de (1978), *L'Analogie en sciences humaines*, Paris: PUF.

Crespi, F. (1983a), *Mediation symbolique et société*, Paris: Librairie des Méridiens.

—— (1983b), 'Le Risque du quotidien', *Cahiers internationaux de la sociologie*, 74.

Dodds, E. R. (1951), *The Greeks and the Irrational*, Berkeley and Los Angeles: University of California Press.

Dontenville, H. (1973), *Histoire et géographie mythiques de la France*, Paris: Maisonneuve and Larousse.

Drot, J. M. (1971), *Le Temps des désillusions, ou le retour d'Ulysse manchot*, Paris: Stock.

Duby, Georges (1971), *Des sociétés médiévales*, Paris: Gallimard.

Dumont, Louis (1966), *Homo hierarchicus*, Paris: Gallimard.

—— (1977), *Homo aequalis*, Paris: Gallimard.

Dupuy, M. (1959), *La Philosophie de Max Scheler*, Paris: PUF.

—— (1982), *Ordres et désordres*, Paris: Seuil.

Durand, Gilbert (1961), *Le Décor mythique de la Chartreuse de Parme*, Paris: Corti.

—— (1969), *Les Structures anthropologiques de l'imaginaire*, Paris: Bordas.

—— (1975), *Un Mésocosme divinitoire: le langage astrologique*, Tours.

—— (1979a), *Sciences de l'homme et tradition*, Paris: Berg.

—— (1979b), *Figures mythiques et visages de l'oeuvre*, Paris: Berg.

—— (1980), *L'Ame tigrée*, Paris: Denoël.

—— (1982), 'Le Retour des immortels', in *Le Temps de la Réflexion*, Paris: Gallimard, vol. 3.

—— (1985), 'Une réponse de la sociologie française', in *Socio-anthropologie des turbulences: hommage à Georges Balandier*, Paris: Berg.

Durkheim, Emile (1892), *Montesquieu and Rousseau: Forerunners of Sociology*, tr. Ralph Mannheim, Ann Arbor: Ann Arbor Paperbacks, 1965.

—— (1893), *The Division of Labour in Society*, tr. W. D. Halls, London: Macmillan, 1984.

—— (1895), *The Rules of Sociological Method and Selected Texts on Sociology and its Method*, tr. W. D. Halls, London: Macmillan, 1982.

—— (1897), *Suicide: A Study in Sociology*, tr. John A. Spaulding and Georges Simpon, London: Routledge and Kegan Paul, 1970.

—— (1898), 'Représentations individuelles et représentations collectives', *Revue de métaphysique et de morale*, 6: 237–302.

—— (1912), *The Elementary Forms of the Religious Life*, tr. J. W. Swin, London: Allen and Unwin, 1915.

—— (1928), *Socialism and Saint-Simon*, tr. Charlotte Sattler, Yellow Springs, Ohio: Antioch Press, 1958.

Ferrarotti, F. (1983), *Histoire et histoires de vie: la méthode biographique dans les sciences sociales*, Paris: Librairie des Méridiens.

—— (1984), *Une Théologie pour athées*, Paris: Librairie des Méridiens.

Feyerabend, Paul (1993), *Against Method* (rev. edn), London: Verso.

Fort, C. (1949), *The Book of the Damned*, New York: Boni and Livenight.

Foucault, Michel (1976), *The History of Sexuality*, vol. 1: *An Introduction*, tr. Robert Hurley, London: Allen Lane, 1979.

Freund, J. (1969), 'Le Révolutionisme', *Respublica*.

—— (1978), 'De l'interprétation dans les sciences sociales', *Cahiers internationaux de sociologie*, 65.

—— (1981), 'Préface' to Georg Simmel, *Sociologie et épistémologie*, Paris: PUF.

—— (1982), 'Préface' to Max Weber, *La Ville*, tr. P. Fritsch, Paris: Aubier-Montaigne.

Freyre, G. (1974), *Maîtres et esclaves: la formation de la société brésilienne*, Paris: Gallimard.

Friedman, Georges (1936), *La Crise du progrès*, Paris: Gallimard.

Gadamer, H. G. (1960), *Wahrheit und Methode*, Tübingen: Mohr.

Gandillac, M. de (1942), *La Philosophie de Nicolas de Cuse*, Paris: Aubier.

—— (1973), 'La Philosophie de la renaissance', in *Histoire de la philosophie*, Paris: Hachette.

George, François (1979), *Pour un ultime image au camarade Staline*, Paris: Julliard.

Girard, P., and Mazol, P. (1980), *Habiter, cuisiner*, Paris: 10/18.

Glotz, A. (1904), *La Solidarité de la famille dans le droit criminel en Grèce*, Paris: Fontemaing.

Goethe, Johann Wolfgang von (1808), *Faust*, tr. Walter Arndt, New York: Norton, 1976.

Goldman, Lucien (1967), 'Epistémologie de la sociologie in J. Piaget (ed.), *Logique et connaissance*, Paris: Bibliothèque de la Pléiade, 1967.

Gracq, Julien (1939), *Au Château d'Argol*, Paris: Corti.

Gurvitch, G. (1967), *Traité de sociologie*, Paris: PUF.

Habermas, Jürgen (1968), *Knowledge and Human Interests*, tr. Jeremy. J. Shapiro, London: Heinemann, 1972.

Hall, E. T. (1977), *Beyond Culture*, New York: Doubleday.

Hesse, Hermann (1922), *Siddharta*, tr. Hilda Rosner, London: Peter Owen, 1954.

Hillman, James (1972), *The Myth of Analysis: Three Essays in Archetypal Psychology*, Evanston, Ill.: Northwestern University Press.

Horkheimer, Max (1930), *Anfänge der bürgerliche Geschichtsphilosophie*, Stuttgart: Köhlamn.

Janneau, E. (1963), *La Philosophie médiévale*, Paris: PUF.

Javeau, C. (1980), 'Sur le concept de la vie quotidienne et sa sociologie', *Cahiers internationaux de sociologie*, 68.

—— (1982a), 'Prolégomènes prétendument méthodologiques à une sociologie du quotidien', Colloque AISLF, Paris, roneoed.

—— (1982b), 'Pour une sociologie de la vie quotidienne: quelques pistes et quelques détours', *Recherches sociologiques*, 12.

—— (1983a), 'La Sociologie du quotidien: paradigmes et enjeux', *Revue suisse de sociologie*, 1.

—— (1983b), 'Compte et mécomptes du temps' *Cahiers internationaux de sociologie*, 74.

Jouvenel, B. de (1972), *Du Principiat*, Paris: Hachette.

Kant, Immanuel (1781), *Critique of Pure Reason*, tr. J. D. Meiklejohn, London: Dent, 1934.

—— (1783), *Prolegomena to Any Future Metaphysics that will be Able to Present itself as a Science*, tr. Peter G. Lucas, Manchester University Press, 1953.

Kuhn, T. S. (1962), *The Structure of Scientific Revolutions*, University of Chicago Press.

Kristeva, Julia (1970), *Le Texte du roman*, Paris: Mouton.

Lafarque, Paul (1883), *Le Droit à la paresse*, Paris: Maspero, 1969.

Lalive d'Epínay, C. (1983a), 'La Vie quotidienne: essai de construction d'un concept sociologique et anthropologique', *Cahiers internationaux de sociologie*, 74.

—— (1983b), *Temps libre*, Geneva: Editions Faure.

Lalli, Pina (1983), 'D'autres médecins: le paradoxe dans le quotidien', *Cahiers internationaux de sociologie*, 74.

Lazega, E., Modak, M. and Lalive d'Epinay, C. (1982), 'Récits de la vie quotidienne et problématique de l'énonciation', *Recherches sociologiques*, 13, 13ff.

Lefebvre, Henri (1958–81), *Critique de la vie quotidienne*, 3 vols. Paris: L'Arche.

Lemos, M. (1924), *Luis de Camoens: Essai historique*, Rio de Janeiro: Forense Universitaria.

Le Roy Ladurie, Emmanuel (1975), *Montaillou: Cathars and Catholics in a French Village 1294–1324*, tr. Barbara Bray, Harmondsworth: Penguin, 1978.

Lévi-Strauss, Claude (1955), *Tristes Tropiques*, tr. John and Doreen Weightman, London: Picador, 1989.

—— (1983), *The View from Afar*, tr. Joachim Neugroschel and Phoebe Hoss, Harmondsworth: Penguin, 1987.

Lewis, Oscar (1962), *The Children of Sanchez: Autobiography of a Mexican Family*, London: Secker and Warburg.

Lukács, Georg (1910), *Soul and Form*, tr. Anna Bostock, London: Merlin, 1974.

Lupasco, S. (1947), *Logique et contradiction*, Paris: PUF.

Lussato, B. (1981), *Le Défi démocratique*, Paris: Fayard.

Maffesoli, Michel (1976), *Logique de la domination*, Paris: PUF

—— (1978), *La Destruction utile*, in Maffesoli 1984.

—— (1979a), *La Violence totalitaire: essai d'anthropologie politique*, Paris: PUF.

—— (1979b), *La Conquête du présent: pour une sociologie de la vie quotidienne*, Paris: PUF.

—— (1980), 'Le Rituel et la vie quotidienne comme fondement des histoires de vie', *Cahiers internationaux de sociologie*, 69.

—— (1981a) 'La Démarche sociologique ' *Revue européenne des sciences sociales*, 19.

—— (1981b), 'Pour une sociologie relativiste', *Cahiers internationaux de sociologie*, 71.

—— (1982), *L'Ombre de Dionysos: contribution à une sociologie de l'orgie*, Paris: Librairie des Méridiens.

—— (1984), *Trois Essais sur la violence*, Paris: Librairie des Méridiens.

Mann, Thomas (1947), *Doctor Faustus*, tr. H. T. Lowe-Porter, Harmondsworth: Penguin, 1991.

—— (1933–43), *Joseph and his Brothers*, tr. H. T. Lowe-Porter, London: Secker and Warburg, 1981.

Mannheim, Karl (1936), *Ideology and Utopia*, tr. Louis Wirth and Edward Shils, London: Routledge and Kegan Paul.

Maquet, J. (1949), *La Sociologie du quotidien*, Louvain: Nauwelaerts.

Marie, M. (1982), *Le Territoire sans nom*, Paris: Librairie des Méridiens.

Matta, R. da (1983), *Carnavals, bandits, et héros*, Paris: Seuil.

Mauss, Marcel (1979), *Sociology and Psychology*, tr. Ben Brewster, London: Routledge and Kegan Paul.

Miller, D. L. (1979), *Le Nouveau Polythéisme*, Paris: Editions Imago.

Moles, A. (1982), *Labyrinthes du vécu*, Paris: Librairie des Méridiens.

—— (forthcoming), *La Vie en contrabande*.

Morin, Edgar (1969), *La Rumeur d'Orléans*, Paris: Seuil.

—— (1977–80), *La Méthode*, 2 vols, Paris: Seuil.

—— (1979), *L'Esprit du temps*, Paris: Livre de poche, 1983.

—— (1980), *Pour sortir du XXe siècle*, Paris: Nathan.

—— (1983), *De la nature de l'URSS*, Paris: Fayard.

—— (1984), *Le Rose et le noir*, Paris: Editions Galilée.

Moulin, L. (1981), 'La Personnalité narcissique, *Revue générale*.

Noschis, K. (1982), 'Identité et habitat', *Cahiers internationaux de sociologie*, 72.

Pareto, Vilfredo (1914), *Il mito virtuista e la letteratura immorale*, Rome: Lux, 2nd edn.

—— (1923) *The Mind and Society: A Treatise on General Sociology*, tr. Andrew Buongiorno and Arthur Livingstone, London: Cape, 1935.

Pennachionni, I. (1982), *La Nostalgie en images: une sociologie de la bande dessinée*, Paris: Librairie des Méridiens.

Perniola, M. (1980), *La società dei simulacri*, Bolgona: Capelli.

Perrot, P. (1981), *Les Dessus et les dessous de la bourgeoisie*, Paris: Fayard.

Piaget, Jean (1950), *Introduction à l'épistémologie génétique*, Paris: PUF.

Pieyre de Mandiargue, André (1967), *La Marge*, Paris: Gallimard.

Popper, Karl (1934), *The Logic of Scientific Discovery*, London: Routledge, 1992.

—— (1992), *Unended Quest: An Intellectual Biography*, rev. edn, London: Routledge.

Poulat, E. (1977) *Catholicisme, démocratie et socialisme*, Paris: Casterman.

Poulot, Denis (1980), *Le Sublime*, Paris: Maspero.

Puech, H. C. (1978), *En Quête de la gnose*, Paris: Gallimard.

Renan, Ernest (1921), *Essais de morale et de critique*, Paris: Calman-Lévy.

Renaud, Gilbert (1984), *A l'Ombre du rationalisme. La Société québecoise de sa dépendance à sa quotidienneté*, Montreal: Martin.

Retz, Cardinal de (1984), *Mémoires*, Paris: Bibliothèque de la Pléiade.

Rist, G. (1984), 'La Notion médiévale d'habitus dans la sociologie de Pierre Bourdieu', *Revue européenne des sciences sociales*, 22, 201–12.

Rousseau, Jean-Jacques (1755), 'A Discourse on the origin of inequality', in *The Social Contract and Discourses*, tr. G. D. H. Cole, new edn, London: Dent, 1973.

Sansot, P., Strohl, H., Torgue, H. and Verdillon, C. (1979), *L'Espace et son double*, Paris: Champ Urbain.

Schopenhauer, Artur (1819), *The World as Will and Idea*, tr. R. B. Haldane and K. Kemp, 3 vols. London: Kegan Paul, Trench, Trübner, 1891.

Schutz, A. (1953), 'Concept and theory formation in the social sciences', in *Collected Papers*, vol. 1, The Hague: Martinus Nijhoff, 1960.

—— (1960) 'The problem of rationality in the social world', in *Collected Papers*, vol. 2, The Hague: Martinus Nijhoff, 1964.

*'Science et conscience': Actes du Colloque de Cordoue* 1981), Paris: Stock.

Sennet, Richard (1977), *The Fall of Public Man*, New York, Knopf.

Shibutani, T. (1966), *Improvised News: A Sociological Approach to Rumour*, Indianapolis: Bobbs Merrill.

Simmel, G. (1898), 'Comment les formes sociales se manifestent', *L'Année sociologique*, 1.

—— (1980), *Essays on Interpretation in Social Science*, tr. Guy Oakes, Manchester University Press.

Sironneau, J.-P. (1982), *Sécularisation et religions politiques*, Paris and The Hague: Mouton.

Six, J. F. (1983), 'Le Christianisme au banc des accusés, *Etudes*, April.

Slama, A. G. (1980) *Les Chasseurs d'absolu*, Paris: Grasset.

Sorel, Georges (1908), *Illusions of Progress*, tr. J. and C. Stanley, Berkeley: University of California Press, 1970.

Spengler, O. (1922–3) *The Decline of the West*, tr. Charles Francis Atkinson, London: Allen and Unwin, 1926–8.

Starobinski, Jean (1982), *Montaigne en mouvement*, Paris: Gallimard.

Steenberghe, E. van (1974), *Le Cardinal de Cues*, Geneva: Slatkine.

Tacussel, P. (1982), *Culture et politique: le processus métanoiaque et l'imaginaire social*, Grenoble: Université des sciences sociales, roneoed thesis.

Thomas, L. V. (1976), *Anthropologie de la mort*, Paris: Payot.

—— (1980), *Le Cadavre*, Brussels: Complex.

—— (1982), *La Mort africaine*, Paris: Payot.

—— (1983), 'Mort et vie quotidienne', *Cahiers internationaux de sociologie*, June.

Tönnies, Ferdinand (1887), *Community and Association*, tr. Charles P. Loomis, London: Routledge and Kegan Paul, 1955.

Touraine, Alain (1981), 'Le Retour de l'acteur, *Cahiers internationaux de sociologie*, 71, 243–55.

—— (1985), 'La Société a-t-elle un centre?', in *Socio-anthropologie des turbulences: hommage à Georges Balandier*, Paris: Berg.

Vattimo, G., and Rovatti, P. A. (1983) (eds), *Il Pensiero de Bole*, Milan: Feltrinelli.

Vincent, G. (1983), 'Sociologie de l'orgie ou débauche de la parasociologie', *Parole et société: Revue du christianisme social*, 1–2, 89–106.

Watzlawick, P. (1978), *La Reálité de la réalitè: Confusion, désinformation, communication*, Paris: Seuil.

Weber, Max (1904), ' "Objectivity" in Social Science and Social Policy', in *The Methodology of the Social Sciences*, tr. Edward A. Shils and Henry A. Finch, New York: Free Press, 1949.

—— (1904–5), *The Protestant Ethic and the Spirit of Capitalism* tr. Talcott Parsons, London: Routledge, 1992.

—— (1913), 'Über einige Kategorien der verstehenden Soziologie', *Logos*, 4.

—— (1921), *The City*, tr. Don Martindale and Gertrud Neuwirth, London: Heinemann.

—— (1928), 'Science as a Vocation', in H. H. Gerth and C. Wright Mills (eds), *From Max Weber: Essays in Sociology*, London: Routledge and Kegan Paul, 1970.

—— (1983), *De la liberté intellectuelle et de la dignité de la vocation universitaire*, ed. Michel C. Martin, Toulouse: Presses de l'Institut politique.

Williame, R. (1973), *Les Fondements phénoménologiques de la sociologie compréhensive: Alfred Schutz et Max Weber*, The Hague: Martinus Nijhoff.

Worringer, E. (1916), *Abstraction and Empathy: A Contribution to the Psychology of Style*, tr. Michael Bullock, London: Routledge and Kegan Paul, 1963.

Yates, Frances (1966), *The Art of Memory*, London: Routledge and Kegan Paul.

Zola, Emile (1885) *Germinal*, tr. Havelock Ellis, London: Dent, 1933.

# Index

Abelard, P., 34
abstraction, 5, 151, 153
action research, 148
Adorno, T., 32, 43
aestheticism, 15–16, 19, 48, 143
agglutinative structure, 99–105, 157
Alembert, J. le R. d', 49–50
Alexander the Great, 114
allegory, 17
alterity, 37, 50–2, 141, 157
altruism, 60
ambivalence, 36–7, 42, 50, 161
amnesia, 21
analogical method, 86–105
analogy, 13, 17, 86, 88, 92–3, 104, 127
animism, 96–8, 100–1
anomalies, 135–6
anomie, 90, 121
antagonistic values, 90, 111
anthropology, 9, 56, 95, 102–3, 172n
antinomy of values, 35, 123–4, 153–4
aphorism, 17
Apollonian research, 20
appearances, 75, 77, 82, 130
approximations, 36, 82–3, 146
Aquinas, T., 48, 63, 76–7, 165–6
archetypes, 11, 68, 75, 96–7, 98
architectonic, 9, 79, 165
Aron, R., 42

'as if' attitude 56, 90–3, 171n
astrology, 104, 108
atomism, 156
Auclair, G., 22, 136
Augé, M., 175n

Bachelard, G., 130, 149–50
Baeta Neves Flores, L. F., 51
Balacz, E., 80
Balandier, G., 7, 20, 36, 40, 61, 70, 93, 104–5, 160, 171n, 175n
banality, 21, 70, 73, 120, 139
  and form, 79
  style of, 128
Barel, Y., 58, 117
Barrès, M., 107
Baudelaire, C. P., 22, 24
Baudrillard, J., 40, 174n
Beigbeder, M., 12, 31, 90, 103
being-together, 72, 155, 157–8
Belassi, P., 141, 167
belief, and illusion, 71
Bénigni, G., 170n
Benjamin, W., 18, 45, 160, 163
Bergson, H., 43
Bertaux, D., 17, 42, 137–8, 164
bestiary, 116
*Bildungsroman*, 74
biographical method, 7, 15, 157, 158, 162–7
  *see also* life stories